CRITICAL ISSUES IN CURRICULUM
John Willinsky, EDITOR

Reading and Writing the Self:
Autobiography in Education and the Curriculum
Robert J. Graham

Understanding Curriculum as Phenomenological
and Deconstructed Text
William F. Pinar and William M. Reynolds, Editors

UNDERSTANDING CURRICULUM
as
PHENOMENOLOGICAL
and
DECONSTRUCTED TEXT

EDITED BY
William F. Pinar
AND
William M. Reynolds

TEACHERS COLLEGE, COLUMBIA UNIVERSITY
NEW YORK AND LONDON

Published by Teachers College Press, 1234 Amsterdam Avenue, New York, NY 10027

Library of Congress Cataloging-in-Publication Data
Understanding curriculum as phenomenological and deconstructed text /
    edited by William F. Pinar and William M. Reynolds.
        p.   cm. —(Critical issues in curriculum)
    Includes bibliographical references and indexes.
    ISBN 0–8077–3114–5.   —   ISBN 0–8077–3113–7 (pbk.)
    1. Education—Curricula.   2. Phenomenology.   I. Pinar, William.
II. Reynolds, William M., 1953–   III. Series.
LB1570.U45   1991
375—dc20   91–27223

Printed on acid-free paper

Manufactured in the United States of America

99 98 97 96 95 94 93 92   8 7 6 5 4 3 2 1

Contents

Preface

The phenomenological movement continues to grow in Canada, and its influence is increasingly felt in the United States. However, that work remains "marginalized" in the American curriculum field, partly due to the legacy of positivism in the traditional field, partly due to the hegemony of Marxism in the reconceptualized field. Perhaps its marginalization also follows from its academic center being in Edmonton, Alberta, a city remote from most American cities, at least in imagination. Finally, even within Canada, phenomenology has struggled against other traditions in curriculum, and like many such struggles, there is an institutional element. Perhaps the central institutional rivalry in Canada is between the University of Alberta and the Ontario Institute for Studies in Education in Toronto.

For all of these reasons the phenomenological tradition—while strong in Canada and worthy of the attention of all curriculum specialists, even by those who will reject it—remains vague in the minds of American students of curriculum. It is long overdue that illustrations of this work be collected for the convenience of students and scholars. Additionally, it is helpful—given recent genealogical research in the American field (Schubert, Schubert, Herzog, Posner, & Kridel, 1988)—that the story of phenomenological curriculum research in North America be chronicled. We were not clear about the story of phenomenology in Canada. Several scholars who are most identified with the movement and who have played and continue to play important roles in it kindly wrote to us regarding the history of the movement and its institutionalization at the University of Alberta. The genealogy contained in the Appendix is derived from this correspondence; it is information that, to our knowledge, has been collected nowhere else.

Superficially one might be tempted to contrast phenomenology as English Canada's counterpoint to Quebecois post-structuralism, but this ignores that a Dutch emigré (van Manen) brought European phenomenology—especially that of the Utrecht School in the Netherlands—to Canada, and that a Japanese-Canadian, Ted Aoki, has done more than anyone other than van Manen to articulate its contributions to understanding curriculum topics. Post-structuralism in education is in a much earlier stage of development. Cherryholmes's *Power and Criticism: Post-Structural Investigations in Education* (1988) has done and will do much to inform the field. Daignault's work (Chapter 11, this volume) will take decades, we suspect, to be interpreted and its significance understood and appreciated. A second generation of post-structuralists will contribute much, we suspect, to understanding post-structuralism in general and the work of Daignault in particular. A genealogy of post-structuralism appears in the Appendix.

We have always been curious and appreciative that these European traditions—phenomenology is German, French, and Dutch; post-structuralism is French—come via Canada. Due to its history and its economy, Canada is closer to Europe and, some would say, to the world, than is the United States. (Our size and [self] importance lead to a certain provincialism, culturally and specifically intellectually. Certainly this provincialism is clear in the social sciences, and particularly in education. Phenomenology and post-structuralism will continue to be marginalized due to the legacy of Anglo-positivism in the American social sciences.) Writing this on June 15, 1990, we are struck by how these traditions represent two distinct societies in Canada, societies sufficiently distinct that—in the aftermath of the failure to ratify the Meech Lake Accord—Quebec may secede. Of course phenomenology is not of English origin, and recall that a Japanese-Canadian and a Dutch-Canadian imported it to the fertile soil of the prairies. It has taken root, however, and many in the second generation of phenomenologists are indeed Anglo-Canadians. Post-structuralism is hardly the mainstream tradition among education faculties in Quebec. The second generation seems to be American.

There is no homologous tension between phenomenologists and post-structuralists as there is between English and French Canada. Indeed, Ted Aoki has spoken of the importance of post-structuralism. David Jardine's scholarship exhibits post-structuralist influences; indeed, it occupies, we have suggested, a "location" between the two discourses (although closer, perhaps, to phenomenology). Nor does the appearance of post-structuralists in education represent the "discursive shift" from phenomenology and Marxism that it did in France twenty years ago. Phenomenology will continue to find a constituency disenchanted with the objectification and depersonalization of contemporary public education. The future of post-structuralism is more difficult to discern. However, one feels assured it will "territorialize sectors of the curriculum terrain," even as it decries the process.

We thank our Canadian colleagues for their exciting contribution to the curriculum field worldwide.

REFERENCES

Cherryholmes, C. H. (1988). *Power and criticism: Post-structural investigations in education*. New York: Teachers College Press.

Schubert, W., Schubert, A., Herzog, L., Posner, G., & Kridel, C. (1988). A genealogy of curriculum researchers. *Journal of Curriculum Theorizing, 8* (1) 137–183.

UNDERSTANDING CURRICULUM
as
PHENOMENOLOGICAL
and
DECONSTRUCTED TEXT

Curriculum as Text

WILLIAM F. PINAR AND WILLIAM M. REYNOLDS

To narrate is to give an account of something, in one sense to tell a story. The history of curriculum studies is the story of competing efforts to *develop* curriculum. Within that paradigm of the field as curriculum development, the social-efficiency advocates narrate a story of curriculum as an assembly line, children as raw material, and graduates as marketable products. The classicists told a story of curriculum as "windows of the soul." Child-centered progressives told a story in which the child was the central character, sometimes achieving mythical status. Counts and the social reconstructionists told a story in the form of exposé, charging that schools were controlled by the privileged who used the schools to maintain their privilege. Dewey and Deweyan progressives told a story in which experience and education are inseparable characters.

These curricular orientations have their contemporary "children" and "stepchildren," if you will. Eisner's (1979, 1985) work on aesthetic evaluation exhibits a Deweyan appreciation for art as experience; Clandinin and Connelly's (1990) narratives of educational experience suggests Deweyan influences; Apple (1988) and Giroux (1988) repeat Counts' famous question; van Manen (1988) focuses upon the child. Each of these contemporary curriculum discourses is larger and more complex, however, than its antecedent orientation.

CURRICULUM AS A PHENOMENOLOGICAL TEXT

Curriculum understood as a phenomenological text communicates a story in which quantitative social science is an evil character whose effort to quantify the immeasurable is unethical and epistemologically unsound. Those elements of experience that are observable and measurable tend to be rather small and specific. The firmament in the positivist sky twinkles with precision and rigor. However, the spaces between stars and those hidden by clouds recede and disappear. Phenomenology seeks to name those spaces, their relation to the stars and to us. The unity of the epistemological whole resides in ourselves. Merleau-Ponty writes:

> We shall find in ourselves and nowhere else the unity and true meaning of phenomenology. It is less a question of counting up quotations than of determining and expressing in concrete form this phenomenology for ourselves which has given a number of present-day readers the impression, on reading Husserl or Heidegger, not so much of encountering a new philosophy as of recognizing what they had been waiting for. (1962, p. ix)

This embodient of knowledge and knowing in the human self led—for some—to autobiography, an interest in telling stories of life history in order to reconceive the relation of self to knowing, a relation at the center of curriculum understood as *currere,* the running of the course (Pinar & Grumet, 1976). In early versions of this work there was a tendency to dwell on the details of life history, to transfer the quantitative project of adding up bits of information to the qualitative project of understanding their meaning (Pinar, 1980b, 1981). This tendency occurs in autobiographical literary criticism (Pinar, 1988). The error was superficial, we believe, as we were always clear that the relation of knower to the known (Pinar, 1980a) was more essential than the concrete incidents and bits of information that express the themes of the "intentional arc."

We shared the sense Merleau-Ponty describes of having "found" something or, rather, of having been found. Phenomenology—Husserl and the early Heidegger—communicates a nostalgia for an earlier time in which (it is alleged) the sky was visible in its entirety, as were we. Heidegger's pastoral themes provide a counterpoint of comfort to his sense of being "shipwrecked" on the shore of Being, of *Dasein* as being-toward-death. Unlike the empty evasive chatter of everyday (urban) life, the pastoral seemed to suggest a "being in time" conscious of its ontological limits and possibilities. Merleau-Ponty returned Heidegger's head to the body and inscribed on the body of phenomenology gesture and sensuality. In French philosophy, this version of phenomenology dominated the Parisian scene in the 1960s, triumphant over classical Marxism ("history is dead," it was asserted), having incorporated dialectics within its own epistemology, and specifically its view of language. Its preeminence would be short-lived, as the political and cultural maelstroms of the decade would result in a resurgence of Marxism (as neo-Marxism and Maoism) and the appearance of the so-called post-structuralism.

In North American curriculum studies, the sequence of events is quite different. Phenomenology was introduced to curriculum studies by Dwayne Huebner (1975). It was imported from philosophy of education via the work of Maxine Greene (1975). Huebner's presentation at the 1967 Ohio State University Curriculum Theory Conference (published in 1975), entitled "Curriculum as Concern for Man's Temporality," represents the first major phenomenological curriculum statement, still the last such word, if you will, on the relation of time and curriculum. During the early 1970s, while Madeleine Grumet and William Pinar were studying phenomenology's relation to autobiography, Max van Manen was reading phenomenology in Holland before emigrating to Canada. Van Manen introduced phenomenology to Ted Aoki, who, as chairman of the Department of Secondary Education at the University of Alberta, created conditions in which phenomenological curriculum study flourished. A genealogy of phenomenological curriculum studies can be found in the Appendix.

CURRICULUM AS A DECONSTRUCTED TEXT

Post-structuralism surfaced in American curriculum studies first in a 1979 University of Rochester doctoral dissertation by Peter Taubman (Taubman, 1982). Taubman explicated Foucault's epistemology, from which he reconfigured current gender and feminist debates. At the 1980 Curriculum Theory Conference (now called the Bergamo Conference) sponsored by the editors of *The Journal of Curriculum Theorizing* (now *JCT: An Interdisciplinary Journal of Curriculum Studies*), held that autumn at the Airlie Conference Center in Virginia, Jacques Daignault and Clermont Gauthier dramatically staged a critique of the reconceptualist movement, decrying the effort—to use a post-structuralist phrase—to reterritorialize the curriculum terrain as "reconceptualization." Daignault has emerged as the major post-structuralist in education on the continent. His complex and elusive essays have deconstructed a number of important curricular themes, including theory, practice, and research. Even before it has been widely understood, post-structuralism has been endorsed (Wexler, 1987) and attacked (Brodriff, 1988).

At the outset it must be said that post-structuralism is an umbrella term of convenience. For instance, while the work of Foucault, Serres, and others can be linked to structuralism (a lineage Cherryholmes [1988] accessibly explains), the work of Derrida—perhaps the most visible "post-structuralist" today—is much more associated with phenomenology, especially with Heidegger (Caputo, 1987; Descombes, 1980). (Certain forms of phenomenology can be argued to exhibit structuralist qualities, of course.) At the outset it is important to acknowledge the volume and complexity of the work associated with the term. Furthermore, any effort to "explain" post-structuralism distorts it, for it is clear that it is a mode of cognition more than a set of propositions that can be listed in linear, logical fashion.

After having struggled to understand Daignault's important work, Pinar made an initial attempt to think post-structurally in 1985 in "Autobiography and the Architecture of Self" (published in 1988). Relying on Megill's lucid tracing of aesthetic themes through what he termed the prophets of extremity—Nietzsche, Heidegger, Foucault, and Derrida—Pinar worked to recast the issue of autobiography as relationality. The Foucauldian endorsement of marginality and the Derridean notions of trace and absence enabled him to conceive of storytelling as a firmament in which the spaces between stars were as crucial to acknowledge and portray as the stars themselves.

The famous phenomenological dictum "back to the things themselves" suggests a "preconceptual" realm in which experience is yet to be articulated. Merleau-Ponty quotes Husserl approvingly: "It is the pure and, so to speak, still dumb experience which must be brought to the pure expression of its own meaning." This phenomenology is said to call us back to "lived experience," those spheres of time, space, and experience that ontologically antedate all conceptualization. There is a purity, innocence, and authority that accompanies phenomenological work; these are evident, we believe, in phenomenological curriculum scholarship (van Manen, 1988). These qualities are simultaneously aspects of its appeal and its rejection by the mainstream research community in North America.

Phenomenological curriculum research calls us back to the body (Grumet, 1988), back to primordial experiences of childhood. Illustrative phenomenological themes include Langeveld's depiction of the "secret place," "bodyreading," "life's original difficulty," curriculum built from the "ground up." More synoptic and inclusive of political themes, Aoki's work calls readers to a mindfulness and clarity accomplished by contemplation and meditation, one which excludes instrumentalism in research or professional relationships (Pinar, 1987). The integrity and moral force of the phenomenological tradition hold enormous appeal, despite criticisms from critical theorists (Bernstein, 1976).

Post-structuralists challenge the ontology and epistemology that ground phenomenology. The binary distinction between experience and language, experience and conceptualization, is denied. The phenomenological dictum that the conceptual sphere rests upon and derives from a preconceptual, antepredicative sphere is denied. To be described, even "dumb" experience, Derrida observes, becomes discourse. Original purity of experience cannot be achieved; while it is implied, it does not exist as text. In the beginning was the flesh, but the flesh became word. Lyotard writes:

> In so far as this life-originating world is ante-predicative, all predication, all discourse, undoubtedly implies it, yet is wide of it, and properly speaking nothing may be said of it. . . . The Husserlian description . . . is a struggle of language

against itself to attain the originary. . . . In this struggle, the defeat of the philosopher, of the logos, is assured, since the originary, once described, is thereby no longer originary. (quoted in Descombes, 1980, p. 161)

Lyotard does not deny that experience and discourse are distinguishable. He does insist that for "dumb" experience to speak—in language, in the look, in the gesture—it becomes discourse. Discourse represents meaning latent in experience but inarticulated.

Meaning is discursive. It can represent only approximations of original experience. Language occupies the space between experience and the word, or *logos*. Lacan locates metaphor "precisely at the point where meaning is produced out of non-meaning" (Lacan, 1977). Merleau-Ponty anticipated this view:

> It is true that we should never talk about anything if we were limited to talking about those experiences with which we coincide, since speech is already a separation. . . . [But] the primary meaning of discourse is to be found in that text of experience which it is trying to communicate. (1962, p. 388)

Discourse as speech or writing occupies that which separates us, that space which is termed the "social." Thus "the word" is inextricably human, thus inextricably political, as Foucault documents in his studies of the discursive systems associated with madness, sexuality, and knowledge (Foucault, 1979, 1980a, 1980b). Merleau-Ponty anticipates this view also: ". . . in the use of our body and our sense in so far as they involve us in the world, we have the means of understanding our cultural gesticulation, in so far as it involves us in history" (1964, p. 82).

"Deconstruction" is the term, first proposed by Derrida, to denote the inextricable relation between experience and language. The concept appears in Heidegger's *Being and Time*. Derrida insists that it is not to be understood in any negative or destructive sense; rather, deconstruction means to circumscribe. Before Derrida's employment of the term, grammarians had used it to refer to the analysis of sentence construction. To deconstruct in the Derridean sense is to lay bare the construction of discourse. Deconstruction shows how a discursive system functions, including what it excludes or denies. Describing his own study of madness, Foucault explains: "I have not sought to write the history of that [medical] language, but rather the archaeology of that silence" (1973, p. xi). In this sense deconstruction is a political activity that exposes the ideological function and content of discursive systems (Descombes, 1980).

The work of deconstruction indicates that connotations, or what Barthes terms "secondary meanings," characterize human language. Bluntly stated, it is contended that there are no primary texts, only interpretations of interpretations. The concept of primary text is implied, as is the concept of original and pure experience, but it cannot be expressed linguistically. Any text is laced with human purposes and crosspurposes, motives and countermotives—what is stated and what is not.

> Interpretation can never be brought to an end, simply because there is nothing to interpret. There is nothing absolutely primary to be interpreted, since fundamentally, everything is already interpretation; every sign is, in itself, not the thing susceptible to interpretation but the interpretation of other signs. (Foucault, quoted in Descombes, 1980, p. 117)

The origin is already "theater," already a staging. There is always, in Derrida's words, an originary delay. This "originary difference" is expressed as "differance," from the French verb *differer,* meaning both "not to be identical" "to defer." "Differance" produces history and knowledge, as it creates disjunctions or spaces among past, present, and future, spaces to be occupied by language. The present is always delayed (Descombes, 1980). The present always contains traces of what is absent. Deconstruction works to show the infinite regress and arbitrariness of interpretation, not for the sake of epistemological or ethical relativism, but in the interests of setting the reader free, of setting the text free. Derrida writes to exemplify these movements and crossmovements in text as he puns and parodies himself (Megill, 1985).

CURRICULUM AS TEXT

Husserl's phenomenology attempted to order and stablize the flux of experience via the eidetic reduction, by bracketing that flux and discerning its essences (Caputo, 1987). Heidegger invoked deconstruction to violate the everyday, the taken-for-granted sphere we construct and employ to evade the ontological facts of our fallenness, our being-toward-death. In *Being and Time* deconstruction functions to disrupt mindless tradition and thus acts in service of the recovery and retrieval of Being. Deconstruction functions in the hermeneutic circle to set free the primordial (Caputo, 1987). In this movement Heidegger sets the stage for Derrida.

Derrida radicalizes deconstruction so that hermeneutics itself is deconstructed. For Heidegger "understanding" sets free what is hidden from view by overlays of tradition, prejudice, and evasion. "Interpretation" represents movements toward such understanding. For both Heidegger and Husserl phenomenological understanding moves from originary experience through language and back again. For Heidegger, originary experience does not preclude the linguistic. He acknowledges discourse as an essential constituent element of the "there." Interpretation is the conceptual working out of preexistent understanding, coming to know what we "knew" already, albeit obscurely. Empirical "proofs" have no place in hermeneutical understanding; to know phenomenologically is to allow to unfold what is already present but not yet seen (Caputo, 1987).

Derrida repudiates Heidegger's epistemology; he has no interest in the language of "homecoming," "mystery," "unfolding," and "Being." Derrida views Heidegger's epistemology as nostalgia for a time past, a time that never was. Derrida insists that hiding in the mist of nostalgia is a metaphysics of order in which the reality of flux becomes tamed and distorted. Derrida suspects any moves that slow movement, arrest the play of language and experience. Caputo observes that Derrida is more faithful to Nietzsche than to Heidegger; Derrida insists that we always remain aware of the fragility and contingency of what we think and do (Caputo, 1987).

Curriculum as a deconstructed text acknowledges knowledge as preeminently historical. Here, however, history is not understood as ideologically constructed, rather as a series of narratives superimposed upon each other, interlaced among each other, layers of story merged and separated like the colors in Jackson Pollock's paintings. The stories we tell in schools, formalized as disciplines, are always others' stories, always conveying motives and countermotives, dreams and nightmares. To understand curriculum as a deconstructed (or deconstructing) text is to tell stories that never end, stories in which the listener, the "narratee," may become a character or indeed the narrator, in which all structure is provisional, momentary, a collection of twinkling stars in a firmament of flux.

Studies of curriculum as phenomenological and deconstructed texts present the multivocality, multiperspectivity, and "lived" aspects of textbooks and of classrooms. Such studies resemble imaginative fiction more than the reviews of the journalist/art critic or the numbers of the quantitative researcher. Such studies will not function as evaluations, of course, or pretend to be "truth" in some final, contextless sense. However, in the project *to understand the curriculum*, phenomenology and post-structuralism play interesting, important, and controversial roles. This collection of essays composed by leading phenomenological and post-structuralist scholars portrays these roles.

The phenomenological voice of the distinguished T. Tetsus Aoki opens the collection, a voice quietly questioning the meaning of teaching. Here the emphasis is upon the teaching as lived, as experienced prior to the conceptualizations layed over raw experience as parking lots over organic soil. The method is storytelling, stories which act as passages (in Daugnault's sense) to a more primal, authentic sense of teaching as lived. The phenomenological method thematizes that lived experience revealed in story, and Aoki identifies teaching as watchfulness and teaching as thoughtfulness. These phenomenological truths are a far cry from microbehaviors observers can presumably identify in any lesson anytime, anywhere. The truth and competence of teaching resides in phenomenological wisdom, not imitation of preestablished behaviors. In Aoki we hear the voices of teachers as human beings. Aoki's voice is at once powerful and beautiful.

From phenomenological voice we move to explication, creating another order of passage, this time back from primal, preconceptual experience to the universe of learned, logical scholarship. Grumet's essay explains phenomenology to those whose epistemological commitments require resistance to notions of the "lived." Even so, the phenomenological voice is strong and melodious in this cogent argument. Characteristically Grumet achieves a "middle way," linking the silence of the antepredicative with the language of academic argument. As she notes: "the path . . . leads us inward, to individual experience, and outward, to metatheory." The supreme pedagogue, Grumet illustrates as she explains, welcoming the initiate as she reasons with the experienced. Nearly twenty years ago Grumet and Pinar slipped from phenomenology to autobiography, as self-report seemed an obvious means to retrieve phenomenological experience educationally. The reasons why, as well as those reasons why phenomenology remains an integral element of her curriculum theory, become evident in Chapter 2.

Robert Brown usefully reviews the work of Max van Manen, editor of *Phenomenology + Pedagogy,* phenomenologist par excellance. He traces the origins of van Manen's phenomenology in the Utrecht School. Brown identifies the following themes in van Manen's opus: the pursuit of everydayness, the discovery of the primordial, his critique of mainstream instructional theory and practice (including the mainstream misunderstanding of theory), pedagogic tact, and the centrality of the child. With the assistance of van Manen, Brown has usefully summarized and reviewed the enormous contribution of Max van Manen to understanding curriculum and pedagogy as phenomenological texts.

A significant theme in the phenomenological tradition is that of time. In Chapter 4 Margaret Hunsberger carefully describes "the time of texts." She begins by criticizing mainstream conceptions of time as "segmented, invariant, and linear." She points out that this school time does not necessarily depict our experience of time as lived. To illustrate the experience of time while reading, Hunsberger conversed with readers. Via conversation she describes "entering the world of the text," including what she typifies as the habit of reading. In addition to attending to the reader's experience, Hunsberger describes "time in the text itself." Finally, Hunsberger sets phenomenological time in not-time, recalling Heider's (1965, p. 28) poem:

> Wild geese, suspended
> Float in mid-air stillness, thus
> Time rests in not-time.

Hunsberger concludes: "Reading gives us an opportunity to experience time in various ways, to start difficult but significant thinking, to glimpse not-time, and to stretch our imaginative limits." Hunsberger's essay deftly illustrates a phenomenological understanding of an activity only recently conceived by the school community as a "whole" endeavor, not technical decoding.

After leaving phenomenology proper for autobiography almost twenty years ago, I (Pinar) rediscovered the power of phenomenology during the 1980s. I suppose it was my regular visits with the University of Alberta faculty and students that reminded me of the power and potential beauty of a phenomenological voice. Like time, death has been a major phenomenological theme, and my father's death in 1988 forced an encounter, about which you can read in Chapter 5.

Terrance Carson's essay illustrates how phenomenology construes action research as research on fundamental pedagogical issues. As well, the essay nicely illustrates how phenomenology might convey a political agenda, as he employs phenomenology to advance the cause of peace education. The questions Carson poses of the peace education group (CARPE) are indeed phenomenological questions:

1. How can we discover hope after all?
2. What to do when the global encounters the local?
3. What is a project anyway?
4. What is a community?

Understood phenomenologically, Carson characterizes action research as a hermeneutics of practice. Such research, and peace education in particular, are said to "awaken us to a deeper layer of experience—how we live authentically with our colleagues and students."

Hermeneutical method is evident in David Jardine's superb essay. After David Smith, Jardine posits as a central educational question: "How are we to respond to new life in our midst in such a way that life together can go on, in a way that does not foreclose on the future?" Radical hermeneutics is about this process, Jardine tells us; its task is "to bring forth the presuppositions in which we already live." Clear here is the phenomenological view that we live prior to language in a preconceptual substratum. The project of radical hermeneutics, according to Jardine, is to "re-collect the contours and textures of the life we are already living." He relies on Gadamer, Heidegger, Caputo, and Nietzsche in his movement toward an authentic conversation between young and old. In the modern world of technical manipulation, Jardine tells us, "life becomes haunted by an unnamed grieving for what is lost." What is lost, he suggests, is the opportunity "to actually *face* the troublesome character of life . . . in such a way that new life, liveliness, some 'movement' might be possible." For Jardine "life dwells in an original difficulty," and efforts—for instance, at mastery—only mask this fundamental truth and lead to either immobility or exhaustion. Dwelling in difficulty, in "the inner tension between illumination and concealment," there is a possibility of authentic understanding. "Hermeneutically conceived, the task of inquiry is not to dispel this tension, but to live and speak from within it." David Jardine achieves this sense of tension, difficulty, and lifefulness in this essay, and in so doing he occupies, we believe, a space on the edge of phenomenology, toward post-structuralism, to which—in Section II—we turn next.

Rebecca Martusewicz opens the post-structuralism section with her succinct and accessible review of post-structuralism and, in particular, French feminist post-structuralism. Her question—what does it mean to be an educated woman?—is a phenomenological question, but in seeking an answer she turns to post-structuralism. As noted earlier, French philosophy also turned from phenomenology to post-structuralism.

Martusewicz begins with a brief review of structuralism, including selected concepts associated with Sassure, Levi-Strauss, Barthes (like other structuralists, also considered post-structuralists), and the early Foucault. From structuralism she moves to Lacanian and Derridean post-structuralism, setting the stage for her discussion of post-structuralist feminism. Reviewing Cixous, Irigarary, and Kristeva, Martusewicz describes the effort to reclaim "woman" from male discourse and locate her in desire and difference. The "feminine" is not the reverse of "masculine"; indeed, post-structurally it represents a denial of the concept of identity (a phallic principle) and the assertion of a multiple, indeterminate female subject. As well, Martusewicz reviews criticism of post-structuralist feminism, that is, the concern over essentialism. From feminism Martusewicz moves to Foucault, particularly feminist analyses of Foucault's understanding of knowledge and gender. From Foucault she moves to Walkerdine, Gore, and Lesko, illustrating the impact of post-structuralism upon the study of education and gender. She concludes this accessible introduction to post-structuralism by answering her opening question: "[T]o live as feminist educators is to live a tension between a critical theoretical space and an affirmative political space. It is within this in-between, this 'elsewhere,' that we must seek the educated woman."

jan jagodzinski's essay exemplifies several post-structuralist characteristics, including imagistic reorderings of words intended to challenge taken-for-granted decodings. For instance, jagodzinski employs lower case letters to spell his name and to refer to himself ("i"), spells woman "wo(man)" to indicate man's origin in the womb, uses the word "Gaia" for earth to indicate that the planet is a living entity. jagodzinski explains these usages in the beginning pages of his essay, before identifying what he characterizes as six layers of aesthetically embodied skin. These are (1) line, (2) color, (3) texture, (4) size, (5) mass, and (6) space. He suggests that a radical restructuring of the curriculum might support the dismantling of male dominance and technical rationality via these six aesthetic layers. jagodizinski's dazzling essay carries the reader into a post-structuralist universe in which reality is discursive.

The concept of action research that Terrance Carson interpreted phenomenologically and hermeneutically is cogently analyzed in post-structuralist fashion by Clermont Gauthier. The English translation still carries echoes of the original French, echoes which suggest the in-between. Gauthier lays out issues of theory, practice, and research in logical fashion, but it is a logic transported from a translogical, post-structuralist space. Several of Gauthier's statements regarding action research illustrate this: "there are only theoretical problems," "[action research] can take place anywhere: in one's office, in one's mind," "action research is above all a matter of language." Like crystal and smoke, Gauthier's analysis is symmetrical and hierarchical while simultaneously being unstable, asymmetrical, and uncontrollable.

Jacques Daignault reflects on traces at work in several senses: traces of Serres, Deleuze, Foucault, Rousseau, Nietzsche, Plato, among others, in his understanding of curriculum as passage. There are other traces as well: his life in schools, the music of Steve Reich, a lost "t" in France, which travels the Atlantic to appear in his published dissertation, an arbitrary event, it would seem, but one which provides a multiplicity of new meanings. More than that of any scholar, Daignault's writing illustrates the "method" and themes of post-structuralism: the anagrams; the echoes and traces from one modality (the body) to another (the mind); themes hitherto unknown to educators, such as fissures, flashes, intensities. From "ad" to "id," Daignault mythologizes "wounds" and healing.

We live, Daignault says, in a flattened world in which our insistence on accuracy destroys fantasy and pleasure. Knowing in this definitive sense represents a kind of death, as it forecloses possibility, playfulness, movement. Our efforts to know are like hunts ("guess what am I thinking? what is the right answer?") in which the prey is killed. "To know is to put to death—to kill the lamb, deep in the woods, in order to eat it." Daignault quotes Serres approvingly and adds: "To know is to kill. . . . Thinking is still alive." What is thinking? Daignault comprehends it as "the in-between," the mediation between suicide and murder. (Virginia Woolf once commented that there are no deaths, only murders and suicides.) The insistence on making reality conform to expectation (objective) leads to terrorism, to murder, as the subjectivity, the fiction of the other, is eradicated. To give up, to turn one's ideals into empty fictions, to have no hope for the world is nihilism. "The passage is really hazardous. . . . I am in danger." To live with hope, yet with respect for what is, requires a complexity of thought Steve Reich's music suggests. Sometimes cacophonous, sometimes melodious, such thought fills up the space between terrorism and nihilism, affirming the complexity of being human, extending our capacity to keep on, to not give up, to love ourselves. "The soul can dress . . . his wounds, benefit from a rest." That of which Daignault speaks cannot be understood in a narrow cognitive sense of decoding. It requires a passage, a translation from this life to another, a movement that he characterizes as curriculum. There is no guarantee of success, even with an event that has a high "passage value." Further: "Curriculum translation is always plural: WAYS; neither definite nor indefinite."

There is humor as well as complexity in Daignault's essay. For those readers for whom post-structuralism is unfamiliar, Daignault's essay will be inaccessible, at least at first reading. Persevere. And chuckle. Education is crossing frontiers, Daignault reminds us; it is not filling the attic with useless possessions, ideas we smugly know are "accurate." As Daignault writes: "An obsession with relating images to their sensible or thought objects, as one would relate a copy to its model, becomes the symptom of an unhappy consciousness that is the victim of a disordered soul—which is the real cause of evil": the terrorist, the nihilist. "Producing sense and enjoying it provide the antidote." Daignault's work, of which the present essay itself is a trace, is such a sensuous text, an invisible skin of the body. Daignault reflects: "I am writing at Nietzsche's dictation: to translate life in joyful wisdom, gay knowledge. Thinking, maybe."

The collection concludes with Peter Taubman's achievement of the right distance. He sketches the distance between teacher and student, teacher and colleague, identity and intention. Relying on Lacan, working autobiographically, Taubman deftly details the experience of coming to teach. The self-identification of oneself as teacher encounters the public conferral of identity. Taubman writes: "The loose identity of teacher formed in the mirror and coalescing conscious and unconscious experience could emerge at the institutional level as castrated. . . . The price for power and control as well as a public identity—castration." The self-relation becomes submerged in the public sphere of the school, repressed but not gone. Accessibly Taubman lays out the dynamics of identity, teaching, and learning, including the teacher's mastery of his or her field. Taubman writes: "To compensate for the unconscious and forever unsatisfied need, the student, knowledge, and the privileged position as the one who knows are substituted. . . . The desire to be, to know, to have is an unending desire that works in the direction of increasing distance between teacher and student." Intimacy with students would require dissolution of identity. Either pole—estrangement or intimacy—is inappropriate. Taubman returns to the question of the right distance, suggesting that it "lies in the middle, at the midpoint." The concept of midpoint he then locates as between Plato and Lacan; the teacher who occupies it "teaches the subject to recognize his own méconnaissance (misrecognition)." Such a teacher—Taubman characterizes him or her as midwife—subverts his or her position as the master, as the one who knows; he or she "assumes an identity that is at a crossroads." At the intersection, he suggests, teacher and student might meet.

REFERENCES

Apple, M. W. (1988). The culture and commerce of the textbook. In W. F. Pinar (Ed.), *Contemporary curriculum discourses* (pp. 223–242). Scottsdale, AZ: Gorsuch, Scarisbrick.

Bernstein, R. (1976). *Restructuring of social and political theory.* New York: Harcourt Brace Jovanovich.

Brodriff, S. (1988). *Nothing matters: A critique of post-structuralism's epistemology.* Unpublished doctoral dissertation, University of Toronto.

Caputo, J. D. (1987). *Radical hermeneutics: Repetition, deconstruction and the hermeneutic project.* Bloomington: Indiana University Press.

Clandinin, D. J., & Connelly, F. M. (1990). Stories experience and narrative inquiry. *Educational Researcher, 19*(4), pp. 2–14.

Derrida, J. (1981). *Positions.* Chicago: University of Chicago Press.

Descombes, V. (1980). *Modern French philosophy.* New York: Cambridge University Press.

Eisner, E. (1979, 1985). *The educational imagination.* New York: Macmillan.

Foucault, M. (1973). *Madness and civilization.* New York: Vintage.

Foucault, M. (1979). *Discipline and punish.* New York: Vintage.

Foucault, M. (1980a). *Power/knowledge.* New York: Pantheon.

Foucault, M. (1980b). *The history of sexuality* (Vol. 1). Ithaca, NY: Cornell University Press.

Giroux, H. (1988). Liberal arts, teaching, and critical literacy: Toward a definition of school as a form of cultural politics. In W. F. Pinar (Ed.), *Contemporary curriculum discourses* (pp. 243–263). Scottsdale, AZ: Gorsuch, Scarisbrick

Greene, M. (1975). Curriculum and consciousness. In W. F. Pinar (Ed.), *Curriculum theorizing: The reconceptualists* (pp. 299–320). Berkeley: McCutchan.

Grumet, M. (1988). Bodyreading. In W. F. Pinar (Ed.), *Contemporary curriculum discourses* (pp. 453–474). Scottsdale, AZ: Gorsuch, Scarisbrick.

Heider, W. (1965). Not time. In P. Dover (Ed.), *Poetry—An anthology for high schools.* Toronto: Holt, Rinehart & Winston.

Huebner, D. (1975). Curriculum as concern for man's temporality. In W. F. Pinar (Ed.), *Curriculum theorizing: The reconceptualists* (pp. 237–249). Berkeley: McCutchan.

Lacan, J. (1977). *Ecrits: A selection.* London: Tavistock.

Megill, A. (1985). *Prophets of extremity.* Berkeley: University of California Press.

Merleau-Ponty, M. (1962). *Phenomenology of perception.* London: Routledge & Kegan Paul.

Merleau-Ponty, M. (1964). *Signs.* Evanston, IL: Northwestern University Press.

Pinar, W. F. (1980a). The voyage out: Curriculum as the relation between the knower and the known. *The Journal of Curriculum Theorizing, 2*(1), 72–91.

Pinar, W. F. (1980b, 1981). Life history and educational experience, parts one and two. *The Journal of Curriculum Theorizing, 2*(2), 159–212; *3*(1), 259–286.

Pinar, W. F. (1987). ". . . Unwanted strangers in our own homeland": notes on the work of T. Aoki. *The Journal of Curriculum Theorizing, 7*(3), 11–20.

Pinar, W. F. (1988). Autobiography and the architecture of self. *The Journal of Curriculum Theorizing, 8*(1), 7–36.

Pinar, W. F., & Grumet, M. (1976). *Toward a poor curriculum.* Dubuque, IA: Kendall/Hunt.

Taubman, P. (1982). Gender and curriculum: Discourse and the politics of sexuality. *The Journal of Curriculum Theorizing, 4*(1), 12–87.

van Manen, M. (1988). The relation between research and pedagogy. In W. F. Pinar (Ed.), *Contemporary curriculum discourses* (pp. 437–452). Scottsdale, AZ: Gorsuch, Scarisbrick.

Wexler, P. (1987). *Social analysis of education: After the new sociology.* New York: Routledge & Kegan Paul.

Part I

UNDERSTANDING CURRICULUM AS PHENOMENOLOGICAL TEXT

CHAPTER 1

Layered Voices of Teaching
The Uncannily Correct and the Elusively True

T. TETSUO AOKI

I have been asking myself twice, three times, and more, "What authorizes me to speak to educators of teaching?"

Could it be that with over forty years of teaching I have become preoccupied with so many answers to the question "What is teaching?" that I have forgotten to question my own understandings of the question itself?

Could it be that in the years of questioning that accompanied my experiences of teaching, I have come to an understanding not so much of what teaching is, but rather what teaching is not? Could it be that this sort of understanding—a negative understanding—is a stage on the way to an understanding of what teaching is? Is this the sort of understanding that allows us to begin to see the uncannily correct but not yet true?

Or could it be that in my questioning, I have become more sensitive to the seductive hold of the scientific, technological ethos that enframes education, and thereby our understandings of teaching? And could it be that because of this sensitivity, I have come to seek a way to be more properly attuned, not only to see but also to hear more deeply and fully the silent call of our vocation, teaching?

LAYERS OF UNDERSTANDING

In our busy world of education, we are surrounded by layers of voices, some loud, some shrill, that claim to know what teaching is. Awed, perhaps, by the cacophony of voices, certain voices became silent and, hesitating to reveal themselves, conceal themselves. Let us beckon these voices to speak to

An early version of this article was presented as an address on the occasion of the "Program For Quality Teaching," a teacher self-development project sponsored in 1987 by the British Columbia Teachers' Federation, Canada.

us, particularly the silent ones, so that we may awaken to the truer sense of teaching that likely stirs within each of us.

Before we visit the place where the silent voices dwell, let us try to uncover layer by layer—three layers—from the surface to the place where teaching truly dwells.

The Outermost Layer: Understanding Teaching as a Black Box

Some of us can remember the days when researchers shied away from the live and complex world of the classroom. These researchers were primarily interested in the outcomes of teaching rather than in the understanding of teaching itself. Likening the school to a factory or a knowledge industry, they assumed that what counts are effects and results in terms of the investments made. Hence, they typically cast their studies into a before-and-after design, concealing the domain of teaching in a black box, nonessential for research purposes, and thereby willfully ignoring the lived world of teachers and students.

Even today the black box image persists, characterized by the yearly visits to schools by assessors—usually measurement experts who style themselves in the language of psychometrics—who seem to revel in their technicized vocation. They heed the call of the instrumental rules of tests and measurements but ignore the call of teachers and students who dwell within the crucible of their own concretely lived situations. Without these voices we lack the understanding of meaning.

I feel that this kind of willful ignoring reflects the hold of an attunement in life, including school life, governed by goals and objectives, and consequently by measures of successful achievement.

In this black box view of teaching, what I resent is the way in which, by ignoring the lives of teachers and students, they are cast into nothingness. That which I consider to be most vital is de-vitalized into nonexistent darkness. For me, the black box reflects a frightening ignorance of so-called educational assessors and researchers, who, as assessors and researchers, are forgetful that they are not merely researchers, but educational researchers. They forget the adjective. And by being forgetful, they deny the humanness that lies at the core of what education is.

We are less naive today. But still we see about us efforts that place teaching in a gray box, if not a black box, wherein teachers are mere facilitators to teaching built into programmed learning packages. These are teacher-proof packages wherein the preference is for noncontamination by teachers' presence. This is akin to a technological understanding of teaching whose logical outcome is the robotization of teaching: schools in the image of Japanese automobile factories—heaven forbid!

The Middle Layer: Understanding Teaching Theoretically and Scientifically

In recent years we have had a surge of interest in expounding what teaching is. Books such as *Life in Classrooms* by Philip Jackson (1972) gave legitimacy to scholars to move daringly into the black box to make sense of the happenings there. Many psychologists, sociologists, anthropologists, and the like have approached the question of what teaching is from their own favored perspectives. Often the psychologists are oriented toward understanding teaching behavior, the sociologists toward understanding the roles of teachers, and the anthropologists toward an understanding of teaching as human activity. In disciplined ways they have attempted to offer complex portrayals, even models, of what teaching is. In so doing they have imposed upon the lived situations of teachers and students abstract, preset categories of their disciplines. Thus a psychological understanding of teaching is popularly framed within the psychological concepts of motivation, reinforcement, retention, and transfer. These are, incidentally, the titles of a monograph series on teaching by Madeleine Hunter (1982). An understanding of teaching framed within the sociopsychological concepts has given birth to a whole array of interaction analysis systems, founded by Ned Flanders (1960); a sociological understanding of teaching based on role analysis often sees teaching in terms of the roles of classroom management, lesson planning, classroom discipline, surrogate parenting, mediating knowledge, and so on, popular themes that occupy a large terrain of the teacher education curriculum and instruction syllabi. An anthropological understanding of teaching frequently sees teaching as cultural activity, enthographically understandable.

As such, all of these are knowledge formulations of behavior, roles, and activities that provide some understanding of human doings: observable, measurable, and within the grasp of reasoned control. They present, indeed, a seductively scholarly and intellectual quality and legitimacy that makes the understanding of teaching uncannily correct. But we must remember that these portrayals, although correct, although illuminative, are all distanced seeing in the images of abstract conceptual schemes that are idealizations, somewhat removed, missing the preconceptual, pretheoretical fleshy, familiar, very concrete world of teachers and students.

The Innermost Layer: Understanding Teaching Techniques, Strategies, and Skills

This understanding of teaching is of special interest to us because it is taken-for-granted hereabouts, popularized in the language of "teaching competence" and "effective teaching."

The notion of "effective teaching" flows from the behavioristic theories of motivation, retention, and the like, transformed into the language of teaching as doing. Within it is the admission that the psychological concept of learning behavior is central and that teaching is the flip side of learning. A proponent of this view, Madeleine Hunter, revealingly states that decisions based on learning theory are decisions of how to teach.

That is quite a sweeping statement to make. The notion of effectiveness that she presents has a sense of practical urgency about it that teachers readily recognize. It is no doubt a word that reminds us that teaching is a deeply practical vocation, that our predicament as teachers is a very pragmatic one.

In the first flush of thought, the notion of effectiveness has a seductive appeal of essential simplicity that suggests the possibility of a focus that can be grasped. It suggests, too, that effectiveness is mainly a matter of skill and technique, and that if I can but identify the components of effective teaching and if, with some concentrated effort, I can but identify the skills, maybe in a three- or four-day workshop, my teaching can become readily effective.

REORIENTING THE SEARCH FOR THE ESSENCE OF TEACHING

All of these scientific and technical understandings of teaching emerge from our interest in intellectual and manipulative grasp and control. But in so understanding, we must be attuned to the fact that while those under-standings that can be grasped are uncannily correct, the essence of teaching still eludes our grasp. What we need to do is to break away from the attitude of grasping and seek to be more properly oriented to what teaching is, so we can attune ourselves to the call of what teaching is. And so, we set aside these layers that press upon us and move to in-dwell in the earthy place where we experience daily life with our colleagues and students, and begin our search for the "isness" of teaching, for the being of teaching. This search calls for a break away from the orientation that may blind us. But what is it to experience a break?

When we are writing and the pencil breaks, suddenly the content of our writing disappears and goes into hiding, and the pencil that we really did not see before comes out of hiding to reveal itself to us. What we see here is how the experience of breaking can help us in breaking out of the seductive hold of an orientation to which we are beholden. I wish to offer short narratives—stories—that point to, more than they tell, what it means to be oriented in a way that allows the essence of teaching to reveal itself to us. I say this because prosaic words are often inappropriate when describing certain phenomena. I find it so when I try, as I am doing here, to talk *about* the essence of teaching. All I can do is point, hoping that the pointing will help us to begin to allow ourselves to hear the voice of the essence of teaching that lurks concealed, but nevertheless calls upon us.

But before I tell the stories, allow me to try to re-understand the question that is holding our attention. I now return to our original question: What is teaching? To this point I have been guided by the question *"What* is *teaching?"* (with the whatness of teaching emphasized). This is the typical way in which most of us understand the question. The question so understood beckoned me to focus on the "whatness" of teaching and yielded to us an understanding of teaching as a black box; as psychological, sociological, anthropological conceptions; and as modes of doing. I wish to ask the same question differently, unavoidably making it a different question. I ask: What *is* teaching? (emphasizing "is").

This new question asks that I reorient myself, that I break from my usual orientation to the question and seek that which not only offers me a different orientation but draws me to a deeper level, a level that allows the essence of teaching to speak to me. With this new question, I feel much more oriented, I hope more properly oriented, to be in the presence of the beingness of teaching.

So placed, I may be allowed to hear better the voice of what teaching essentially is. The question understood in this way urges me to be attuned to a teacher's presence with children. This presence, if authentic, is being. I find that teaching so understood is attuned to the place where care dwells, a place of ingathering and belonging, where the in-dwelling of teachers and students is made possible by the presence of care that each has for the other.

A notion of pedagogy might be helpful here. Pedagogy means, in the original Greek sense, leading children. Teaching is truly pedagogic if the leading grows out of this care that inevitably is filled with the good of care. Teaching, then, is a tactful leading that knows and follows the pedagogic good in a caring situation.

The narratives that follow are meant to point to rather than to describe what teaching more truly is. But this pointing is more an allowing of a concretely lived place to speak to us—a disclosure that allows us a glimmer of the essence of teaching.

Narrative One: A Look That Hears

To help further our effort to reorient ourselves properly, let me tell a story my mother told me years ago. I title it "A Look That Hears."

IN FEUDAL JAPAN there lived a monk, famed for his temple garden of morning glories, and a lord at a nearby castle. The lord, upon hearing of the bountifulness and beauty of the garden, sent forth to the temple a message that on the day following the full moon, he would arrive in early morn to view the garden.

On that appointed day, the monk, upon early rising, went directly to the garden and plucked all the morning glories but one. When the lord arrived, the monk guided him to the garden, fresh-laden with morning dew, beckoning him to savor to the fullest what his eyes could behold.

The mass of foliage denuded of the multitude of flowers he had imaged beckoned the lord to break the silence to ask of the monk, "Where are the morning glories for which you have gained renown?"

The monk, gesturing to the lord to savor the lone flower, said softly, so as not to tread upon the silence unduly, "My lord, if you but allow the morning glory to speak, the flower will disclose to you the essence of the being of the morning glory that it is."

The lord paused, allowing his eyes to rest upon the flower, and listened with care to the speaking of the morning glory. Then he turned to the monk, bowed a little more deeply than a lord typically is wont to bow, and said quietly, "I know better now what it is to hear when I look." With that he left, upon his lips a faint smile.

In a true sense, our monk was a pedagogue, a person who leads. He asked his lord to push aside the seductive hold of those understandings that claim correctness and to approach with bowed humility, with an attitude of surrender, the sound of the voice that calls. What yielded to him was a deep seeing into, an insight, that if he is properly oriented and if he listens carefully—that is, a listening filled with care, the care that brought the lord and flower together—understanding will be granted to him.

The monk as pedagogue taught the lord, a leader of men, what it is to lead—that in a world of beings, to lead is to hearken and to follow the voice of the *logos;* that he who cannot follow the voice of *logos* is not an authentic leader; and that what authorizes him to be a leader is not so much the title or position, but rather his attunement to the care that silently dwells.

Narrative Two: Christa McAuliffe—She is the Teaching

January 28, 1986: the breakdown of the *Challenger.* All of us experienced shock, sorrow, and deep pain. The whole world mourned.

We lost Christa McAuliffe, a teacher and colleague.

In death, life?

I feel personally touched by Christa McAuliffe, whose absence speaks to me with a strong presence of what her teaching essentially was and is.

This social studies teacher, who ventured forth on what is typically understood as a scientific mission, cared about how science and technology, held in objective regard, should be more fully understood in the context of the beingness of humans. Hers was a teacher's hope to break away from the bonds of the technological perspective and to offer to our children and youth a reoriented vision.

But this re-oriented seeing was not so much geared to a seeing of the earth from the perspective of space, although that was a part of her mission, but one more oriented to a deeper sense of seeing. In this regard, we recall her thoughtful words uttered with care, "I want to humanize the technology of the space age." That is what she said.

She planned to do this not so much by observing from high above what she would see below, but by writing in a journal her experiences of what it might mean for her as a human being to be involved in a technological venture. She, indeed, wanted to understand how human beings are embedded in human beingness. Her interest, and this is my interpretation, was to listen to what her writing might say, to listen therein to the voice that called upon her as teacher and as ordinary citizen. She had hoped to seek a deeper understanding of what it means to be beholden to science and technology.

A cruel accident has taken the life of a fellow teacher, but I am sure she is even now very much present in all of us, touching the inner soul and being of each of us. I am convinced that this kind of touching comes from the deep care people have for the teachers in whose trust they place their young. What speaks here in the truest sense is the truest sense of being pedagogues, the being of those who in leading the young abide by the *logos* of care that tells us what is pedagogically good in our relationship with children.

Christa McAuliffe helped me to see a glimmer of the essence of teaching, of what it means to be attuned to the call of care that is present in every authentic pedagogic situation.

Narrative Three: June's Story and Two Pedagogical Themes

The third narrative begins with the story of a bewildered child, as June Aoki recalls a break in the dailiness of her school life as a junior high school student. Drawn into the story, I linger on two themes: pedagogical watchfulness and pedagogical thoughtfulness. Here, then, is June's story: "A Re-Meeting with Mr. McNab, My Grade 7 Teacher."

IT WAS A CLOUDY DAY in early April, 1942. I was thirteen then, going on fourteen, in Grade 7 at Fanny Bay School, a two-room school about forty miles from Nanaimo in British Columbia.

It was a bewildering day for many of us. Our Japanese Language School had already been ordered closed by the Ministry of Education. My father had already been sent to a road camp near Blue River in the far off wilds of the

Rockies. We had been hearing rumors that we were to be moved, first to Vancouver, then somewhere to the interior of British Columbia and possibly beyond. We had been trying not to believe Charlie Tweedie who told my brother, Tim, that all the Japanese would be herded en masse to Hastings Park, and who had said, teasingly perhaps, "That way only one bomb will do it!"

On this day in April, I went to school solely for the purpose of leaving school. As soon as school began, we cleaned out our desks, returned texts that belonged to the school, gathered our books and belongings while our Occidental school mates silently watched our movements. With our arms full, we left our classroom, taking footsteps that seemd to know that these might be the last, at least in this classroom. Cautiously, we moved step by step down two flights of stairs and wended our way along the worn path of the school playground, homeward bound.

The leaving this day was different from our usual taking leave at the end of the school's day. Somehow I felt I was leaving a place to which, like home, I belonged. Why was it that my usually happy feet had no skip to them? I guess we were experiencing emptiness in leaving behind what had become so much a part of our everyday existence. As I walked, I felt the school's tug and this walking home was like hands that slip away in parting, knowing not what to say in a silent farewell.

I was about to leave the school yard. Something called upon me to turn around for a last look. On the balcony of the school stood my teacher Mr. McNab, alone, watching us as if to keep guard over us in our departure.

I almost felt I did wrong in stealing a look, so without a wave of good-bye, I resumed my walk homeward. I wondered, "What is Mr. McNab thinking right now?"

I cannot really recall my other teachers in all the years of my schooling which began in Fanny Bay. But Mr. McNab, I remember. He was the one I recall. He was the teacher who urged us in school to display our Japanese kimonos and to perform some "odori" to Japanese music. He was the one who on the annual district sports day insisted on taking all the students, the athletic and the not so athletic, breaking with the tradition of sports days for elite athletes. For us, the event was something special. It mattered little whether we won or lost. All of us were grateful that Mr. McNab took us— swift ones and slow ones, dumpy ones and lean ones, tall ones and short ones.

Recently, we returned to the Coast, in a way a touching again the earth and water we once knew. Coming home, I wondered if by chance I could make contact with Mr. McNab, of whom I had heard not a thing over more than four decades.

Through the British Columbia Teachers Federation offices we learned that William McNab, a retired teacher, lived in North Vancouver. I felt a stirring in my heart. I phoned him. Most graciously he listened to my story.

For him it must have been puzzling after forty-four years to sort me out from a mountain of memories of hundreds and thousands of students who called him "teacher." But he was my Mr. McNab, my teacher.

He kindly visited us. I experienced a deep inward joy of thanks when my hand grasped the hand of the man [who] silently watched over us as we left his school that April day forty-four years ago. I felt he did not know that over all those years the memory of his watching stayed vividly with me. For me, the singular moment reflected his being as teacher.

I told Mr. McNab how over forty-four years, I often recalled the image of his watchfulness clothed in care. Mustering courage, I asked him if he remembered the moment. There was a moment of silence. Then he simply said, "That was a sad day." That was all he would say. The rest he left unsaid. But I felt that in the silence he said much.

I felt blessed being allowed after forty-four years ago to be in the presence of a teacher whose quiet but thoughtful gesture had touched me deeply. Today I feel doubly blessed being allowed to re-live the fullness of the moment in the re-gained presence of Mr. McNab.

What deeper seeing into, what deeper hearing of teaching does this story allow? I wish to dwell upon two themes that speak to what teaching is: pedagogical watchfulness and pedagogical thoughtfulness.

Theme 1: Pedagogical Watchfulness. What is the voice of teaching that this story speaks? Surely it is more than a nostalgic remembrance of a past. Surely it is more, much more than a recording of a minor historical event in the lives of a teacher and a few students.

Why is this particular story of a single moment worth a re-marking? Could it be that that which is re-markable is the in-dwelling presence of the shimmering being of teaching that is open to those whose listening is attuned aright?

How shall we understand the voice of Mr. McNab's teaching? Could it be that it is not so much what he did—"watch"—but more so the person he was as he watched?

We might see a glimmer of the person he was as teacher if we listen with care to his "watching." His watching was not so much watching as observing, a looking *at* that which is apart from his self, although in part it was, as he watched the students wind homeward. It was a watching that was watchfulness—a watchfulness filled with a teacher's hope that wherever his students may be, wherever they may wander on this earth away from his presence, they are well and no harm will visit them.

Teachers understand the meaning of the presence of absence growing out of their own experiences of watchfulness. Teachers know that pupils come to them clothed in a bond of parental trust, and parents know that they, in entrusting their children to teachers, can count on the watchful eyes of teachers. So, too, teachers know that at the end of the year, they and their students will part, the students to the next grade or to another school. Yet it is their very leaving that allows them the possibility to return—a turning again to the experiences of the present. And the teachers know that watching the students depart at the end of the year is a watchfulness that is filled with the hope that wherever they may be the students will do well and be well, and no harm will befall them.

Authentic teaching is watchfulness, a mindful watching overflowing from the good in the situation that the good teacher sees. In this sense, good teachers are more than they do; they are the teaching. When McNab watched, he was the teaching. No less, no more.

Theme 2: Pedagogical Thoughtfulness.   Let us recall the question put to Mr. McNab: "What were you thinking when you watched us leave?"

June's story speaks also to thinking that was a part of Mr. McNab's watchfulness. But it speaks not of the form of thinking that holds sway in most quarters wherein educators and noneducators dwell—the form of thinking that has kindred modality to what we call rational thinking, logical thinking, or critical thinking, although in part it is. Thinking typically understood in our Western tradition has a seductively intellectual ring to it. As some psychologists tell us, the bulk of the behavior we call thinking is cerebral, all in the head above the neck, as it were, holding in lower regard anything below the neck as being secondary attachments. As analytical philosophers tell us, there is a logic in reason that makes thinking a reasoned forward movement, so that with every click of the synapse, we can hammer out a linear path to a logical conclusion.

"Thinking" so understood is so familiar to us that when we say "thinking," we can think no other thought about thinking but that. In fact, we tacitly subscribe to this understanding of thinking such that we forget that we have been seduced into having a love affair with such an understanding. And in the blindness that usually accompanies such affairs, we fail to see other possibilities of understanding "thinking."

What seems to be concealed and hence unseen and unheard is an understanding of thinking that might be understood as thoughtfulness—thoughtfulness as an embodied doing and being—thought and soul embodied in the oneness of the lived moment.

When Mr. McNab watched his students leave, his watching was a watching with thoughtfulness—a thoughtfulness that spoke silently from deep within, a thoughtfulness that reached out without gesture or motion, a thoughtfulness filled with both hope and sadness: hope for the well-being of the departing student, and sadness that he must now live in the empty presence of his students' absence.

Although he had become attuned to the annual departure of his students at the end of the school year, the departure of these students at midyear must have been for him a different experience. As a teacher, it is likely that for some time he was caught in this living difference, experienced the solitude, and was left alone to make sense of this unwilled break-up that happened in his classroom.

So why was it, when remembering a moment of forty-four years ago, our teacher Mr. McNab merely said, "that was a sad day?"

A LINGERING NOTE

In the foregoing I have attempted to unfold layers of understandings about teaching. I began with an understanding wherein teaching is hidden, willfully ignored, in the dark recesses of the black box.

In the unfolding we explored teaching understood as behavior, as role, as human activity, wherein disciplined abstractions of teaching hold sway, somewhat forgetful of the lived world of teachers and students that was the source of their interest in the first place. We explored, too, understandings of teaching that flow out as applied versions of these abstractions. We noted also the seductive appeal of these understandings—of suggestions of simplicity and pragmatic usefulness—all uncannily correct.

I have suggested that what seems urgent for us at this time in understanding what teaching more truly is, is to undertake to reorient ourselves so that we overcome mere correctness so that we can see and hear our doings as teachers harbored within pedagogical being, so we can see and hear who we *are* as teachers.

I ask you now to think of a really good teacher that you have experienced in your time. Allow him or her to be present before you. I believe that the truth of this good teacher of yours is in the measure of the immeasurable. And, now, say to him or her: he *is* the teaching; she *is* the teaching. And after you have said these words, allow the unsaid to shine through the said. Savor now the elusively true, the mystery of what teaching essentially is.

REFERENCES

Flanders, N. A. (1960). *Interaction analysis in the classroom: A manual for observation.* Minneapolis: University of Minnesota Press.
Hunter, M. (1982). *Mastery teaching.* El Segundo, CA: TIP Publication.
Jackson, P. (1972). *Life in classrooms.* NY: Holt, Rinehart and Winston.

CHAPTER 2

Existential and Phenomenological Foundations of Autobiographical Methods

MADELEINE R. GRUMET

Written in the 1970s, this essay was originally published in Toward a Poor Curriculum, *a collection of essays that William Pinar and I wrote to explore and justify
autobiographical accounts of educational experiences as resources for educational
research and theory. Challenging the prevalence of quantitative methods of inquiry
in education, we explicated the humanities traditions of philosophy and literature
that used narrative to order as well as express experience. Our emphasis then, in
contrast to the anonymity and standardization of the quantitative research model,
was on the biography of the individual writer, on the adequacy of everyday experience as a context for knowledge, and on the capacity of the narrative form to contain
and convey the character of educational experience. The tension that exists between
phenomenological and existential approaches discussed in this essay is one that continues to run through any project related to autobiographical method. Making sense
of our stories summons us to address their contradictions: the intimacy of self-report
and the distancing of reflection; the spontaneity of narrative text and the form of
logic of narrative; the assertion of individuality within the communicative collusion
of conversation with an other. Phenomenology and existentialism offer us no easy
resolutions to these contradictions, no closure. They remind us to be attuned to the
specific and actual situation in which a story is spoken, heard, and answered. They
remain generative resources for educators who work to reveal and transform the
bonds that constrain the human spirit.*

We reconceptualize the ways we know the world not to update our abstractions, but to confirm Sartre's conviction that to name something is to
change the world. Thus to reconceptualize is to reform. When we examine
the ways in which we construct the forms of knowledge, we discover, as
Merleau-Ponty has reminded us, that form is not a physical reality, but an

28

object of perception contingent upon a worldview. We see, in Norwood Hanson's terms, with theory-laden vision.

Whenever we speak of education, we are speaking of a person's experience in the world. Despite the unique specificity of each person's perspective, the intentionality of all conscious acts focuses our gaze on some object, real or imagined; we exist always in context. Colloquial assessments of a person's education are often descriptions of that context, in the field of experience. The judgment that one is "well-educated" may be a measure of social class, literacy, years of schooling, travel, the length and breadth of experience. All or any of these measures describe, if superficially, a person's experience in the world; as such, they are more descriptive of outer status than inner condition. We seek a definition that will diminish the discrepancy between public performance and private experience.

Consequently, when I designate an experience as educational, I imply that its effect upon its subject transcends the immediate encounter; its season passed, a spore remains and grows roots in the psyche, bringing forth new vegetation, nurtured by that singular, inimitable soil. In other words, an encounter with the world is a generative act, a spawning experience, a hybrid of objectivity and subjectivity, whose very birth modifies and extends and finally transcends its inheritance.

Just as art requires the imposition of subjectivity upon the objective stuff of the world, and is embodied in that stuff—in its materials, forms, and limitation—so education requires a blending of objectivity with the unique subjectivity of the person, its infusion into the structures and shapes of the psyche.

Viewed from this perspective, education emerges as a metaphor for a person's dialogue with the world of his or her experience. It is tempting to make the analogy more economical, to eliminate the middleman of dialogue and to speak of education only in terms of experience. But that formula, for all its artful simplicity, would reduce its epistemological subject to an object by reducing the person who is able to interpret, repudiate, or affirm experience to a *tabula rasa* upon which the world makes its marks, a template of societal conditioning. To delete dialogue from this concept of educational experience would be to relegate learning to a series of reactive, conditioned behaviors best described as training. Although that description of existence wherein we become our experience may satisfy the behaviorists, it is rejected by the existential philosophers in their acknowledgment of and commitment to human freedom. In the words of Merleau-Ponty, "I am the absolute source, my existence does not stem from my antecedents, from my physical and social environment; instead it moves out towards them and sustains them, for I alone bring into being for myself the tradition which I elect to carry on" (Merleau-Ponty, 1962). It is this dialogue of each person, of an idiosyncratic history and genetic makeup with situation, place, people, artifacts, and ideas that we call educational experience.

THE DIALECTICS OF EDUCATIONAL EXPERIENCE

Any definition of education requires a definition of knowledge; any consideration of epistemology requires an ontological foundation. The theory base of an autobiographical exploration of education experience is drawn from humanistic philosophy, phenomenology's emphasis on the reciprocity of subjectivity and objectivity in the dynamic constitution of human knowledge, and existentialism's emphasis on the dialectical relationship of persons to our situations. This is to say, educational experience can be approached in a phenomenological examination of the relationship of one person to his or her world.

In order to speak of educational experience, we turn to phenomenology and existential philosophy, whose proponents have wrenched their interpretations of experience away from systems of positivism and subjective idealism in order to render, accurately and specifically, their experience of themselves in the world. The writings of Husserl, Heidegger, Sartre, and Merleau-Ponty describe existence as being-in-the-world. They recognize the existence of the world without explaining its facticity and accept our experience of it without first establishing its causality. The natural and social sciences that attempt explanations of that causality are to them merely second-order expressions of the *Lebenswelt,* the world of lived experience. Thus, for the phenomenologist, knowledge of the world requires knowledge of self-as-knower-of-the-world.

This paradoxical identification of objectivity with subjectivity, each realized through the other, creates an intellectual tension that is as intolerable as it is generative. In seeking to know subjectivity or objectivity, we seek identities that can never be fixed, for our inquiry transforms what it seeks, and in the process discovers worlds it never sought.

Paradox dominates the phenomenological work of Edmund Husserl, whose insistence upon the *epoche* requires that we distance ourselves from our experience in order to come closer to it. Paradox is the very structure of the consciousness that Sartre describes as the being that is what is not and is not what is. The contradictions of paradox preclude certainty, that elusive confirmation of our actions and decisions.

Despite the ambiguity of paradox and the frustrations that it provokes, anthropologist Terence Turner (1973) has resisted applying the developmental schemes of Piaget to studies of ethnography because they lead in a linear trajectory to plateaus of equilibrium, understating the contradictory, irrational characteristics of artistic, religious, and social experience. Piagetian theory has been criticized for providing a goal of decentered cognition that, in its emphasis on abstraction and rational thinking, underestimates the turmoil of desire, the force of ideology, all the conflict and tension in adult cognition. Klaus Riegel (1973) has proposed a further stage of cognitive development, *dialectical operations,* to follow Piaget's final stage of formal operations. Riegel maintains that at the stage of mature dialectical operations, the individual does not necessarily resolve conflicts; rather, he or she is willing to live with contradictions, accepting them as a basic feature of thought. In *Radical Man* Charles Hampden-Turner has argued that a tolerance for paradox and dialectic is essential to full psychosocial development, citing F. Scott Fitzgerald: "The test of a first rate intelligence is the ability to hold two opposed ideas in the mind at the same time and still retain the ability to function" (quoted in Hampden-Turner, 1971, p. 39).

We cannot talk about education without talking about a dialectic between person and world, a dialectic that holds all the mysteries and ironies of paradox. The apparent polarities of subjectivity and objectivity, immanence and transcendence, particularization and generalization, essence and existence dissolve into reciprocity, each constituting the other.

Too often curriculum collapses around one pole of the dialectic or the other as those charged to design curriculum flee from ambiguity to mechanistic and analytic descriptions of the process of education. Although studies of the cognitive processes and the organization of the academic disciplines illuminate parts of the whole, they isolate one agent in the negotiation from others in order to study its activity. And if the world were experienced in discretely organized units by persons who could isolate emotional responses from intellectual ones, past from present, present from future, I from me, and me from us, then programmed instruction, behavioral objectives, and other products of the "divide and conquer" approach to learning might be justified.

They are not; further depersonalization and fragmentation of human experience distort it and estrange us not only from each other but from ourselves as well. When we refuse to reduce the educational process to training, the assembly-line production of skills and socialized psyches standardized to society's measure, we must forsake the statistic and consult the educational experience of one person. Thus my first request of a reconceptualized curriculum is the safe return of my own voice.

Although this appeal to self-support may appear to be an atavistic methodology, it is the logical response to the domination of the empirical paradigm. There is a parallel to this state of affairs in clinical medicine. After treating an ailing patient with drugs, and more drugs to counter the effects of the antidotes, the physician, trapped in a web of treatment, must remove the patient from all drug therapy and start once more from the beginning by taking a history. Our current responsibility is to rescue our patient from the results of our recent attentions.

In *The Explanation of Social Behavior,* Harré and Secord (1972) examine the deficiencies of an empiricism that, striving for objectivity, discounts the distortions of the lab setting, and concentrates on behaviors that are quantifiable and on passive, manipulated subjects who surrender their capacity to direct their own behavior and to report their own experience to the experimenter. Traditional empirical research is designed to describe the behavior of individuals and groups and to ascertain those conditions that inhibit or encourage it. In contrast, the concept of education presented here, although it involves actions, is less concerned with eliciting behaviors than with grasping the actor's understanding of them. Phenomenological reflection is, according to Schutz, a process that simultaneously discovers and constructs meaning:

> Meaning does not lie *in* experience. Rather, those experiences are meaningful which are grasped reflectively. The meaning is the way in which the Ego regards its experience. The meaning lies in the attitudes of the Ego toward that part of its stream of consciousness which has already flowed by. (quoted in Chamberlin, 1974, p. 131)

Admittedly, it is a grandiose ambition to imagine a research method that simultaneously and consistently will embrace both poles of the dialectic and not relinquish subjectivity to objectivity or vice versa. William Pinar's approach is to scale the inquiry down to the experiential field of the individual. *Currere,* the root of the word curriculum, is Pinar's term for educational experience; it describes the race not only in terms of the course, the readiness of the runner, but also seeks to know the experience of the running of one particular runner, on one particular track, on one particular day, in one particular wind. Thus to talk of education as the dialogue of person and world is not to break down this complex interaction into separate parts, subjecting each to a distinct, isolated analysis. Nor are we describing education as a magical transformation, a metamorphosis of self into the forms of the world. Educational experience is a process that takes on the world without appropriating that world, that projects the self into the world without dismembering that self, a process of synthesis and totalization in which all the participants in the dialectic simultaneously maintain their identities and surpass themselves.

Self-report may not insure an accurate description of behavior or identification of its causes. The work of Jones and Nisbett (1974) indicates the disparity between the account of the observer, who tends to attribute the behavior of the actor to his personality traits, and that of the actor, who attributes the cause of his own behavior to the situation in which it occurs.

Nevertheless, the focus of the research described here is educational experience. Rather than attempting to describe or evaluate behaviors or establish their causality, we are interested in determining what it is that the subject makes of them. Indeed, Harré and Secord predict that the "most profound discoveries of social psychology will be made by those who, while playing a part, filling a role and so on, can be their own audience" (1972, p. 231).

If we must calibrate education, then we might say that we are educated to the extent that we are conscious of our experience and to the degree that we are freed by this knowledge to act in the world. By defending education as awareness of one's experience, I am not confining that definition to introspection, for that would assume that experience resides merely inside one's cranium, draping its walls with the voluptuous and decadent hangings of sentiment and libido. Experience is outside and inside, and the skills that are required to know it are as diverse as experience itself: language, logic, the use of tools to scan the skies, the earth, the eye.

PHENOMENOLOGICAL FOUNDATIONS OF AUTOBIOGRAPHICAL WRITING

The first phase of the autobiographical method is writing the world, the creation of a text that brings the subject's experience in the world to words. In the writings of Edmund Husserl, mathematician, psychologist, philosopher, we find a model for the process of disciplined reflection that takes the consciousness of one individual as its data and develops a system of hermeneutics for the explication of that text. The principles and processes of phenomenology that are most pertinent to our consideration of autobiographical method are its emphasis on the reciprocity of subjectivity and objectivity in the constitution of meanings, its attempts to describe immediate, preconceptual experience, and the distancing and bracketing required to accomplish these ends.

The term "constitution" was used by Husserl to describe neither the creation of subjectivity nor the discovery of objectivity. It is founded upon Brentano's postulation of intentionality as a structure of consciousness: All consciousness is consciousness of something; thus, subject, precisely as subject, can be presented to consciousness purely through the object that it intends. The typewriter, this paper, tomorrow's dinner, the Garden of Eden, pain, self are all objects of consciousness. Objective constitution is the life of the subject; knowledge of self becomes knowledge of self-as-knower-of-the-world, not as an expression of latent subjectivity, but as a bridge between these two domains, a mediator. The homunculus of educational experience resides in each cogitation.

Suspending judgment about the "real" world, Husserl directed complete attention to phenomena, objects as they are evident to consciousness as the passive recipient of sense impressions, and the idealism that denies us full knowledge of the world but consoles us with the constructions of our own psyches. Husserl situated meaning in the moment of engagement when significance expresses relation.

> When phenomenology examines objects of consciousness—regardless of any kind, whether real or ideal—it deals with these exclusively as objects of the immediate consciousness. The description—which attempts to grasp the concrete and rich phenomena of the cogitations—must constantly glance back from the side of the object to the side of consciousness, and pursue the general existing connection. (Husserl, 1931/1964a, p. 16)

It was to clarify these connections that he employed the terms "noesis," to describe the quality and kind of psychic activity involved in the act of consciousness—that is, feeling, remembering, imagining—and "noema," the meaning of the intentional act of consciousness that is not tied to that act alone, but to a unifying identity that gives meanings to a series of intentional acts of consciousness. Reliance on the lived experience of the individual in autobiographical methods of inquiry draws support from Husserl's conviction that it was only in the freshness and immediacy of encounter that certain knowledge could reside. To that end Husserl devised a system of disciplined reflection designed to determine the adequacy and fullness of this knowledge. The knowledge would be given primordially, uncontaminated by theories of formal logic or the natural sciences; it would be grounded in the lived experience of the subject.

Nevertheless, the certainty that is the goal of this method brings us, despite its reference to lived experience, to an abstracted, eidetic knowing. The purpose of bracketing the natural attitude is to submit the apprehensions of phenomena as lived experience to an analysis that strips it of all features and qualities that are not absolutely essential to it. In this way Husserl hoped to intuit the essential forms of lived experience, brushed with meaning and scoured by thought.

This idealistic tendency is qualified by another stream in Husserl's thought, one that acknowledges the ways in which all thought, even his own scheme of disciplined reflection, is situated in the history of individual persons and the culture they share. In the *Cartesian Meditations* (1931/1970), consciousness is described as a stream of experience: having its own history, initiated in primal encounters, nonverbal, antepredicative instants of experience in the world, extended into a horizon of confirming harmonious appearances and conceptual syntheses.

In this phenomenology of consciousness the distinction between the terms "encounter" and "experience" is made explicit. An encounter is consciousness of external reality; experience is awareness of immanent objects. What is sensed is not different from the act of sensing. All encounters are known to consciousness through experience as immanent objects, and the transition from encounter in the world to experience as immanent objects is established. In the *Phenomenology of Internal Time-Consciousness,* edited by Heidegger, Husserl (1964b) describes an immanent flow of now-points (also termed "primal apprehensions" and "partial intentions"). Just as he described the identity of a transcendent object as being developed and confirmed through multiple presentations, profiles, and perspectives, he describes immanent objects achieving meaning in a temporal manifold. In this flow of pure subjectivity, we experience a series of now-points, each carrying horizons of past and immanent nows, passing into phrases of retention and extending into phrases of protention. Elapsed now-points are retained and are present in consciousness as part of this temporal manifold.

It is this prereflective flow of now-points that Merleau-Ponty evokes when he speaks of antepredicative experience in the Preface to *The Phenomenology of Perception:*

> to return to things in themselves is to return to that world which precedes all knowledge of which knowledge always speaks, and in relation to which every scientific schematization is an abstract and derivative sign language, as is geography in relation to the countryside in which we have learnt beforehand what a forest, a prairie or a river is. (1962, p. ix)

It is in the silence of primary consciousness that Merleau-Ponty finds essence and existence blending, and reminds us that the "eidetic reduction is . . . the determination to bring the world to light as it is before any falling back on ourselves has occurred, it is the ambition to make reflection emulate the unreflective life of consciousness" (1962, p. xvi).

The theory of inner temporality mirrors the distinction made earlier between experience in the world and education. As there is a double awareness, both of my encounters in the world and of the experience of those encounters extended through my own inner time, so is there the double awareness in autobiographical method, at once a transcendent and an immanent process, constituting meanings in subjectivity of its being in the world. The narrative takes place in time and permits a temporal manifold to reveal itself as the speaker views its events from different temporal perspectives.

Husserl's principles of association and passive genesis link all our synthetic organizations of meaning to the world as we receive it in these primal encounters, and each judgment is both derived from these encounters and subjected to confirmation or repudiation by subsequent encounters—enacting once again the dialectic that is the basis of educational experience: the dialectic between objectivity, the encounter in the world experienced in inner temporality, and subjectivity, the judgment drawn from that encounter.

Research in education has understandably hovered around the end products of that process of consciousness described by Husserl—those synthetic
judgments, concepts, and abstractions that we call knowledge. The writing
and reading of autobiographical accounts of educational experience reach
under these structures to preconceptual encounters that are their foundation
and the processes of interpretation that endow them with significance.

GLIMPSES OF SUBJECTIVITY

Education always refers to the development of some-body. Theories of
consciousness and knowledge must ultimately have reference to the continuous identity of some *one,* and in educational studies and practice the one
who receives our attention is usually the student. But even though autobiography may appear to be a lengthy monologue, it is actually a conversation,
for autobiography is a story that is told to someone. And even if I am the
only reader of my own story, as in the case of a private journal of jottings for
no one but myself, as both the writer and the reader of the tale, I am doubled.

Theories of consciousness rooted in object relations also remind us that
the sense of oneself as a singular identity is derivative, necessarily preceded
by a relation to another, or as Stephan Strasser puts it, "the you is always
older than the I" (Strasser, 1969).

Like identity, pedagogy too is grounded in relation and dialogue. When
teachers and educational researchers employ autobiographical methods of inquiry they too become the subject and the object of research. It is never only
about the other; it is never only about the student. If the *epoche* can, as
Merleau-Ponty maintains, "slacken the intentional threads which attach us to
the world and thus bring them to our notice" (1962, p. xiii), then perhaps
the reflexive process suggested by William Pinar (1988) would also contribute to the developmental capacity to reach back through our experience to
the preconceptual encounter that is the foundation of our judgments. Pinar
suggests that when we misunderstand ourselves, we misunderstand our
world. In "The Method," he describes a research method that would attempt
a phenomenological description of both subject and object, requiring knowledge of self-as-knower-of-the-world and tracing the sinuous path from preconceptual experience to intellection (Pinar & Grumet, 1976).

The journal of William Butler Yeats offers another version of this objec-
tive/subjective symbiosis: by understanding the world, I understand myself:

> The soul becomes a mirror not a brazier. This culture is really the pursuit of self
> knowledge insofar as the self is a calm, deliberating, discriminating thing, for
> which we have awakened our tastes and our criticism of the world as we taste it,

we have to come to know ourselves; ourselves, I mean, not as misers or spend-thrifts, as magistrates or pleaders, but as men, as souls face to face with what is permanent in the world. (Yeats, 1973, p. 159)

Yeats's description of educational experience confirms Merleau-Ponty's conviction that phenomenology puts essence back into existence. Here we meet subjectivity meeting itself through its projection into the objectives of art. Studies of autobiographical accounts of educational experience provide both an encounter with objectivity and a microcosm, which, unlike the real world's constant flux, is fixed in the permanence of the written word, making it accessible to other subjectivities and future encounters.

Even though he distrusted the products of reflection, maintaining that "my 'I' is not more certain for my consciousness than the 'I' of other men," Jean-Paul Sartre did concede that glimpses of the self could be caught hovering on the horizons of one's actions, as projections of self into the world (1957, p.104). Glimpsing the self, as Yeats suggests, in one's response to culture, is phenomenologically mapped out by Sartre in his descriptions of the audience's response to Jean Genet's plays. Although Sartre insists that culture cannot justify man's existence, in *The Words* he also identifies it as a source of self-knowledge; "it is a product of man; he projects himself into it, that critical mirror alone offers him his image" (1964, p. 254).

In autobiographical methods of inquiry, a writer reads his or her own text. As the reader voluntarily re-creates that which the writer has disclosed, once again a fictive world is created, drawn from the substance of the reader's experience and fantasy. Reading is one way of demonstrating the reciprocity of objectivity and subjectivity and their interdependence; it extends to the reader/researcher the artist's awareness that subjectivity transforms any objectivity it seeks to describe.

The writing and reading of phenomenological description share an estrangement, a distancing from the everyday world in order to see the familiar with the freshness and immediacy of the vision that is seeing for the first time. Perhaps you remember the first tour you took of the neighborhood or town where you now live. Sometimes a memory from that first view persists, the outline is there, the silhouette of houses on mazelike streets. The dimensions assumed by the local school, shopping center, or restaurant were comprised even then, as they confirmed, undermined, or surpassed your expectations (reminding us of the impossibility of restoring an absolutely original perception); those perceptions are all transformed now by your associations with the place, the meanings that saturate each landmark. Both the phenomenological and aesthetic processes strip away those meanings not necessarily to repudiate them but to review them and to celebrate our freedom to reject or affirm them once more.

In his study of autobiography, *Metaphors of Self,* James Olney (1972) maintains that while it is true to say that one can see with no other eyes than one's own, it is also true to say that one can, after a manner, see oneself seeing with those eyes. That perspective requires distancing, and it was to this end that Edmund Husserl urged a mental discipline of abstention from the natural attitude.

EXISTENTIAL FOUNDATIONS

The natural attitude is our own common sense: an unexamined orientation to the world that sees the old neighborhood, real rainbows ending in imaginary pots of gold, good men and bad men, facts and lies. The phenomenological reduction or *epoche* brackets our convictions and prejudices so that we may examine the world in its primordialness, as it gives itself to consciousness. The *epoche* is designed to cleanse the field of consciousness so that we may see, feel, imagine the essential form of a thing. The essence embodied in concrete experience is scoured of irrelevancies, distortions, and confusions until only its pure, irreducible, and necessary form emerges. As Olney's study of the autobiographies of Montaigne, Darwin, Mill, and Jung reveals characteristic patterns and symbols recurring throughout them, so may analysis of autobiographical accounts of educational experience reveal essential recurring forms through one's responses to literature, mathematics, or science. An individual encounter in the world is consulted not to reveal the particular truth of its facticity, but its general truth as it emerges in a community of multiple subjectivities and is confirmed by subsequent encounters. In this respect there is no end to phenomenological research. There is always the possible negation of another subjectivity, of a whole new era of subjectivities released from the historicity of the last generation's view. Nevertheless, it was Husserl's aim to go through the particular to the general in order to grasp the essential structures of consciousness and the world.

For Heidegger and Sartre, Husserl's *epoche* was a retreat from the world of experience to a transcendental never-never land of ideal forms. Heidegger rejected any dualism that distinguished consciousness from its objects. Dismissing ego and the cogito, Heidegger asserted *Dasein,* meaning "care" or "engagement," as the only attitude of consciousness, of being-in-the-world.

Merleau-Ponty attempted to rescue the *epoche* from the repudiations of Sartre and Heidegger. He asserted that the essences are located in the existence and maintained that the *epoche* need not divert our attention from being-in-the-world, for what was essential was the lived relation of the body-subject to its situation.

Perhaps the existential position is best described by Maurice Roche when he asserts that phenomenology "helps us to see the ordinary as strange and in need of some explanation" (1973, p. 27). This scrutiny of what is ordinary requires a critical approach to the social and political environment, for the "ordinary" is a social concept, an unquestioned assumption of the natural attitude. For these existential philosophers, the "ordinary" became the sign-post for intellectual, moral, and spiritual morass. Nietzsche, Kierkegaard, and Sartre urged us to reclaim our intuition by wrenching it from the fallacies that parade as society's doctrines, moralities, and intuitions.

Kierkegaard subjected the ordinary to his scathing humor. He saw the social systems and customs of his world as ridiculous structures erected in fear to protect citizens from the anguish of infinite possibility and the terror of faith. In Husserl's scheme, infinite possibility was part of an intellectual process leading to the eidetic reduction; because Husserl directed his inquiry toward knowledge of the world rather than action in the world, infinite possibility held none of the anguish for him that it did for Kierkegaard, or that Sartre's version of infinite possibility, the nothingness that afflicts consciousness, held for him. Kierkegaard's prisoner of the ordinary rushes to identification in the certainty and shelter of type, an ethical, aesthetic, or religious model to guide his choices. Condemned to meaning, we must, as Sartre insists, choose ourselves, and Nietzsche ridicules our cowardice in seeking immunity from choice in the complicity of the herd and the passivity of religion, the ascetic ideal that fabricates the ornate burden of original sin to justify the meaningless suffering of existence. Both Nietzsche and Kierkegaard saw the "ordinary as strange and in need of some explanation" and attacked the rational systems of thought represented in the philosophies of their contemporaries as mass delusion. Nietzsche celebrated the freedom of our will; allowing consciousness to be the author of the ego, he glorified our power to turn in upon ourselves and violently strip away our old values and ideals in order to know our experience of the world.

In the process of designating and ridiculing the misunderstandings that shape our lives, Nietzsche, Kierkegaard, and Sartre exposed and excoriated the myths of culture that lure us away from overambiguous experience to their chimerical certainty. Sartre internalized the conflict even further, identifying our flight from our authentic selves as a flight from nothingness that is our consciousness. Flight into the impostures of bad faith reifies possibilities into habits, rituals that permit us to evade the responsibility for our own existences.

Even if Husserl's initial impulse toward phenomenology was to delve through lived experience in order to salvage certain knowledge in essential forms, the *epoche* is a rationalized version of Nietzsche's and Kierkegaard's rage against the conceptual intrusions perpetrated by society in the name of culture, science, religion, and character. The phenomenological injunction, "back to the things themselves," establishes a perspective that frees us from our common assumptions and presuppositions so that we may see through them to the world of our experience.

The researcher who scrutinizes one person's account of experience must confront the very issues that were debated by Husserl and his existential progeny. To what degree does reflection, even when subjected to rigorous discipline, distort experience to fit idealized forms? Does the distancing required by the phenomenological perspective break the bonds of commitment and action that tie us to the real world? Who is the self that we attend? Is the reflecting self continuous with the acting self? Do our multiple social roles splinter the self into situational poses strung along a temporal chain?

We must be reminded that the methodology of the empiricist does not avoid these quandaries. They are disguised in an empirical ritual that avoids confrontation with the whole by its atomization, a scrutiny of parts, and by a series of controls that create an unreal world as a backdrop for one antic variable.

In contrast, autobiographical methods are rooted in context. They view us, as does existential phenomenology, in situation. Here they confirm the thought of Paulo Freire, who maintains that every aspect of a person's interaction with culture, language, and others is saturated with the political reality of his or her situation. While autobiographical methods of inquiry presuppose a continuity of ego that will justify a concern for the impact of biography upon a person's action and choice (as in existential psychoanalysis), they are also cognizant of the impact of milieu and address the political present and the subjective past simultaneously.

Whereas education has often been described as acculturation, the initiation of the child into the distinctive codes and rituals of the society, a phenomenology of educational experience examines the impact of acculturation on the shaping of one's cognitive lens. Existentialism recognizes culture as the given situation, with all it facticity, through which the individual expresses his subjectivity, embodied in acts in the world. Awareness of self develops not in hermetic introspection, but in the response of subjectivity to objectivity. Thus that culture that we present to our students is in Sartre's dialectic an objectivity to be surpassed, as every one of us is free to make more of what has been made of us. Creative consciousness, which is existence, is, in terms of Hegel's dialectic, a transformation of one objective reality into another.

As phenomenology repudiated psychologism and empiricism, and as existentialism repudiated idealism, autobiographical method repudiates behaviorism and technocracy. Husserl's reply to the determination of psychologism was the individual's intentional consciousness, endowed with the ability to intuit essences, emerging within the integrity of history and character as they develop in the *Lebenswelt*. Sartre's reply to the determinism of the ego and the unconsciousness was to liberate us from the utter determination of history in order to have us realize our innate freedom, first in leaps to nothingness, then in action in the world.

Autobiography's reply to the traditional empirical paradigm is a return to the experience of individuals by respecting all the qualities that disqualify us for consideration in the behavioral sciences: our idiosyncratic histories, our preconceptual foundations, our contextual dependencies, our innate freedom expressed in choice and self-direction.

As educators, we alone must bring into being the tradition that we elect to carry on; existential phenomenology requires action as well as theory. Levinas's criticism of Husserl's pursuit of certain knowledge is pertinent here:

> Is our first attitude in the presence of the real attitude of theoretic contemplation? Does the world not manifest its very being as a center of action, a field of activity or concern . . . ? (quoted in Kocklemans, 1967, pp. 104–105)

If the philosophies of phenomenology and existentialism cannot, by definition, prescribe our actions, they can inform them.

CONCLUSION

The path of reconceptualized inquiry leads us inward, to individual experience, and outward, to metatheory. Employing the critical distance of the *epoche*, research into the experience of education reaches back first to the antepredicative encounter, the lived sense that is a *sine qua non* for a conceptual ability. It then reconstructs the pathway to the present choice by digging back under the layers of one's biography to identify the encounters that led to it.

The other, broader application of phenomenological description is proposed in Maurice Roche's examination of the social sciences and in Habermas's *Knowledge and Human Interests* (1971). The theory-laden perspectives of sociology and psychology, disciplines strongly influencing educational theory, relinquish their basic assumptions to phenomenological probing. We will attempt to describe educational experience in its most particularized incarnation, the history and response of the individual, and in its most general expression, the interpretations of human experience that characterize the conceptual frameworks of the disciplines that shape educational research.

Finally, for practitioners, actors in a world that requires choice and deed, the debates of Husserl and his existential commentators suggest the following concerns: How does educational experience shape the cognitive lens, change the vision so that the world is, in fact, encountered differently? If one could, and that is questionable, alter another's world view (the kind of conceptual organization described by Norwood Hanson [1958]), on what grounds, if any, is that intrusion justified? How can the educator reconcile the phenomenologist's call for detached speculation with the existentialist's emphasis on situation and action in the world?

Autobiographical method may not effect the total reconciliation of objectivity and subjectivity in educational research, but it does commit us to acknowledge the paradox, if that is our experience. In *The Ethics of Ambiguity* Simone de Beauvoir praises paradox, its mysterious freedoms and awesome responsibilities: "[T]he antimonies that exist between means and ends, present and future, they must be lived in a permanent tension" (1948, p. 133). Employing the *epoche,* she urges the kind of cruel scrutiny that reading our own autobiographical accounts of educational experience requires: "In setting up its ends, freedom must put them in parentheses, confront them at each moment with that absolute end which it itself constitutes and contests in its name and means it uses to win itself" (1948, p. 134).

REFERENCES

Beauvoir, S. (1948). *The ethics of ambiguity* (B. Frechtman, Trans.). New York: Philosophical Library.

Chamberlin, L. G. (1974). Phenomenological methodology and understanding education. In D. Denton (Ed.), *Existentialism and phenomenology in education* (pp. 119–138). New York: Teachers College Press.

Habermas, J. (1971). *Knowledge and human interests* (J. Shapiro, Trans.). Boston: Beacon.

Hampden-Turner, C. (1971). *Radical man.* New York: Doubleday.

Hanson, N. (1958). *Patterns of discovery.* New York: Cambridge University Press.

Harré, R., & Secord, B. F. (1972). *The explanation of social behavior.* Oxford, England: Basil Blackwell & Mott.

Husserl, E. (1964a). *The Paris lectures.* (P. Koestenbaum, Trans.). The Hague: Martinus Nijhoff.

Husserl, E. (1964b). *Phenomenology of internal time-consciousness.* Bloomington, IN: Midland Books.

Husserl, E. (1970). *Cartesian meditations* (D. Cairns, Trans.). The Hague: Martinus Nijhoff. (Original work published 1931)

Jones, E., & Nisbett, R. (1974). The actor and the observer: Divergent perceptions of the causes of behavior. In E. Jones et al. (Eds.), *Attribution.* Morrison, NJ: Greater Learning Press.

Kocklemans, J. J. (Ed.). (1967). *Phenomenology.* New York: Doubleday.

Merleau-Ponty, M. (1962). *Phenomenology of perception.* London: Routledge & Kegan Paul.

Olney, J. (1972). *Metaphors of self: The meaning of autobiography*. Princeton, NJ: Princeton University Press.

Pinar, W. (1988). Whole, bright, deep with understanding: Issues in qualitative research and autobiographical method. In W. Pinar (Ed.), *Contenporary curriculum discourses* (pp. 134–154). Scottsdale, AZ: Gorsuch, Scaribrick.

Pinar, W. F., & Grumet, M. (1976). *Toward a poor curriculum*. Dubuque, IA: Kendall-Hunt.

Riegel, K. (1973, January). Dialectical operations: The final period of cognitive development. *Research Bulletin*. Princeton, NJ: Educational Testing Service.

Roche, M. (1973). *Phenomenology, language and the social sciences*. London: Routledge & Kegan Paul.

Sartre, J. P. (1964). *The words*. (B. Frechtman, Trans.). Greenwich, CT: Fawcett.

Sartre, J. P. (1957). *The transcendence of the ego* (F. Williams & R. Kirkpatrick, Trans.). New York: Noonday Press.

Strasser, S. (1969). *The idea of dialogal phenomenology* (Duquesne Studies, Philosophical Series No. 25). Pittsburgh: Duquesne University Press.

Yeats, W. B. (1973). *Memoirs* (D. Donoghue, Ed.). New York: Macmillan.

CHAPTER 3

Max van Manen and Pedagogical Human Science Research

ROBERT K. BROWN

"The end of phenomenological research is to sponsor a critical educational compe-tence: knowing how to act tactfully in pedagogic situations on the basis of a carefully edified thoughtfulness."

Max van Manen, "Practicing Phenomenological Writing"

This essay explores the particular educational theorizing of Max van Ma-nen, who is recognized as a foremost contemporary curriculum theorist in North America. In recognition of his work, van Manen received the 1988 Canadian Association of Curriculum Studies Award for Outstanding Inter-national Accomplishments in Research in Phenomenology and Pedagogy. He is the founding editor of the human science journal *Phenomenology and Peda-gogy* and has authored various hermeneutic-phenomenologically oriented ar-ticles. Van Manen has authored two books. The first, published in 1986 and entitled *The Tone of Teaching,* was written as a pedagogic text for parents and teachers. The second, published in 1990 and entitled *Researching Lived Ex-perience: Human Science for an Action Sensitive Pedagogy,* was written as a guide to conducting hermeneutic phenomenological research in education. A third book will be published in the summer of 1991 entitled *The Tact of Teaching: The Meaning of Pedagogical Thoughtfulness.* I will reflect on particular mo-ments of the rethinking of educational research and practice as revealed in van Manen's writings.

Emphasis will be placed on four aspects of van Manen's work. The first will be that of the philosophic tradition upon which van Manen has founded his work. In this section I will briefly describe the philosophy and methodol-ogies associated with the Utrecht School that have provided much of the theoretical grounding for van Manen's work. Second, I will discuss those elements of van Manen's writings that distinguish it as hermeneutically "phe-nomenological." Discussion will center upon some of the major premises of hermeneutic phenomenology and how van Manen has employed them in his work. Third, I will discuss the primary themes discernible in his writings. The final section of this essay will be devoted to a summary discussion of his work in which implications and practical applications will be examined.

THE UTRECHT SCHOOL AND MAX VAN MANEN

Van Manen's Academic Influence

Max van Manen first studied phenomenology in 1962 while engaged in undergraduate study at the State Pedagogical Academy in the Netherlands, his homeland. It was there that he studied the works of phenomenological educational theorists such as Martinus J. Langeveld and N. Beets and received an initial understanding of the relationship between phenomenology and pedagogy. Langeveld and Beets developed a phenomenological view of pedagogy and pedagogical research in the 1950s at the Institute for Didactic and Pedagogic Studies at the University of Utrecht, which has become known as the Utrecht School. Its founder and principal pedagogue was Langeveld himself, and his work alone exemplifies the educational endeavors for which this school of phenomenological thought has become noted (van Manen, 1979a).

Van Manen emigrated to Canada in 1967. He began his graduate studies at the University of Alberta, where he studied with T. Tetsuo Aoki. Because it had not yet been introduced in Canada, van Manen did not study phenomenology at the University of Alberta. Not until he encountered a "crisis of relevance" while working on his dissertation did he bring to the forefront the phenomenological views of pedagogy he had learned previously in his undergraduate studies in Europe (van Manen, 1988a). An important methodological and programmatic source for his master's thesis as well as his Ph.D. dissertation became an edited volume by J. H. van den Berg entitled *Person and World*. Described as one of van Manen's earliest and favorite phenomenological texts, it is a collection of works that reflect the phenomenologically grounded pedagogical, psychological, and social perspectives of the Utrecht School (van Manen, 1988a).

Van Manen's Theoretical Influences

Though van Manen has been influenced by and has incorporated ideas from other theorists, such as Gadamer and Habermas, in the formation of his ideas, it has been primarily the Utrecht School that has served as the basis of his work. Central to understanding the contributions of the Utrecht School to van Manen's work is their distinctive usage of the terms "phenomenology" and "pedagogy."

The Utrecht School and pedagogy. The European notion of pedagogy includes both education and childrearing (van Manen, 1979a, p. 49). In the Utrecht view, pedagogy encompasses the entire realm of lifeworld issues that are encountered in teacher/student/adult/child relationships. The concerns of these relationships can range from questions of curriculum and learning methodology to what it means to be a parent with a pedagogical responsibility to a child. A term given to anthropological and ontological significance, it reflects the view that pedagogy is not just an activity carried out in schools. Pedagogy is a particular normative stance one takes in the world toward children. Van Manen writes:

> As new parents, before we have a chance to sit back and reflect on whether we can accept this child, the child has already made us act. And, luckily for humankind, this spontaneous needfulness to do the right thing is usually the right thing. As we reach to hold the child (rather than turn away and let it perish), we have already acted pedagogically. This is our practical "knowledge" of pedagogy. . . . In other words, as soon as we gain a lived sense of the pedagogic quality of parenting and teaching, we start to question and doubt ourselves. Pedagogy is this questioning, this doubting. We wonder: Did I do the right thing? Why do some people teach or bring their children up in such a different manner? (van Manen, 1988b, p. 447)

For van Manen, the meaning of pedagogy is not derived from some systematic view of philosophy, politics, or culture. Instead, pedagogy receives its meaning from its own anthropological nature. To define pedagogy is to identify ways of being in concrete situations. It is to refer to "something that lets an encounter, a relationship, a situation, or a doing be pedagogic. . . . [I]n short [it refers to] a relationship of practical actions between an adult and a young person who is on the way to adulthood" (van Manen, 1982b, pp. 284–285).

The Utrecht School and phenomenology. According to Langeveld, "phenomenology" has been applied in two directions since Husserl introduced it in 1913. One is the philosophical sense in which emphasis is given to understanding as a logical system of thinking about the world. The other sense is that of "methodology" that attempts to use the attitude of phenomenology to construct patterns of research that reveal the lived formations of meaning. It is the latter that the Utrecht School has sought to develop.

Utrecht researchers employ a method of structural exposition known as "situation analysis." Adherents of this investigative procedure believe that it is possible to obtain insights into the meaning structures and relationships of pedagogical experiences from a careful study of concrete examples supplied by experience or imagination. According to Beekman and Mulderij (1977), phenomenologically oriented pedagogical analysis of lifeworld experiences consists of three primary components. The first stage of analysis involves the accumulation of life experience material. This phase comprises the gathering of descriptions given by individuals using everyday language to describe specific experiences. The second stage of investigation engages the researcher in the task of examining the lifeworld description for the structural elements contained within the description. This involves searching the description for language clues that perhaps signal deeper conceptual structures of meaning associated and consistent with that particular experience.

The third stage of situation analysis calls for recommendations and practical applications that can be derived from a deeper understanding of the experience studied. It is this difficult issue that has caused pedagogical phenomenology to receive much of its criticism. Criticism for being subjective and lacking generalization has caused many to disregard this form of analytical research (Bernstein, 1976). It is the achievement of a practical phenomenological method with concrete applications to pedagogy to which van Manen has devoted much of his energies during his 15-year tenure (as of 1991) at the University of Alberta. He writes:

> Some argue that phenomenology has no practical value because "you cannot do anything with phenomenological knowledge." From the point of view of instrumental reason it may be quite true to say that we cannot do anything with this knowledge. But to paraphrase Heidegger, the more important question is *not*: Can we do something with phenomenology? Rather, we should wonder: Can phenomenology, if we concern ourselves deeply with it, do something with us? (1982b, p. 297)

The Influence of Langeveld

The work of the Utrecht School and its guiding purposes are suggested in the following passage by Langeveld:

> As we all know, nothing is so silent as that which is self-evident. Thus it becomes our task to render audible, readable, articulate, that which is silent. As we all know too, humans are not simply born; they do not just grow up into mature adults. For what we call a child is a being that calls to be educated. (1983, p. 5)

Here Langeveld reflects two aspects of the phenomenological approach taken toward pedagogy. The first is the imperative of the phenomenologically oriented individual to make "audible, readable, and articulate" the realm of the silent "self-evident" (Langeveld, 1983, p. 5). This entails a continual process of interpreting the everyday world around us. Hermeneutic phenomenology is the process of describing the "essence" of something or, in van Manen's words, describing "that which makes a thing what it is (and without which it would not be what it is)" (1990, p. 177). It has been the project of the Utrecht School to develop this activity of pedagogical interpretation into a "science" of the self-evident, a *lifeworld science*. The effect of such a science would be the elucidation of those elements of our existence with which we are in contact most, our everyday lived world, those of which we are the most illiterate. Having practical ways of investigating our lifeworld would put us subjectively in touch with the knowledge of what it is to be-in-the-world instead of separating and alienating us from it by objectification. Objectification is the act of making the world fit into distinct dichotomous realms of subjects and objects. This dualism stresses the independent existence of things in the world and obscures the interactive, holistic existence of reality asserted by phenomenology. The latter is what Merleau-Ponty (1983) refers to as the "embodied" nature of existence.

Second, because children are not born knowing what it is to be human, and because they did not ask to be born, it behooves us as adults to assume a pedagogical role with children that assumes a determination "to bring into being for the sake of this child and with the help of this child, all that is essential to its being human" (Langeveld, 1983, p. 5). Van Manen comments on the importance of Langeveld's view of human nature when he writes:

> Humanness is not something with which a child is born but rather something to which a child is born, he [Langeveld] says. The human child is born to the promise of educational potential; it is this "potential of educability" that distinguishes a young homo sapien from the newly-born among the rest of the animal species. A human child is not just someone who can be educated, says Langeveld, it must be educated, by virtue of its need for extended care, security, and the need for growth opportunities to become an autonomous human being. Every child wants to become someone, him or herself: a person—that is, someone with personality. (van Manen, 1979a, p. 50)

According to the above statements, children come into the world by the willful acts of others and bring with them the innate need to become who they can be. As the volitional beings who have made their existence possible, adults are to assume the pedagogical purpose of assisting children through the self-formative process of possible ways of being-in-the-world. This view stresses that the possibilities of being are structured by the child's experience and therefore lie within the child's world, not the adults' world. Subsequently, the child assumes a primary, not secondary, place in pedagogical activity. Instead of being solely the recipient of instruction, the child also serves as its source. Phenomenological pedagogical investigation is therefore not only *for* children, but also *by* children. Adults provide the occasion for the lifeworld of the child and the potentiality that lies therein to appear.

According to van Manen, van den Berg's edited work *Person and World,* "contains some of the best contributions to the phenomenological enterprise of the Utrecht School" (1979a, p. 58) The foreword of that work, written by van den Berg and Linschoten, summarizes the program of the Utrecht School:

> We want to understand man from his world, that is, from the meaningful ground structure of that totality of situations, events, cultural values, to which he orients himself, about which he has consciousness, and to which his actions, thoughts and feelings are related—this is the world in which man exists, which he encounters in the course of his personal history and which he shapes through the meaning he assigns to everything. Man is not "something" with characteristics, but an initiative of relationships to a world which he chooses and by which he is chosen. (van den Berg & Linschoten, 1953, p. i)

HERMENEUTIC PHENOMENOLOGY AND MAX VAN MANEN

Hermeneutic phenomenology is often as varied an approach as those who choose to follow it and the interests to which it is applied. Rather than being a liability, this heterogeneity suggests the usefulness afforded by viewing the world from such a perspective. Phenomenology is a supple mold of investigation that allows itself to be in some respects recast by the subject it is committed to understanding or "seeing." While this is disdained by those who seek to order the world in tightly bounded and stable categories, it affords to others the tools of research necessary to allow the world to remain in its labyrinthine form and yet reveal the rich meanings of the lifeworld that is common to the researcher as well as the researched.

Due to this diversity, it is necessary to understand phenomenology as it is conceived by the particular researcher employing it. The following discussion of van Manen's view of phenomenology and phenomenological research may be helpful in introducing and discussing some of his unique emphases later.

The Pursuit of Everydayness

Following the lifeworld theme of Husserl, van Manen holds that the subject of phenomenological viewing is that of the everyday experiences of those in the world. Of special importance to him, of course, are those everyday experiences that relate to the pedagogical concerns and activities of parents, teachers and children. He writes, "phenomenology does not offer us the possibility of effective theory with which we can now explain and/or control the world but rather it offers us the possibility of plausible insight which brings us in more direct contact with the world" (1984a, p. 38). Emphasizing the need for "contact" rather than manipulation destabilizes the traditional, detached, and almost voyeuristic role of educational researchers and places them more in the posture of active participant.

Curriculum research that employs a phenomenological approach is a self-reflective process that seeks to give us a sagacious knowing of the mundane that affords enlightened pedagogical actions. The purpose of educational research is not to put us in command of our own or others' educational lives but instead to put us in "touch" with those lives. Phenomenology has historically been metaphorized as a "seeing" and a "hearing," which is a useful and significant characterization. Yet more than sight or hearing, it also involves the sense of "touching" or "being in touch" with those lifeworld experiences we seek to understand. Phenomenology brings a required sensitivity to understanding the pedagogical relationships that exist among parents, teachers, and children, sensitivity that, according to van Manen, has been lacking in much educational research.

The Discovery of the Primordial

The universal aim of phenomenology is to discover the primordial nature of ideas and the intended object of those ideas before "words" or language captured it (van Manen, 1984a). Phenomenological research assumes a "standpoint" that attempts to reveal meanings and understand how they are connected to lived experience. Phenomenology, however, is not an attempt at giving meaning to lived experience. Meaning is already existent and found in the "things" that make up our everyday world. Phenomenology proposes to describe the revealed meaning in its most essential form.

According to van Manen, the phenomenological question is not, "How do these children learn this particular material?"; it is, "What is the nature of the experience of learning (so that I can now better understand what this particular learning experience is like for these children)?" (1984a, p. 38). This paring to the very essence of a pedagogical experience is only achieved when the basic existential nature of that experience is understood. The result of this understanding is the possibility of a more informed response to that particular pedagogical experience.

In one sense, phenomenology can be understood as the philosophical examination of lived experiences. Reflecting Merleau-Ponty's influence, van Manen frames this conceptual exploration in poetic terms when he writes that phenomenological research is "a heedful, mindful wondering about the project of life, of living, of what it means to live a life" (1984a, p. 39). In fact, he encourages us to see that this whole process of wondering about life is itself a poetizing activity. In this sense, language is engaged as "a primal incantation or poetizing which hearkens back to the silence from which the words emanate" (1990, p. 13).

Contextualized Humanity

While Husserl contended that by use of "reduction" or "bracketing" one could somehow distance oneself objectively from that which was to be phenomenologically investigated, later theorists, especially Heidegger (1962), disagreed. They argued that such abstraction from the world was impossible because being-*in*-the-world and being-*of*-the-world meant to exist in constant interactive relationships with the world. It was impossible to abstractly assume a position that put one out of the context of the whole. Phenomenological investigation illuminates contextualized humanity. The primary phenomenological pursuit became to describe what it is to be human with the understanding that the phenomenological standpoint was not one of detachment. Max van Manen's research reflects this existential legacy when he writes:

> As we research the possible meaning structures of our lived experiences, we come to a fuller grasp of what it means to be in the world as a man, a woman, a child, taking into account the sociocultural and the historical traditions which have given meaning to our ways of being in the world. (1984a, p. 38)

Phenomenology is an investigative process that restores to the subject the autonomy of subjectivity and yet locates quintessential humanity in the descriptive interpretation of individual experience. It is not an analysis of subject-object encounters in the traditional Aristotelian sense, but more similar to an inquiry into what Whitehead refers to as the "ego-object amid objects" (1925, p. 151).

Phenomenology Is a Human Science

Van Manen chooses to characterize his hermeneutic phenomenological methodology as "human science research." He prefers to classify his work as "human science" because of how the term was employed by William Dilthey (van Manen, 1990). Dilthey denotes human science, or *Geisteswissenschaften,* as investigation concerned with those areas of human existence involving consciousness, purposiveness, and meaning. For van Manen, these areas of human existence are the necessary fields of pedagogical inquiry. In contrast, Dilthey posits the notion of natural science, or *Naturwissenschaften,* as research preoccupied with "objects of nature, things, natural events, and the way that objects behave" (van Manen, 1990, p. 3). Van Manen regretfully acknowledges that the methodology of "natural science" predominates in North American educational research.

Van Manen synthesizes contributions from the theoretical fields of phenomenology, hermeneutics, and semiotics. According to him, these are not used due to personal preference but because each is required to understand fully the phenomena of pedagogy. He writes that:

> pedagogy requires a phenomenological sensitivity to lived experience (children's realities and lifeworlds). Pedagogy requires a hermeneutic ability to make interpretive sense of the phenomena of the lifeworld in order to see the pedagogic significance of situations and relations of living with children. And pedagogy requires a way with language in order to allow the research process of textual reflection to contribute to one's pedagogic thoughtfulness and tact. (1990, p. 2)

MAJOR THEMES IN VAN MANEN'S WORK

Van Manen's work can be seen as phenomenological research into the concrete relationships encountered in educational practice. His desire to understand more about the existential relations experienced in pedagogical acts can be thematized as follows: (1) the interconnection between theory and research, (2) the place of "tact" in pedagogy, and (3) the place of the child in pedagogy.

The Role of Theory and Research

The decentering and isolating of the child.   For Max van Manen, much of current educational research suffers from a disinterested view that lacks a "practical pedagogic orientation to children in their concrete lives" (van Manen 1988b, p. 438). This lack of a pedagogical perspective and child orientation can be noted in various ways. One is the way in which curriculum theorists refer to themselves. Van Manen finds disturbing the trend among theorists to classify themselves as other than educators. He writes:

> Educational theorists exemplify their unresponsiveness to pedagogy in their avoidance of it. They would rather think of themselves as psychologists, sociologists, philosophers, ethnographers, critical theorists, and so forth, than as educators oriented to the world in a pedagogic way. (van Manen, 1988b, p. 438)

For him this reflects an attitude that shows educational researchers as being overconcerned with how they perceive and position themselves within the profession at the expense of the child and teacher/parent pedagogical relationship. He argues that studies emanating from the field give evidence to the professional posturing and primacy assumed by many researchers through their claims of being able to control educational settings by their research methodologies.

The assumption of manipulative roles by researchers in educational research exemplifies how contemporary research lacks a true pedagogic orientation to children. The result of this has been the decentering and discrediting of the relationship between the child and those significant others who approach the child in a pedagogical way. These "significant others" include teachers, administrators, and parents. Van Manen argues that the way that we as researchers position children within our research reveals our intentions toward them and identifies the relationship we have with them. He maintains:

> Rather than teaching us to live our lives with children more fully, educational research so often seems to be cutting us off from the ordinary relation we have with children. (1988b, p. 439)

He particularly criticizes ethnographical researchers who mistakenly assume that they capture the "true settings" of children and teachers through their research methodology. He writes:

> But what we are offered on the basis of these studies are texts of lives of children, teachers, administrators, and so forth that distance and estrange us from those lives rather than bringing these lives closer into the field of vision of our interest in children as teachers, parents, educational administrators, and so on. (1988b, p. 439)

According to van Manen, it is a misguided endeavor to isolate moments of educational activity between children and educators. It is a commonly held assumption that isolation from as many intervening variables as possible will make the activity under investigation clearer and more verifiable. In van Manen's view, what is accomplished by such practice is the constitution of an unnatural pedagogical setting. The scene of the pedagogical act becomes a contrived world fashioned after the interests of the researcher, not the researched. It is an investigation that lacks the moral presence of the children researched. He states:

> The children may be there as objects of our human science interest in them—but they are not morally present in that they force us to reflect on how we should talk and act with them and how we should live by their side. (1988b, p. 439)

How damaging a critique of modern educational research one regards van Manen's statements depends of course, upon one's epistemological view. Scientific realists, with their contention that the world is nothing but the sum of its parts, have no epistemological difficulty in attempting to isolate parts from the whole in order to understand the independent identity vs. dependent relation those parts have to the whole.

Human scientists, such as van Manen, instead stress that the world is the experiential domain of "being" and interminably connects with the experiential domain of other "beings." Understanding of what it is for human beings to be-in-the-world is possible by a descriptive phenomenological analysis of the nature of concrete experience. As a result of such analysis, it makes no sense to imagine that one can sever pedagogical experience (or any experience) from its highly complex and interwoven context. Although experience cannot be severed, it can be understood. To do so involves a phenomenologically empirical methodology that recognizes this contextual complexity and works hermeneutically within its existential framework.

Van Manen asks:

> Is it ever possible to observe a child closely and to see the child's experience in a pure way? Outside of our relation to this child? Is it possible to describe a child, and his or her lifeworld, in a fashion that is disinterested, that lacks orientation? (1988b, p. 439)

Van Manen's answer to his last question is, of course, no. Since it is not possible in the mainstream research paradigm, another theoretical model is necessary that understands a child's experience without reducing that experience to one's own (van Manen, 1988b). What we need is "edifying theory" (van Manen, 1982a, p. 41).

The misunderstanding of "theory."   For van Manen, educational theorists are raising many questions about educational theory but are missing the most essential one. It is the question of "how the subject of (educational) theory should even be spoken" (1982a, p. 41). According to him, we have lost the vision of the initial purpose of reflecting on pedagogical practice. A major cause of specious educational research is the misguided desire to conceptualize, and even reconceptualize, educational experience. Instead of approaching pedagogical practices directly in the original context of the lived experience, the majority of educational theorists are satisfied with manipulative reconstitutions of experience. Modern curriculum theorists attempt to capture conceptually the replicative essence of pedagogical practice. The common result of their efforts is existential alienation because, as he writes, modern theorists attempt to exchange the living rationality of the spontaneously experienced with a reconstructed rationality derived from a theoretic (reconstructed) account of desirable (because more rational) practice. (1982a, p. 46)

It is theory construction that seeks as its primary task to "find the permanent in the fleeting, the commensurable in the incommensurable, the conceptual in the unique, the measurable in the poetic" (1982a, p. 46).

Van Manen argues that practically all modern curriculum theorists fail, to some degree, in capturing the nature of pedagogy. This failure occurs because research into curriculum theory development is seen as an epistemological—not ontological—inquiry. It is a search for the theoretic principles of knowledge that succumbs to an emphasis of "method, certainty, . . . structure and rigor" (1982a, p. 46). For van Manen, strong curriculum theory is not that which philosophically and conceptually analyzes curriculum and pedagogy. Instead, strong theory is that which is committed to the orientation to or edification of the pedagogic good. By pedagogic good, he refers to "the end . . . from which all our hope, love and inspiration for our children draws its meaning" (1982a, p. 47). He contends that curriculum theory's role is not to inform us as much as it is to remind us and position us toward the pedagogic good of the student. Good curriculum theory, or *curriculum theory of the good,* helps us as pedagogues build a place, or *edifice,* for students to experience being-in-the-world in all its dynamic variances. He writes:

> As the poet poetizes to create speech which we experience as poetry, so the theorist edifies (builds, speaks, theorizes) in order to create theories which we may experience as edifying pedagogic consciousness. (1982a, p. 44)

Pedagogical theorizing takes on the hermeneutical role of interpreting the spontaneously experienced meanings found in the relationships that teachers, parents, and administrators have with children in specific pedagogical moments. It is reflective and interpretive and not manipulative or condescending, keeping in mind that pedagogical practice as an event is prior to pedagogical theory. Considering this van Manen writes that

> curriculum theory could be seen as edifying displays of examples of pedagogic praxis: relations and situations of thoughtfully "leading" the child into the world, by mediating tactfully between the original self-activity, the deep interest of the child, and the spiritual, cultural meanings and objectifications of the world. (1982a, p. 47)

What edifying theory pursues and provides for those involved in the activity of educating children is "pedagogic wisdom" or "tact."

Pedagogic Tact

The technical versus the nontechnical. Pedagogic capability or competence has been conventionally approached from positivistically oriented
research paradigms that use means-end methodologies to enhance the technical aspects of teaching. The objective is to create improved teaching competence in the classroom that will make learning more efficient and systematic. New teachers are annually ushered into classrooms with a myriad of
learning and student management strategies. They have been given preservice
practice as well as continuing inservice training in various new technical skills
that research has shown to be effective. What the research does not show, but
teacher experience soon acknowledges, is that teaching is much more than
the dutiful execution of technical acts. While most involved in education
would agree that good teaching is more than technical skill and performance,
van Manen questions why research has not attempted to investigate the nontechnical dimensions of teaching. By the nontechnical, he means those aspects of teaching where the issue is not skill-based strategies but the necessity
for "pedagogic tactfulness" or the "sensitivity or sensitiveness to a situation
that enables me to do pedagogically the right thing for a child" (1984b,
p. 158).

For van Manen, such tactfulness is not so much "a body of knowledge"
one possesses but rather "a knowing body," a way of being with students that
recognizes the pedagogical actions that are appropriate in a given moment
with a particular child. It is an improvisational thoughtfulness that involves
"the total corporeal being of the person; an active sensitivity toward the subjectivity of the other, for what is unique and special about the other person"
(1988c, p. 5).

A teacher who exercises tact is one who recognizes the highly subjective
nature of learning and is responsive to the uniqueness of the student. A tactful teacher is also one who knows when to exert influence and when to with-
hold it and enjoy a continuing sense of pedagogic confidence and capability
in spite of the varying learning situations they encounter (van Manen,
1988c). For van Manen, tact is pedagogically vital because it maintains the
child's preeminence in the learning environment; it strengthens what is good
and enhances what is unique in the child. Tactfulness is also important because with it, teachers are suspicious of that which could hurt the student,
and yet tact also "heals (makes whole) what is broken" (1988c, p. 6).

The pedagogue has opportunity to implement tact in speech as well as
in silence, in a particular glance or gesture as well as by example. Obviously,
tactfulness is not something that can be inserted into the daily lesson plan.
Van Manen emphasizes that although it cannot be planned for, one can prepare or ready oneself for it. This readiness demands engagement in a "pro-

found process of humanistic growth, education and the development of thoughtfulness" (1988c, p. 2). This process should lead to an ability to "read" and interpret the social context enveloping the relationship between the child and the teacher. Such reading is possible only by learning the language of unique experience. As van Manen writes:

> From a phenomenological point of view, to research is always to question the way we experience the world, to want to know the world in which we live. . . . Phenomenology is, in a broad sense, a philosophy of the unique, it is interested in what is essentially not replaceable. . . . Phenomenological research sponsors a certain attentiveness to the details and seemingly trivial dimensions of our everyday educational lives. (1984b, pp. 160–68)

Pedagogic tact as "resistance." For van Manen, the greatest enemy of pedagogical tactfulness is "the hegemony or desire for control" (1984b, p. 164). Agreeing with critical theorists such as Apple and Giroux, van Manen asserts that this desire for control encourages research methodologies and classroom practices that emphasize rigid educational outcomes as well as manageable behaviors:

> This process often turns politicians into educational powerbrokers, academics into pedagogic entrepreneurs, educational administrators into so-called executives, and teachers and other subordinates into replaceable workers, who now merely carry out what the technological educational bureaucracy has blueprinted. Insofar that creative technique, skill and tact are still required in the execution of externally planned and organized curriculum or social service programs, they are now interwoven in the methodological apparatus of the rational planning system (1984b, p. 164)

Unlike critical theorists who emphasize neo-Marxian critique as a tool of social and thereby educational reform, van Manen's emphasis on moving to resistance and reform from technicratization lies within the broader adoption of hermeneutic phenomenological research in educational theory and practice.

> Phenomenological research into the so-called theoretical basis of pedagogic tactfulness is a way of resisting the technologizing effect of pedagogic lifeworlds by claiming and exercising personal autonomy over our pedagogical actions. This personal autonomy is authorized, not primarily by the legal-rational power structures of bureaucratic institutions, but by our very pedagogic commitment to children. (1984b, p. 164)

Van Manen describes phenomenology as a "philosophy of action" well suited to radically reforming educational practice (1984b). His argument is

that phenomenology, because of its ontologically oriented methodology, provokes serious and original thinking about the world. It raises radical questions concerning preconceived ideas of what it is to be-in-the-world and what
is the nature of truth. A deeper understanding of the lifeworld of the student
through phenomenological research precipitates a greater likelihood of one
actively articulating questions and dissent concerning ideas and programs
that violate the good of the student. "It is on the basis of understanding what
serves the human good of this child or these children in need that one may
engage in collective political action" (van Manen, 1984b, p. 165).

Secondly, phenomenology is active, not passive, especially in the pedagogic setting, because pedagogy is the practice of action (1984b). Pedagogy,
by its nature, calls for active involvement in the lives of others. It is a way of
being-in-the-world that interactively responds to the way of being-in-the-
world of others, primarily children/students. Pedagogical tactfulness respon-
sively manifests itself only after others have acted. It is therefore a life of
action that is primarily one of re-action. Phenomenology aids the parent/
teacher/administrator by providing for informed pedagogical action/reaction
based on a greater understanding of what it means to be-with-the-student in
a pedagogical way.

A third and final reason van Manen cites in his argument for phenomenology as a philosophy of action is that phenomenology requires a sense of
situated personalness (1984b). The commitment to the child inherent in
pedagogy is underscored by the personal engagement required in doing phenomenological research. Van Manen writes:

> When I act towards a child I feel responsible that I act out of a full understanding
> of what it is like to be in this world as a child. And so, for the sake of this child
> or these children, I want to be suspicious of any theory, model, or system of
> action that only gives me a generalized methodology, sets of techniques or rules
> for acting in predictable or controllable circumstances. (1984b, p. 165)

For van Manen, what is needed most from educational research and
training is not the enabling of teachers with the ability merely to think but
also to be *thoughtful,* that is, pedagogically tactful (1988c). The personal
commitment to the child reflected in the above passage echoes the following
third major theme of van Manen's theorizing.

The Place of the Child in Pedagogy

The child's orientation.   In his view of educational research, Max van
Manen supports allowing the child to dwell in his or her proper place. He
contends that mainstream educational theorizing and research have decen-

tered the child and his or her perspective of the world, instead emphasizing the values and goals of the observer of the child, that is, teachers, curriculum theorists, administrators, and researchers. What he holds as essential is for educational research to orient its observation to view principally the "meaningful" experience of the child (1990). For van Manen, true pedagogically oriented observation assumes this type of relational emplacement in the child's life. Van Manen writes:

> The . . . pedagogue is oriented toward the child in a special way. While being concerned with maturation, growth and learning, I do this: I immediately enter a very personal relationship with the child. There is a fellow feeling between us but at the same time another and new distantiation which makes me "his observer." Since I "know" this child I can hold back superficial judgments about him. And in this holding back I create another "distance," but now of a different order of objectivity than the distance of the outside observer. "Simultaneously I stand closer but also further away." There is a maximal closeness with the maintenance of distance. This is what Beets means when he says "pedagogic observation is: discovering and meeting the other in the heart of personal existence." (1979b, p. 14)

Parents and teachers are given a unique opportunity of relationship with children. Their eyes, if properly focused, can see children in ways other adults cannot. A striking example of this is offered by van Manen in the *The Tone of Teaching* (1986). In a section entitled "Pedagogy Is Child-Watching," van Manen describes a story of how two people, one a passerby who has stopped for a moment to enjoy watching children play in a schoolyard, and the other, the children's teacher who is supervising the children at play, experience seeing a girl skipping rope. The passerby quickly looks past the girl in his mind and sees himself skipping rope as a child at play at school. He senses regret, for seeing her has stimulated a desire to revisit his childhood days. He knows, however, that those days are gone and so he too goes by. Van Manen then shows us the same child skipping rope in the schoolyard but this time through the eyes of her teacher. The teacher is also touched with remorse, as he watches the girl jump rope, but for entirely different reasons. He senses regret because he knows the child. He sees and hears the anguish of the child's life in every skip of the rope caused by an overdemanding mother and the consequential loneliness that haunts the child.

For van Manen, it is important to note that both adults saw the child, but only the teacher saw the person. The passerby saw the child as an opportunity to see himself and remember his past, whereas the teacher saw the child and found an opportunity to be even more aware of this girl and her needs. It is too easy for professional educators to assume the orientation of the passerby, especially when traditional research paradigms encourage such a nonpersonal view. He warns that educators must not adopt a control-oriented observational style that displaces the child into categories of adult interpretation. Instead, educators must adopt the child's orientation (1973, p. 181). For van Manen,

> The theoretical language of child "science" so easily makes us look past each child's uniqueness toward common characteristics that allow us to group, sort, sift, measure, manage, and respond to children in preconceived ways. . . . Putting children away by means of technical or instrumental language is really a kind of spiritual abandonment. (1986, p. 18)

To be oriented to the lifeworld of the child is to discover what a particular experience is like for the child. Van Manen contends that knowing what a particular pedagogical situation is like for a child is the first question that educators should seek to answer (1986). Such knowledge is vital because it gives to the teacher a clearing through which to approach the child. The clearing sets the tone and prepares the way for an educative encounter between the teacher and the student. This encounter is founded on the student's view of her world and establishes a relationship that is more prone to recognize what is pedagogically good for the child (1989).

The teacher's orientation. In view of van Manen's emphasis on the experience of the child in directing the pedagogical relationship, it follows that, for him, the place of the child in pedagogical research is not just the place of a student but also that of a teacher. He writes:

> Parents and teachers are good pedagogues when they model possible ways of being for the child. They can do that if they realize that adulthood itself is never a finished project. Life forever questions us about the way it is to be lived. "Is this what I should be doing with my life? Is this how I should spend my time?" No one can reawaken these questions more disturbingly than a child. All that is required is that we listen to children and learn from them. In this, children are our teachers. (1989, p. 13)

To van Manen, children serve as a type of primordial form of adult existence. Children are seen as archetypal beings disclosing primordial human existence. By approaching the world through the experiences of a child, we not only learn what it is like for the child in that situation, but the essences of human existence are also discovered.

> "I wish I could be young again but know what I know now." Many of us are nostalgic about our childhood, and not because we want to be children again. What we really want to do is be able to experience the world the way a child

does. We long to recapture a sense of possibility and openness—a confidence that almost anything is possible. . . . All kinds of things are possible when one is young, and the reward for both parents and teachers is the presence of hope. That is what a child can teach us. It is what a child must teach us if we are to be true and good parents and teachers. (1986, p. 29)

Van Manen criticizes educators who see themselves as competent and superior in their adult understandings of the world. Their attitude is one of not needing anything from children in the pedagogical relationship but their devotion, diligence, and cooperation. Such educators contend that children have no lessons to teach them other than possibly those of patience and the professional reward found in self-gratification when the students perform as predicted and desired. To van Manen, such educators turn education into a "pedagogy of oppression—an authoritarian form of domination of adults over children" (1986, p. 15).

CONCLUSION

Van Manen is a strong advocate for the voice of the child to be heard in research, in theorizing, and in everyday pedagogical activity. His writings reflect a deep sensitivity and commitment to children that are foreign to many adults. In part, his work attempts to give administrators, teachers, and parents a way to begin developing and extending their understanding of children. Though very beneficial, van Manen's work is restrictive in the sense that it articulates the young child's voice only as the voice of the student. Noticeably absent are distinctive student voices of adolescents and young adults. The factors contributing to this emphasis are possibly two. One involves van Manen's close relationship with his own child, and the second is his view of children as an expression of the primordial essence of human existence. In fairness, van Manen has never maintained that his research addressed all of the complexities of pedagogy. By insightful descriptions into the nature of pedagogical relationships with children, he indirectly reveals the need of phenomenological research that describes pedagogy in the context of older students; that is, secondary, college, vocational, and so forth.

Another strength of van Manen's work is its responsiveness to the criticism that phenomenology is too elitist in its methodology. Van Manen admits that for "newcomers to the enterprise of phenomenological method, such [phenomenological] descriptions are virtually impossible to reconstruct" (1979a, p. 57). He has sought, therefore, to make phenomenology more accessible and to extend the work of the Utrecht School by developing more explicit procedures for doing phenomenological research. His latest book, *Researching Lived Experience: Human Science for an Action Sensitive Pedagogy,* is an effort to accomplish these aims. This book is clearly written and includes a glossary to aid those not familiar with the vocabulary of phenomenology. Within the text, van Manen identifies six dimensions of conducting phenomenological research. Part of his discussion includes advice in formulating a human science research project and how to outline it in a research proposal. This book is beneficial to educators because it uniquely contextualizes phenomenological research and pedagogy as one and the same project.

Van Manen's book is also helpful in examining the status of phenomenological literature. Many of the phenomenological research works available to newcomers are essays published in various phenomenologically oriented educational journals. Many of these essays rightfully give explanation and defense of the value this type of research affords to our understanding of the world. Other essays give us the results of phenomenological study in beautifully written prose and poetic descriptions. The difficulty for interested readers is that these essays usually shield them from the concrete processes the researcher may engage in conducting the study. Van Manen recognizes that the processes of phenomenological research and writing are messy and difficult (1990). His book gives an "inside" perspective into the basic philosophical and methodological processes constituting this type of research and writing. Such insight aids in understanding the phenomenologically oriented reasons behind the various twists and turns taken by the researcher in framing the final description. Without this type of assistance, inquirers into phenomenological research often leave an encounter with a phenomenological text perplexed. The lingering impression is that to do this type of research, you need only be a "sensitive person" in the colloquial and not the phenomenological sense of the term.

Simply stated, Max van Manen has contributed immensely to curriculum and, more broadly, to educational theorizing and research by his explanation and application of phenomenology to pedagogy. Hopefully, in the years ahead, more of his work will become known to a wider and more diverse population of North American educators.

Acknowledgment. I wish to thank Professor van Manen for his criticism of this paper. His suggestions were most helpful; they have since been incorporated into the text.

REFERENCES

Beekman, A. J., & Mulderij, K. (1977). *Beleving en ervaring: Werkboek fenomenologie voor de sociale wetenschappen*. Amsterdam: Boom Meppel.

Bernstein, R. (1976). *The restructuring of social and political theory.* New York: Harcourt Brace Jovanovich.

Heidegger, M. (1962). *Being and time.* New York: Harper & Row (1927).

Langeveld, M. (1983). Reflections on phenomenology and pedagogy. *Phenomenology and Pedagogy, 1*(1), 5–7.

Merleau-Ponty, M. (1983). *The structure of behavior.* Pittsburgh, PA: Duquesne University Press.

van den Berg, J. H., & Lichschoten, J. (1953). *Persoon en Wereld: Bijdragen tot de Phaenomenologische Psychologie.* Utrecht: Erven J. Bijleveld.

van Manen, M. (1973). *Towards a cybernetic phenomenology of instruction.* Unpublished doctoral dissertation, University of Alberta.

van Manen, M. (1979a). The Utrecht School: An experiment in educational theorizing. *Interchange, 10*(1), 48–66.

van Manen, M. (1979b). The phenomenology of pedagogic observation. *Canadian Journal of Education, 4*(1), 5–16.

van Manen, M. (1982a). Edifying theory: Serving the good. *Theory Into Practice, 21*(1), 44–49.

van Manen, M. (1982b). Phenomenological pedagogy. *Curriculum Inquiry, 12*(3), 283–99.

van Manen, M. (1984a). Practicing phenomenological writing. *Phenomenology and Pedagogy, 2*(1), 36–69.

van Manen, M. (1984b). *Action research as theory of the unique: From pedagogic thoughtfulness to pedagogic tactfulness.* Paper presented at the Annual Conference of American Educational Research Association, New Orleans, LA.

van Manen, M. (1986). *The tone of teaching.* Richmond Hill, Ontario: Scholastic-Tab.

van Manen, M. (1988a). Personal communication to William F. Pinar.

van Manen, M. (1988b). The relation between research and pedagogy. In W. F. Pinar (Ed.), *Contemporary curriculum discourses* (pp. 437–452). Scottsdale, AZ: Gorsuch Scarisbrick.

van Manen, M. (1988c, October). On the tact of teaching. *Canadian Association For Curriculum Studies (CACS) Newsletter,* pp. 2–9.

van Manen, M. (1989). *A childhood reading.* Manuscript submitted for publication.

van Manen, M. (1990). *Researching lived experience: Human science for an action sensitive pedagogy.* London, Ontario: Althouse Press.

van Manen, M. (in press). *The tact of teaching: The meaning of pedagogical thoughtfulness.* New York: SUNY Press.

Whitehead, A. N. (1925). *Science and the modern world.* New York: Macmillan.

CHAPTER 4

The Time of Texts

MARGARET HUNSBERGER

"Time is one of the fundamental and most pervasive phenomena of our lives. Yet, unlike a thing, it cannot be tasted, seen, smelled, heard or touched. It has remained a perplexing and problematic phenomenon for human understanding."
Donald Polkinghorne, *Narrative Knowing in the Human Sciences*

It is a commonplace for us to speak of time as quantified, segmented, and invariant. We learn in school that a second is a small unit of fixed duration, that sixty of them make a minute, and that every minute is equal in length. This conceptualization is made manageable by, and dominated by, clocks and calendars. In our language, time becomes a sort of commodity; we recognize that we have a limited "amount" of it and so we "spend" time and we "buy" time or we "waste" a bit of it. The underlying analogy of money is very strong here, since the terms seem to be "borrowed" from talk about money. But then we also say, do we not, that "time is money"? And although, according to the clock, each individual has the same twenty-four hours available, some people appear to have more time at their disposal than others. To limit and constrain time in this way is regarded as a convenience to make it manageable. "The very concept of an *event* in nature is the result of the human programme of cutting nature up to make it intelligible" (Spurling, 1977, p. 39). Intelligible, that is, according to certain objectified criteria that prefer to examine segmented and isolated pieces.

Perception of time as segmented, invariant, and linear is cognitive, school-based knowledge that is thoroughly ingrained into us. But this learned knowledge does not necessarily reflect our inner sense of reality. As we experience it, a half-hour spent in the dentist's chair is longer than two hours spent over dinner with a close friend, no matter what the clock may say. Our colloquial language reflects this state. We say both that "time drags" and that "time flies" and see no contradiction or inaccuracy there. Interestingly, it typically does one or the other: "Time always seems to tease me, going either too slow or too fast" (Nureyev, 1963, p. 128). Thus we are caught in a dichotomy in which we know, cognitively, that hours are invariant and linear, but we simultaneously know, experientially, that hours vary greatly and that segmentation feels superimposed upon us. "People simply do not experience time as a succession of instants" (Polkinghorne, 1988, p. 127). The cognitive view is the way we are taught to think and speak, so that we have words for this scientific knowledge of time, but about inner time we are less articulate. Awareness of inner time may be realized initially as nothing more than a vague sense of unease or incompleteness about the scientific assessments of time. The two perceptions of time may be described as objective, or clock, time contrasted with experienced, or inner, time.

William James identifies one contrast between them as being that the present as we experience it has duration, even though in a scientific sense the present is only a flash. When we hear a song we experience all the notes, the whole song, as being sung in the present. James thus finds two kinds of present: the split-second one and the one that is experienced as having some duration. "The practically cognized present is no knife-edge, but a saddle-back, with a certain length of its own on which we sit perched, and from which we look in two directions at once" (1890, p. 609). In a sense the present is forever because we live exclusively in it. The past and the future are like the horizon—always there in the distance but never reached. And yet, like the horizon, they are very much with us, part of the landscape in which we are situated. Just as the horizon is needed in order to locate ourselves in space (being in a thick fog is disorienting), so the past and future are a necessary part of our sense of the present and of our sense-making.

> The future and the past are experienced as the horizons of my living present. The future is that towards which my task and projects are directed, and hence it is that which makes sense of my present since it defines the orientation, or at least the style, of my present actions.
>
> The past is an ever-receding platform to my present situation, yet which is subject to continual re-interpretation in the light of my present and future projects. Future and past are not points on a line, but intentionalities that anchor me to my environment. (Spurling, 1977, p. 40)

If time is truly a flux of intentionalities, then future and past are inseparably involved in the present, and the three divisions do not always serve us well.

Given the complexities of thinking about—and living in—time, what then happens to time during reading? How is it experienced? And how does our experience of time in reading relate to our experience of time in other ordinary activities? In order to pursue these questions, I asked several readers to talk with me about their experience of time in reading and what they feel happens to time as they read. Each of these people is university affiliated, and each reads both professionally and by personal choice in leisure time. They are identified here by first names only.

ENTERING THE WORLD OF THE TEXT

First there is the matter of entering the world of the text. Two acts of the will are implicit in the process of getting into the text. We must make the decision to "spend" some time with a particular text. That choice is made in clock time; it is the using of time: "I'll read for an hour," "I'll finish this book this evening," "I'll get as far as I can before it's time to leave." The second act of the will is a commitment to become involved with and open to the text. The moment of letting go of the reality of physical surroundings and entering the world of the text is the moment of transition from clock time to inner time and to a different sort of reality. This transition is made fairly easily by people who like to read or by anyone who is eager to become acquainted with the particular text in hand. But it is precisely that moment that can so easily become the barrier to reading. People who do not enjoy reading find that when they sit down and pick up a book they promptly think of several other things they would prefer to be doing. Just at the point where yielding to the text is required, they resist. Clock time is not suspended. A similar barrier is encountered when the text does not appeal but is "required reading" or when time suspension is not possible because we are really waiting to be called to an appointment and so are not permitting ourselves to slip entirely into the world of the text.

As Ian's statement implies, the transition to the inner world is clear, but is easily lost:

> I guess when something happens that brings me to the attention of the world, only then do I realize that I have half an hour to get somewhere. Clock time recedes, but how far? I guess it's always there ready to be brought forward. It's very easy to get back into. In my day-to-day existence I'm guided heavily by a sense of reserving an hour of this time for some purpose.

The tension between clock and inner time is becoming apparent. As readers we find it most enjoyable to be lost in the text, but that can only happen when we are free to let go of the clock and attend whole-heartedly to the text. As long as clock time retains its grip, we must be careful as we read not to slip too fully into the text. Reader after reader testifies to the experience of moving easily into the text and feeling world time recede, but not recede very far if responsibilities call. Doug notes the contrast:

Clock time is my work day. I'm tired, I try to squeeze more and more into it. Time is a real consideration for me. I try to use my time efficiently. So I'm aware of work occurring in world time and of what I can squeeze into half an hour here and there. For reading occurring in inner time, I think of losing track of time. When I'm really caught up in a book I like, I lose sense of time. But I've got to have a more extended period of time to get me out of time. It doesn't happen that often. If I'm in the library with twenty or thirty minutes before a class or a meeting, I keep an eye on the time so I won't be late. But as soon as that pressure is taken away, there are all kinds of things I can get into for fifteen or twenty minutes. Things can capture you.

People who enjoy reading are acutely conscious of the lack of synchronization between being lost in a book (time is irrelevant) and being aware of the clock in order to manage time efficiently (time is very relevant). In this way, time is experienced as disjointed.

> Temporality is an intrinsic property of consciousness. The stream of consciousness is always ordered temporally. . . . The world of everyday life has its own standard time, which is intersubjectively available. This standard time may be understood as the intersection between cosmic time . . . and inner time. There can never be full simultaneity between these various levels of temporality, as the experience of waiting indicates most clearly. (Berger & Luckmann, 1966, p. 27)

Heap (1977), based on Schutz, claims that reading occurs at the intersection of clock and inner time and that the essential requirement of clock time is existence, but the essential requirement of inner time is meaning and relevance. Within clock time, existence is basic. Text and reader must both exist. And as Berger and Luckmann indicate, awareness of time necessitates consciousness, essential in reading. But existence and consciousness are not enough. In inner time, the fixed temporal order of the world time becomes insignificant as our remembrances of past experiences, knowledge of the world, and predictions about the future, along with our values and visions— our reality—can all simultaneously be brought to bear on the making of a text interpretation. This inner reality is a constantly shifting vantage point, however, as life flows on, and so exactly the same factors will not be involved again should we choose to reread the text. The interpretation is thus bound to shift as well, whether slightly or significantly.

There seems a useful analogy here between the sense of time and that of space.

> Objective space lies on the horizon of every existential space, so that, for example, the space peculiar to dreaming must still work on and refer to the spatially

distinct objects of the real world. Indeed, the loosening of existential space from its anchorage in physical space is the defining characteristic of hallucinations. (Spurling, 1977, p. 37)

Similarly, in reading, clock time lies on the horizon of inner time. Clock time must recede to the horizon, but not disappear out of sight entirely. To live exclusively in inner time is a mark of illness; to live exclusively within world time and have no inner reality, no vision, may be just as disturbed, although less likely to end in hospitalization. Reading is at the intersection, encouraging and necessitating the two kinds of time, even if the movement between them is a little disjointed. And reading allows swings deep into the territory of inner time, just as some very routine tasks occupy the hands while allowing the mind to forage off toward inner reality.

Ultimately, however, we are clock-watchers, and in spite of our brief escapes we always feel the pressure of time at our backs creeping up on us. And that consciousness leads to two opposite concerns about reading and time. On one hand, we are eager to "save" time and hence to make the reading go as quickly and efficiently as possible. On the other hand, we sometimes use reading as a way to "kill" time, make it pass by.

SPEED READING

In our efficiency-conscious society, the possibility of speed reading has proven very attractive to many people. When there is a great deal of paper sitting on one's desk waiting to be dealt with, it is an advantage to get through it quickly. When professional journals arrive each month and one wants to keep abreast of ideas but not read what is mundane or familiar, skimming and scanning are useful skills. For such purposes, rapid reading is helpful. And acute awareness of the clock is one way to get work done.

But, of course, to go too rapidly is to miss many details. If details are important, it is usually necessary not only to go very slowly but to reread. If we are in a very great hurry to understand a text, we may go so rapidly that we understand virtually nothing and are not really reading at all. This is particularly so if the message of the text has great personal import in our lives. Jane Austen illustrates that situation in her description of a young woman, very much in love, who was badly upset by a quarrel with her lover, so that when she received a letter from him: "She read, with an eagerness which hardly left her power of comprehension, and from impatience of knowing what the next sentence might bring, was incapable of attending to the sense of the one before her eyes" (Austen, 1813/1972, p. 233). There are times when speed just is not helpful, and it is necessary to force ourselves to slow down.

Those instances in which saving time is important turn out to be related to work, business, getting the job done. What about personal reading? A significant difference between reading for information and reading for pleasure is that with the former the intent is to finish the reading in order to utilize the information gained; whereas, in reading as a leisure activity, the pleasure is in doing the reading itself, and it makes no sense to speed read. Part of the enjoyment of leisure reading is in savoring the richness of the language and the descriptive detail, in letting the world of the text rest gently on the mind and be envisioned, and in freeing the imagination to build on the proffered account. Such activities take time. Davies pours full dramatic scorn on the notion of speed reading in his discussion of

> the actual business of reading—the interpretive act of getting the words off the page and into your head in the most effective way. It is not the quickest way of reading, and for those who think that speed is the great good, there are plenty of manuals on how to read a book which profess to tell how to strip off the hulk and guzzle the milk, like a chimp attacking a coconut. There are remedial reading courses for adults who are dissatisfied with their speed, which show you how to snatch up clumps of words with your eyes, and how to bolt paragraphs at a glance, so that a determined zealot can flip through *War and Peace* in five hours, and like a boa-constrictor, gobble up all Plato in a week. But if you read for pleasure, such gormandizing will not appeal to you. What musician would hastily scan the pages of a sonata, and say that he had experienced it? (1961, p. 11)

The comparison to music is insightful. Just as the written notes are only a score and must be played or sung to become music, so a text must be savored by a thoughtful reader in order to be brought to life and fruition. Neither score nor text was intended to lie dormant or to be hastily devoured.

We have a great concern for speed and efficiency. But it was not ever thus. In the 1600s it was said: "Learn to read slow; all other graces will follow in their proper places."

THE READING HABIT

If we regard that advice with some amusement and skepticism, perhaps we should take a similar stance toward the popular attitudes of our own era. It is clear that not all reading is particularly informative or inspirational, nor is it meant to be. Some of it is done just to kill time while waiting or trying to unwind. And perhaps reading too much can on occasion induce a kind of dull-wittedness. Heather, who loves to read, admits that it is not an entirely unmixed blessing: "I've often been depressed by reading, too. You can read yourself into a sort of stupor. If you spend a great deal of time reading, you sometimes feel kind of numb, as if somebody'd hit you over the head." How can that be so? How can an activity that can be so insight-giving, so much a stimulant to the imagination, lead to numbness and stupor? Perhaps there is a clue in that word "stimulant." Perhaps reading, like a drug, can produce a variety of effects, depending on the way in which, and the purpose for which, it is taken. How does reading to kill time differ from reading to learn or to enjoy the encounter?

In reading such texts as mystery stories or romances, we feel the fascination of wanting to know "who done it" and how it comes out, but when we get to the end there is a certain emptiness. And mindlessness. People speak of reading such books when "I'm too tired to think" or "when I want to unwind, so that I can sleep" and add that such stories are immediately forgotten. "It's not the kind of meaning that stays in my mind. It's rather ephemeral, so that I can read the same thriller a couple of years later and not remember that I've read it until I'm well into it, unless it has been something that has intrigued me very much." For Nancy, there is a kind of immediate relief, but little lasting value, in such reading. This is not to say that she regards it as undesirable. There is, indeed, a place for ephemeral things. But the pleasure derived is temporary and superficial. It is reading done, as she says, "on the very surface of my mind."

The reading that is done solely for an ulterior purpose such as getting to sleep or killing time in an airport or doctor's office does not originate so much from a wish to become acquainted with a particular text as from a desire to make the time pass, since what we are really doing in those circumstances is not reading, but waiting. As long as the mind attends to the clock rather than the text, the waiting continues and the minutes drag, as the voice of the text is submerged. However, if we become involved in the text, then we are actually reading, and only incidentally waiting, instead of vice versa as before. At such times we may even go so far as to hope not to be called to the appointment for a few minutes, or we may quickly skim the article before an interruption occurs. The very term "interrupt" indicates the shift. On those occasions on which we look at the text but continue to wait, being called is not an interruption but a release.

Reading while waiting may be easier than living creatively inside one's own head. According to Nancy:

> I can't go very long without reading. That's why I think in some ways reading may be a drug. "Hooked on books" is an apt phrase. In our family reading was a good and appropriate thing to do. I had a friend whose mother was always telling her not to waste any more time reading. But I'm almost certain that in our family it was that you couldn't sit doing nothing. So what one did was to read.

Sometimes the reading, or at least the appearance of reading, is done for the sake of appearances. Being seen to be reading may be regarded as acceptable behavior. In those instances we make certain we have a book open in front of us. But it can just as well be that the reader is hooked and is virtually unable to sit empty-handed.

In a conversation between historian Arnold Toynbee and his son Philip, this same notion of being hooked arises:

> PT: I read them [thrillers] with half my mind and I never puzzle out who has done it, or anything like that. I think I read them because it is easier to be reading something than nothing. I think there's a disease of reading. I can't sit in a railway train without reading something. Even if I have to look through the advertisements in the back of a newspaper, I find myself reading. It's a very bad thing.
>
> AT: It is a disease that an Indian would despise one for. One ought to be able to contemplate, and to do that at any time and under any conditions.
>
> PT: I sometimes look out the window and think how pretty it is, but I find myself getting a bit nervous if I haven't got some print in front of me. (Toynbee, 1963, p. 94)

Why one ought to be able to contemplate anywhere is not very clear. Presumably contemplation, like any other activity, is facilitated by appropriate circumstances. But what emerges strikingly in this conversation is the strength of the "habit" or reading. It is almost stated in terms of a drug habit. "I get nervous without print" has overtones of needing a fix. Habits, of course, can be very strong and deviation from them quite uncomfortable. To contrast this view of reading as habit (disease, drug, compulsion) with the view of reading as an experience of understanding (meaningful dialogue) is to see how focal attention on time interferes with an open encounter with the text and how dependent reading is upon the reader's purposes and circumstances.

TOWARD MATURITY

The reading encounter also changes as the reader grows older. Becoming older is very much a matter of the calendar and invariant time, but how our thinking and attitudes change and develop is in the domain of inner time. Doug discusses the change he sees in how he experiences reading:

> I think I've become more tentative as I've experienced more, but I'm not sure about that. I'm also more definite about things. I guess I see

things less in simplistic terms and realize that they are more complex. I know I've become more definite about my political and moral views. There are things I reject out of hand. But in other ways—I recently read an essay which made lots of sense, but it had a new point in it that I'd never encountered before and I was tentative about accepting it. But then, as I thought about it and had a chance to talk it over, that seemed to help clarify it—it's a pretty definite fixture in my thinking at this point. So at first I wondered, but then as I lived with it awhile and talked a bit about it, I finally came to accept it.

The sense that Doug expresses of feeling both more definite and more tentative is familiar enough and is confirmed by other readers. As we mature, we become more aware of complexities and less ready to leap at new ideas. So when a new concept is presented to us, we are more tentative, less likely to accept or reject it out of hand. In being slower to make up our minds, we are more thoughtful—or at least, we give ourselves the opportunity to be more thoughtful—about the new idea. This attitude of tentativeness allows for greater tolerance than we had when making the quick judgments of our youth, and greater tolerance is supposed to be an attribute of increasing maturity.

At the same time it also allows for more critical judgment. Betty is very much aware of that aspect:

When I started university, anything that was in a textbook that looked knowledgeable pretty well had to be true. I would read and accept without question. Also whatever meaning came to me as I was reading, I would accept unless I was forced to go back. I think I still tend to do that with novels, but with textbooks I used to accept my first interpretation whereas now I'd be more inclined to do some other reading to see if I could get further clarification. I'm definitely more critical now.

It is interesting how a measure of tentativeness in interpreting and responding simultaneously promotes more critical judgment and more tolerance. For both take some time and thought. Snap judgments preclude both. The reader who is willing to consider an idea, temporarily accept it perhaps while playing with it, has a good chance of understanding it, seeing why it appealed to its writer, and finally responding in an intelligent and logical way. This tentativeness may allow not only for more tolerance of the views of others but also for more understanding of their situations and their reactions in those situations. So the attitude toward text may have implications for interpersonal relationships, which is to say that it has implications for personal maturity and character development, a concern Heather raises:

Reading was more of an escape for me at one time. Now that I'm older I don't like romances; I like stories that are more in touch with what's really happening. But I read less fiction than I used to; I find it more important to read books that touch on some philosophical or spiritual dimension. One hopefully is changing as a person. I like to think that I'm becoming more understanding and more knowledgeable. Therefore, our reading should be a part of that.

Heather's daily round and her reading are coming closer together. Integration is a dimension of maturity. She is less likely to wish to escape into a rose-tinted world where the text makes all too clear the barrier between itself and experience, and more inclined to seek texts that speak directly to her daily life and its concerns.

Yvonne also feels less separation between reading and daily routine than in her youth, so that now she is conscious of reading happening within time and within life. This gives her more perspective on the text and allows her to be both cooler and more appreciative in her responses than was previously possible:

As I've grown older, reading has a different dimension in my life. I think when I was young—I guess I began seriously reading when I was 12 or 13—reading was realer than life. The characters in books and their situations were realer than in life. Part of that was that I had the feeling, although I didn't articulate it until I was in my 20s, that people were more open in books. People in the books talked about and lived through things that I had no part of. And they weren't bizarre books. These were books about rather ordinary people, and the thoughts were legitimately in those books, whereas those things couldn't have been discussed at home. And I don't think we were a particularly rigid family that way.

Now I'm much more conscious of time and much more objective about it than when I was young. Then time was a much more subjective experience. I don't identify with the characters as much now. I think, essentially because I have so much more experience than I did when I was a kid, that I'm more appreciative of what the writer has been able to convey. I'm influenced by having studied university English, and if something really strikes me I'm intrigued by how it was achieved. Then I'll go back and think of it that way. I don't see that as being particularly intellectual. If anything, it deepens the enjoyment. But the time dimension has changed for me.

Since Yvonne's life experiences, including her university study, are no longer so much cut off from reading experience, she can bring them to bear

on her interpretations and understanding and hence enter into a fuller dialogue, be more sensitive to and appreciative of text and its detail, style, turn
of phrase, and story. When reading was "realer than life" it was another world
and she was aware of distinction and contrast between the two. As they partially merge and influence each other, the impulse is toward integration.

TIME IN THE TEXT ITSELF

But the reader's sense of time does not form independently from the text
that influences how time is experienced. Some texts use time much more
overtly than others. Yvonne points out that:

> some authors leave us much more aware of time than others. I'm think-
> ing of *War and Peace,* where it seems to me you were very much aware
> of the time element. He would say, "Late that October . . ." and then
> give a description of the city in October and the leaves whipping
> around in the streets so that you were much more aware of time. One
> of the cleverest stories I ever read as far as time was concerned was one
> by Doris Lessing. She talks about this marriage and there's nothing in
> the marriage except they celebrate Christmas and they go away for two
> weeks every summer. And the whole story just moves like that—6
> o'clock, 12 o'clock, 6 o'clock, 12 o'clock. There are two points in the
> lives of those two people.

A text can explicitly create the sense of time passing or time dragging
emptily if that is important to the theme being presented. But a novelist is in
an interesting predicament in this regard. For the seeming length of time
alters when recollected from what it was when lived. "In general, a time filled
with varied and interesting experiences seems short in passing, but long as
we look back. On the other hand, a tract of time empty of experiences seems
long in passing, but in retrospect short" (James, 1890, p. 624). During the
act of reading, which experience is the reader having? There is an immediacy,
and often an involvement, in the story that is very much present time, but it
is like past time in that the reader is thinking about the action rather than
doing it. A text that tries to show emptiness in a character's life by dragging
it out in the text risks boring the reader, but how else to show it? Fortunately,
in most stories the attempt is to show something rather than nothing, action
rather than emptiness. It is difficult to write interestingly about emptiness.
But it can be done. Yvonne continues:

In many novels there is a sense of both kinds of time operating on two different levels. In *War and Peace* that one winter seems to last and last because it's so cold and desperate. So that there is also a clear sense of inner time in which time doesn't pass evenly and certain seasons are very long. Probably the clearest example is Solzhenitsyn's *One Day in the Life of Ivan Denisovich*. It starts at 6:00 A.M. and literally tells about every hour in the day. And yet there are, within that, inexorable days that go on and on and on, so empty, dull and endless, forever.

An hour can be experienced as lasting indefinitely. And there is no connection between this sense of duration and the time actually spent reading.

Authors can also manipulate time in fiction in a way that is so unrealistic and contrived as to be disturbing to the reader, as Alice observes:

In fiction especially time gets turned around so much, and people in novels behave in a certain way which sometimes is so manipulated by flashbacks or whatever that it doesn't seem to have a reality of its own; it's just something that can be moved around for purposes of plot or whatever. It's not suitable at all. People don't always behave exclusively because of past experience.

Writers of fiction cannot assume that because the world they are creating exists only on paper, they have a freedom to arrange the time and characters as they please. Certainly flashbacks and other such devices can be used, but the resulting flow of time in the story must seem to the reader to be natural and appropriate to the story. Manipulation that is apparent fails. The characters cannot be seen merely as puppets pulled by strings of their past—influenced by their past, yes, but not automatically responding based on a flashback conveniently inserted. Time is experienced in many variations, but it has its own constraints.

The type of narrative also affects the experience of time. Jeff notes that when he reads a mystery story his feeling is a great desire to whip through it and find out what happens. The reading is fast and the feeling somewhat superficial. "The story is trivial, and I know that when I eventually do find out what happens I'm going to wonder why I got excited in the first place." Although the long-term results may not be very satisfying, the story is, for the moment, fast and exciting. Other sorts of narrative call up different responses. Jeff speaks of one novel that created for him "a remarkable sense of stillness." To read this story was to leave behind his own world with its particular distractions and pressures and enter one with a very different rhythm and pacing to it:

Far Tortuga is about turtle fishing. For the first 300 pages it's as if you were on this turtle fishing boat with nine other men and doing the chores of running the boat and talking during their mealtimes and idle hours about life back home, talk of the most trivial and unimportant kind. It's as if you are there living with the men, doing what they do at the pace they're doing it. Movement stops. Your life is sort of suspended and you simply readjust your rhythms to the rhythms of turtle fishing. What I learned about turtle fishing is that not much happens! At least until you actually do the fishing, then it's difficult, hectic, and even dangerous if the seas are rough. So for 300 pages very little happens except that nine people live out their lives for three weeks. It's tranquil and still and timeless. Then in the last sixty pages everything comes together. It took me as long to read the first 300 pages as it did those turtle fishermen to do the nothing that they did for three weeks, then the last sixty pages went fast because everything ends with a great swoop.

A reader who wants constant action will probably skip through those 300 pages and concentrate on the last bit as the only "good part" of the book. A reader who is willing to adapt to the text's pace and enjoy the tranquility has the opportunity to slow down, perhaps pause, daydream a little. If texts can create tense, high-action worlds that make the heart beat faster, they can also create a stillness that gives reprieve. The text can create the mood, but the reader must be vulnerable to it and willing to join in.

While Jeff is pointing out stylistic distinctions within one text, Yvonne is aware of the effects of different writers on the reader's inner time:

It seems to me that different authors have a different pace. I think for example of someone like Alice Munro. I read her very slowly because I don't want to miss any detail. I read her the way you look at wallpaper with a lot of detail and you just have to look a long time and you go slowly, but it's not slowly in the sense of tediousness. It's like a summer's day—you just savor it. And then you think of *The World According to Garp* and there's no other way to read it except to romp. He uses every trick in the book to keep that pace up for 500 pages. There are times when he doesn't do it, but you can't slow down. You're either romping or skipping.

How is the text able to prod the reader toward that variation in pacing? It would be possible to list stylistic devices such as sentence length that affect the reader's pacing and are a necessary part of the writer's craft, but they are only the skill, not the art. Part of the art is the text's ability to create its own world; the world may be real or fantasy, inside or outside of the reader's experience, present day, past or future, big or little, described at great length or evoked in a phrase. It can be a huge world of battlefields and continents filled with thousands, or it can be as small as one person, but it must be clear, so clear that the reader sees it and feels it intimately and fully and can know it well. The text must create its own world, make it come alive and open the door to invite the reader in. The reader can always decline, but people who like to read are rather willing to be lured in. And the world can be tranquil or cataclysmic or anything in between and can move during the story from one to another. If the text can evoke its own special world in the first place, it can also alter it to one with quite different inner time. Readers are not only willing, but eager, to be involved in other than personal experiences and to feel the different time, clock and inner; that is one of the reasons for reading.

Jeff makes a comparison between effective narration and the passing of ordinary life:

> The way we live our lives day by day, we can't accelerate events. Events have their own kind of volition and life unfolds. We don't try to accelerate it to see what's going to happen. Yet in mystery stories we want the whole thing to unfold so we can see what's going to happen, then discard that book and begin on the next one. It's only a diversion, and not at all like living. Whereas more thought-provoking books *are* life, and events unfold as life unfolds. They'll end, we know that, but there's no hurry to get there.

In fact, in life there is normally a distinct wish not to get there.

Included in this sense of no hurry for the text to end is having the time and the wish to daydream. Reading can trigger the imagination not only to visualize what is being read about but to extend the story or the ideas in various directions, or to shift, perhaps through metaphor or analogy, to a different topic, or even just to digress through a whim of fancy into another interesting area.

Narrative, discursive writing, and poetry each have somewhat different relationships to time. One of the essential characteristics of narrative is that it includes change. If anything at all is to happen in the story, change must occur. And change takes time. In a narrative the timespan encompassed can be anything from a second to centuries, but there is recognition of time passing. The other two types of text require no such assumption. They may imply or discuss the passing of time, but they need not do so in order to be what they are. Discursive writing, however, is dated. When we read it, we want to know when it was written and take the time of writing into account as we read. Some discursive writing quickly becomes outdated and is read, if at all, largely for historical interest. That which remains relevant, however, still requires a date of writing as a guide to the context within which it must be interpreted. Neither of these conditions is necessary for poetry. To the extent that a poem deals with universalities, it is eternity in a moment.

So texts influence inner time by their style, structure, topics, and worlds. A strong constraint on texts is that by their nature they are presented as linear, flowing in a continuous line from beginning through middle to end, moving along through clock time. The story or argument must be made to flow along that same line whether or not it is itself linear and whether or not it was written in that order. This can be a point of tension between clock and inner time. The layout is linear. But the reading . . . ?

SEQUENCE AND ENDINGS

The logical way to read a book, as any schoolchild knows, is to start at the beginning and progress systematically line by line, page by page, to the end.

But is that how we usually read? Dictionaries, for example? Or sources when we are reading about a topic in preparation for writing a paper? Discursive writing is typically read very selectively. With reference books (telephone directories, recipe books, atlases), our attention is confined to the item we are concerned with at the moment. In professional reading, such as journal articles, we select by title, skim rapidly any parts containing familiar ideas, or consider only those sections that seem relevant at the moment. A common practice is to read the summary first and use it in deciding whether to backtrack and to what. Jeff claims, somewhat tongue in cheek, that his professional reading:

> is done by osmosis. Somebody comes in to my office and will be talking to me, and it will become important to check something out and we'll look it up and read a page or two. Who knows, maybe over the course of 20 or 30 years you do read all of the book, at least all the good ones.

This sense of being pragmatic and, incidentally, nonlinear is very strong and is experienced as being "only common sense" in reading for information. Among people who do a great deal of professional reading, discursive writing is so commonly, almost predictably, not read straight through that it is remarked upon when an able reader is found who does proceed that way. This is the case remarked on in a biography of Pierre Trudeau:

> Even more than his body, Trudeau disciplined his mind. Blessed with an exceptional memory, he read omnivorously and with a ferocious, head-down tenacity.

"I was never satisfied with reading eight chapters of a book, I had to read twelve."
Even when teachers recommended it, he never skipped. He has never altered this
linear approach. Early in 1979, when members of the Task Force on National
Unity gave Trudeau an advance copy of their report and met with him privately
to discuss it, he asked them questions only about the first three chapters—all
he'd had time to read. By contrast, Marc Lalonde at the same meeting hopped
all over the map because, as most of us would when pushed for time, he had read
only the summary of recommendations. (Gwyn, 1980, p. 32)

The fact that such a comment is included indicates how exceptional this reading pattern was thought to be. And while Trudeau is known to be an able
student, this approach to discursive writing is not particularly efficient, nor
advisable to teach children to use.

Teachers have a tendency to advise students to be linear in their reading.
As a result, many of us read that way until we stumbled across the discovery,
possibly about first year university, that it is not possible to prepare term
papers that way. Impending deadlines forced skipping. And gradually we figured out how to select articles, which parts to read, how to use an index most
effectively, and so forth. More teaching about alternate ways of reading
(other than "straight through") would not be amiss. Even young children
should not be taught that linearity is necessary or automatically desirable.
Indeed, changing the order is one strategy that may help to clarify when we
are having trouble understanding. Skipping back and forth sometimes helps,
as later text is used to inform earlier text: "Now I understand what is meant
back there."

But stories are different. They have a sequence that builds through crisis
points to a climax. Is it important to read them in the order given? Readers
disagree and tend to form two groups: those who read in a fixed order and
those who skip around in the text. With this difference of view, it is interesting to examine both reading approaches and the reasons given for them.

First, those who keep in line. Pat sees herself as a systematic person and
rejects skipping ahead:

I try not to do that; that's cheating. Cheating myself, I mean. The author has a structure and a reason for organizing that way. I only skip a
section or read the ending if I'm bored; otherwise I read in order. I
think that's because of the kind of person I am—very methodical.

Yvonne indicates that to read the ending early on is to "break the trust" with
the author. Jeff holds a similar view:

I have a rule of thumb; I'm absolutely ethically bound that I'll never
turn to the end and find out how it ends. Sometimes I'll sneak ahead

and see if the name of the person I'm most interested in appears on the last page. That's the closest I'll come to cheating.

(That is also about as close as it is possible to come to doing something while still claiming not to do it.) Terms such as "sneak," "cheat," and "trust" indicate the moral/ethical force that these readers give to this decision. They are content to wait for completion and wholeness of text. Paul suggests that the reason it feels like cheating to him is that in real life we cannot look ahead, cannot see endings in advance of their happening. Inner time permits skipping around; clock time does not. Because reading is one form of real-life experience, reading ahead feels like trying to cheat life, or "cheat myself." This implies that to know the ending may ruin a good story, that the enjoyment is in the suspense and the living out of a story. A strong sense of story structure and of how stories ought to be told and experienced seems a good reason to leave the outcome to the end. Not everyone shares that feeling about stories, however.

Does knowing the ending really spoil a good story? If it is important not to know, why did *The Day of the Jackal* become a best-seller? It is a fictional account of an assassination plot against Charles de Gaulle. Most readers know before picking up the book both that there were a number of attempts on de Gaulle's life and that they all failed. Thrillers are the sort of story in which it is supposed to be crucial not to know. Why read this one? Well, of course, the plot and characters are still unknown. And the story is fast paced and action filled. But it also seems that sometimes knowing the outcome adds to, rather than detracts from, the enjoyment.

Some readers, in contrast to the former group, read the ending early in an attempt to achieve unity of text and to do it as soon as possible. As Cathy says:

> When you do reach the end and reflect on what you've read, there's a wholeness there. But I don't know if it's at the end in particular. I read the end of the novel first anyway, so that puts it into a whole framework for me, and I can see if there is a logical unity there.

Later text can, and in effective reading will, always be used to influence the interpretation of earlier text. If the text is read in sequence, the earlier text must be reinterpreted in light of later text in a gradual building of understanding; if later text is read first it can be used immediately, although there is a risk of misinterpretation because of missing parts. In a sense the future is being used to influence the past in a way that it never can be in daily life. Some of the benefits of rereading may become available on first reading.

Cathy adds that "reading ahead is one of my major strategies in whatever

I read." The term "reading ahead" is almost self-contradictory. How can we be reading ahead of where we are actually reading? But the fact that such a term makes intuitive sense demonstrates the breakdown of linearity and the forming of something much more interactive and intertwined.

Alice also reads ahead: "I read the last page early, depending on what kind of novel it is. I admit it unashamedly." Although Alice is very free to make this statement and smiles as she does so, her use of the words "admit" and "unashamedly" conveys a sense that there may be something to be ashamed of, but she has sufficient confidence and bravado not to be. She is also very clear about her reason:

> It keeps me from rushing. Sometimes I find myself galloping through something just to find out what happened, so that way I can read and enjoy the author's attention to detail. If the author is literate and enjoying the historical part of it, then I can enjoy it also. Whereas if I'm reading to find out who gets the girl or how she outwits the wicked uncle, I miss all kinds of richness. I don't do this with everything, but I do with that type of romance or mystery that hinges on something. I don't have to know how the detective or whoever works things out because I like to see that progressing, but I do like to know who wins at the end.

Alice is saying that knowing at least a piece of the ending, rather than detracting from the story in any way, enhances her ability to appreciate the story, since it frees her to attend more widely to a variety of aspects in the writing and to understand the text more fully. And she specifically uses this strategy on "light" reading, romances and mysteries, the very type that are often thought to be spoiled by knowing how it comes out.

But there is more to a story, even to a thriller, than knocking the ending. It can be read as a puzzle to see if the pieces fit together. (Mystery stories are often not quite that cleverly crafted, and discrepancies frequently appear.) Or it may be read just for the thrill, a thrill that our routine does not provide and that we would not want anyway, but which is fun as long as we really know that we are safe in our own homes. When we feel ourselves genuinely threatened, such stories become distasteful very quickly. Even as a thrill, this is a chance to see life through another lens and extend our view.

With series stories, it does not matter when the ending is read, because even before starting we already know that the protagonist is going to survive and win. (On one of Wayne and Schuster's comedy records, they do a mock adventure story sketch in which the hero gets into a mess from which there seems no escape. At that point he says, "But I'm the hero, I have to survive." To which his partner replies, "Oh no, you don't. This isn't a series, just one little old LP.") The knowledge that a hero will not die means that it is safe to feel an identification. In those stories where the ending is not known there is great risk in linking our own fate too closely with that of someone who may not survive. Maybe that is another reason for looking ahead. But the limitation of such series is at exactly the same point. The fact that the main character will always triumph keeps the stories from being taken seriously. And if it is what makes identification safe, it is also what makes it difficult. How can we, with our personal doubts and struggles, identify with the always smooth, smiling, invulnerable protagonist? Our lives contain hopes, but little certainty.

Another support for using any order the reader chooses is given by Ingarden (1973) in his observation that the objects portrayed in a text gain a different order from the sequence used in the text. People, events, and objects are organized and seen in the reader's mind in a different order from that in which they are told or described. The writing has to be linear to some degree, but the reader's understanding does not.

And when the text, in whatever order, is ended, what then? What is the experience of coming to the end?

> With a really good book I have this terrible conflict when the ending comes because I want to see some closure in terms of the story, but I don't want the book to end. And I certainly have experienced with some stories a tremendous sadness because it's over and you know you can't pick up the book again. Not in the same way you did the first time.

For Yvonne the arrival at the last page of a book involves a sense of separation that comes with any parting and the ambivalence that is common to separations. On the one hand there is a desire for the conclusion of one phase, a sense of completion and an impetus to move on to something else; but simultaneously there is regret at having to let go and leave the world of the text, in which we have participated and which contains people whose association we want to keep. But the text, like life itself, pushes us ever onward. There is no more sheltering under the umbrella of the story-world. It is, of course, possible to reread the book and to recapture some of the pleasure, but as Yvonne indicates, it is different. It will now be a conscious going back to something known and enjoyed, not a striding forward with vulnerability to new experiences.

But even if it is not quite the same, to reread is one way to extend the experience and live in the world of the text a little longer. Rereading at least makes the breaking off from the text more gradual. "Nina had finished the journal Sunday night. And because she couldn't bear it to be finished, started

all over again, seeing ever more deeply into Odile and her feelings for K"
(Cameron, 1968, p. 89). The seeing more deeply and understanding better
is a chief benefit of rereading, but it may not always be the reason for starting
to reread. It is that bittersweet feeling that we cannot "bear it to be finished."
Naturally we do not wish to see the end of a world in which we have lived
happily. Actually, we know it is still there and we can revisit or recommend
it to friends. But we have to reassure ourselves of that. In the moment of
running out of text, there is still the sense of loss.

Jeff feels a similar reluctance to let go, but his desire for "this new world
to go on" is more specifically focused on those texts which create a community he has joined:

> Every now and again I read a book that I don't really want to end. I
> have that feeling in reading Tolkien. I didn't want to finish *The Lord of
> the Rings*. In fact, I don't know if I did finish it. I know how it ends.
> I've read all but the last eight to ten pages probably. I remember that I
> didn't want to see the breakup of the fellowship. In a sense I know that
> that's what had to happen, but I didn't want to be a part of it. It was
> inevitable, but I loved the book so much that I didn't want to see it
> happen.

This sense of participating in a fellowship points up one of the paradoxes
of reading. Reading is essentially a solitary activity best done by one person
in a quiet room, but the experience of reading is frequently the alleviation of
loneliness, the moving into a fellowship. And if the ending of the story shows
the fellowship dissolving, the reader can never return to it without being
influenced by that knowledge.

But a wise author is able to let a reader go at the end. That may be as
much a part of writing well as is catching the reader's attention at the beginning. For Yvonne that is important:

> I think at the end of a good novel there is a psychological resolution of
> some sort, more than just a resolution of conflict in the story. There is a
> peacefulness. The author lets you go. If the author ensnared you at the
> beginning, then it seems to me there is a letting go.

Part of the letting go is in the presentation of a story that illuminates our
lives, that does not produce a sense of jarring irrelevance, and that can become an integral part of life.

And, for all the reluctance we feel to be faced with the end of a good
story, readers do find a certain satisfaction in the final pages of a text. Reading

any story involves succumbing to an eagerness to find out what happens next. It is important that the story comes out "right." And a right ending involves going in the direction we have been led to expect, perhaps with a twist to make available any subtleties, such as those of symbols, that we may have missed. That is, the reading has a trend, so the ending must take us down the road we thought all along that we were on; but the author is welcome to put a little bend in the road and give a bit of surprise. Thus, as noted above, Jeff says of the ending to *The Lord of the Rings,* "I knew it had to happen. . . . It was inevitable." He did not happen to like it, but that did not keep him from recognizing that it was "right." However, Jeff also notes that:

> sometimes the writer saves the final surprise so that ideas don't fully come together until the very end. I have thought I was fully under-standing the message that the writer was pointing toward, and then all of a sudden in just the last page or two I've seen that the message, the truth, had really been slightly escaping me and I'd not really been fully appreciating what the writer was trying to say until the very end. That hidden kind of message wasn't revealed until the end. It's not until you see the whole that you can really understand what the work is about.

Jeff recognizes the contradiction in his statements of saying on the one hand that he occasionally does not quite finish a story and on the other hand that the story cannot be fully understood apart from the ending. He admits he may be missing some final surprise by not reading the last few pages of *The Lord of the Rings* but says he was completely satisfied with the story as he had experienced it and felt no need to attend to the ending. The contradic-tion may be more apparent than real. For the story in question makes a difference. Some stories have unexpected or particularly powerful endings that really are a twist of the tale and strongly influence our understanding of the whole story. They build to a crescendo and final crash of strong chords. But other stories wind down gradually, almost drift to a close. The impact of such stories is made subtly and gradually throughout.

When the text presents us with a world that appeals as resonant of real life, it is understandable that we should want to stay in it as long as possible and that we should find the ending illuminating both for insight into the whole text and for reflection upon our own experience. And sometimes the text world lives on after reading. "Sometimes when I'm reading I'm only getting the overt significance of what has happened, but later on upon reflec-tion things spring forward and a whole new meaning arises." Alice's experi-ence often happens to readers. If the text has really made an impression, it mulls around in the mind, forming and reforming itself. Some details fade, others emerge from different parts of the text and link themselves together. A bowl of flowers with petals falling described near the end becomes a symbol for a portrayal near the beginning of a comfortable way of life about to be disrupted. And in the linking the meaning of both flowers and prerevolutionary life changes. Part of the pleasure of reading is in that process of integrating the text afterwards:

> When I'm reading there's a sense of moving into a new realm. At the same time there's a going back between what I'm reading and the things I've already read. What I'm reading now has a sense of projection into the future, but is very much tied to the past. That which I read in the past is changing because of what I'm reading now. There's constant reinterpretation of what I've read in what I'm reading now. So in that sense the meaning of the text to me is constantly changing. Even when I read the last page and put the book down, the meaning is still changing. As I take up the book again at some future point, I'm constantly changing, so I see it in that light. I find fascinating that sense of living with what the author has said.

In the moving vantage point Ian describes, divisions such as past and present become inappropriate. Out of the changing and modifying interpretation and reinterpretation, text influences text and text influences life. Any text may be modified by another read later, so that it is not possible to say that one text has its fixed and final interpretation. Also, a text may continue the reading dialogue by its effect on us and our thinking—an aspect important to Cathy:

> In a sense I suppose a text is finished when I close the book, but it's not finished inside of me. If it's had an impact on me, it's something that I think about and ponder, go back to again. It's never finished. It's part of who I am.

The phrases used by these readers—"with some texts the reading never ends," "it's growing older together," "it's part of who I am"—show the very strong and lasting impact they perceive reading to have on their imaginations and their lives. This points out the importance of what is read and accepted and shows also the continual impulse toward making sense, unity, and, hence, integrity in our lives.

SEEKING UNITY

The understanding that is necessary for such wholeness emerges in two aspects of time: that which occurs during the reading as it flows along, and that which comes together afterward to form a new kind of unity. Ingarden identifies the two phases in general time:

> First, the reading of a specific literary work, or the cognition of that work which takes place during such reading, and second, that cognitive attitude which leads to an apprehension of the essential structure and peculiar character of the literary work of art as such. (1973, p. 10)

Frye also distinguishes between the passage of time during the reading of a text and the holistic consideration of it afterwards, but gives a fuller description of these phases:

> While we are reading a poem or listening to a play on the stage, we are participating in a linear narrative: this linear participation is essentially pre-critical. Once finished, the poem or play tends to freeze into a single simultaneous unity. This sense of simultaneous unity is what is symbolized by "recognition," which may be a crucial point in the play towards the end or some crucial emblematic image, like a scarlet letter or a golden bowl, and which is usually indicated in the title. It is in this sense of total comprehension of structure, or "verbal icon," that the critic can begin. (1969, p. 5)

In an earlier essay Frye described the first response as "direct experience of the work itself, while we're reading a book or seeing a play, especially for the first time. This experience is uncritical, or rather pre-critical, so it's not infallible" (1963, p. 44). Such a response is frequently described by readers in terms of their enjoyment of the text as they read.

> JEFF: It's the language, the imagery, the characters, the day-by-day, page-by-page things you read about. I savor the experience as I go along.
>
> YVONNE: A shared insight with the writer seems to me to be fairly instantaneous; as soon as the idea is read or the phrase decoded, the insight is there almost instantly. The meaning may be at a very inarticulate level. But there is that flash of recognition.

The phase that leaps off the page and lands fullblown in the reader's mind is difficult to illustrate because it varies so much from one reader to another. A turn of phrase that seems so apt to one person may seem rather ordinary to another. And to quote such a phrase out of context also reduces its vivacity. The reader must be willing to attend carefully, think, and become involved before this can be expected. But one of the delights of reading is suddenly coming across a detail or picture or expression that is striking. It catches us unawares, and that knowledge that a little gem can pop up at any second during the reading adds greatly to the pleasure. Sometimes the expression needs mulling over and improves with consideration. Other times, as Yvonne says, it comes in a flash.

Yvonne's awareness that this response may be fairly inarticulate and Jeff's picture of "savoring" the experience, drifting along in it, both illustrate Frye's view of this experience as "precritical." It is not that critical and thorough assessments of the text cannot, or will not, be made. It is rather that experiencing the text is a key aspect if the reader is to have anything to be reflective or critical about. Iser, in discussing the sense we have as readers of moving along through the text, observes that Henry Fielding in *Tom Jones* and Sir Walter Scott in *Waverly* both use a metaphor comparing the reader to a traveler in a stagecoach. The traveler:

> has to make the often difficult journey through the novel, gazing out from his moving viewpoint. Naturally, he combines all that he sees within his memory and establishes a pattern of consistency, the nature and reliability of which will depend partly on the degree of attention he has paid during each phase of the journey. At no time, however, can he have a total view of that journey. (Iser, 1978, p. 16)

During the act of comprehension, with its "moving viewpoint," the whole work is not available to the reader, so the reader must build consistency of interpretation, modify accordingly, and be patient about reaching a unified whole picture of the text.

The second form of response happens at the end of or after a reading, when a "simultaneous unity" occurs. Time is made irrelevant as parts of the text influence one another in the reader's mind and become a unity. There is a kind of circle of understanding operating here, so that the ending, or perhaps a reference to a symbol or a particular metaphor used (the "verbal icon"), illuminates an earlier part of the text, which then sheds more light on the later text itself; out of the circularity emerges a richer, fuller interpretation.

However, it is at precisely this point of unity that a major problem in reading can occur. If the "simultaneous unity" does not form, serious misinterpretations are likely. Sometimes due to a text's length or complexity or the reader's limited knowledge about the topic of the text, the reader will make a very incomplete or inadequate interpretation of the text. The text does not become a unity, but remains a series of bits. Time is not suspended, since each piece of text or idea must be considered in turn. The reader is thus reduced to thinking about or discussing words, sentences, or paragraphs separately, without being able to interpret them from the viewpoint of the whole text. Rereading will facilitate synthesis of some of the pieces, but if the fragmentation is severe, unity is unlikely. This segmentation will affect the reader's interpretation, since any piece of text is context dependent and to alter the context or to remove it is to change the function and significance of the segment. When Dylan Thomas describes a town as "bandaged," the phrase in isolation could have a variety of meanings, including an attempt by the town to recover from a disaster, an interpretation sometimes made by readers. But taken in the whole context of a joyful celebration of Christmas and winter, it becomes apparent that "bandaged" is a metaphor for snow-covered. All the implications of the expression cannot be determined, how-ever, unless "bandaged" is integrated with its context.

When the unity does form, it has implications for the interpretations made earlier during the "moving viewpoint" of the various parts of the text, as Yvonne illustrates:

> I think it's at the end of the book where you see a coherent whole.
> Then it takes shape. In any good story I think it is critical what happens
> to a character in the story generally. Scobie in *Heart of the Matter* kills
> himself at the end. Well, I don't think you can really appreciate the
> book, or really understand the book, or the book has much meaning
> unless you take that fact into account. There's lot of foreshadowing, but
> it's in the last two pages that it happens. I don't see how you could
> have a real understanding of that character otherwise.

The situation at the end, in this case, influences the interpretation of former text. It may also lead to rereading the text in light of the ending. Sometimes the adjustments in our interpretation are readily made by thinking through the story. Other times the whole does not quite synthesize; details have been shaped in our memory by how we were interpreting at the time, and it is necessary to go back and reread in order to sort out "what I thought" from "what the text actually said."

But the unity at the end has implications not only for the interpretation of earlier parts but also for the interpretation of the whole text, an experience Alice identifies:

> When I've finished reading, what I remember is not little bits of things
> or progressions, but a feeling about the whole thing. And if somebody
> says to me, "What was it like?" I don't answer them that this happened
> and that happened, I give them a feeling about the book.

It is not only a matter of all the pieces falling into place, but also of a creation of a complete picture that has no pieces and is no longer divisible into parts, even though it may once have been.

Out of the gradual buildup of many impressions and partial interpreta-tions arises an understanding that is much more than the sum of its parts and that even allows the distant and the recent past to be equidistant. Vanauken describes this fusion in reading a novel like *David Copperfield* that covers many years. In that book one follows the boy David running away to his Aunt Betsey Trotwood, the youth David loving Dora, the mature David with Agnes. While one reads, chapter by chapter, even as one lives one's own life week by week, David is what he is at that particular point in the book's time. But then, when one shuts the book at the end, *all* the Davids—small boy, youth, man—are equally close: and, indeed, are *one*. The *whole* David. One is then, with reference to the book's created time, in an eternity, seeing it all in one's own Now even as God in His eternal Now sees the whole of history that was and is and will be. (1977, p. 186)

That is part of the meaning of wholeness: not being subjected to the sequence and fragmentation of time, but being, with reference to some person or story, in an eternity. To be human is to be subject to the constraints of time, but there are specific exceptions where it is possible to break these shackles in some aspect of life. "*All* the Davids . . . are *one*. The *whole* David." How frequently is wholeness available in daily experience? Reading provides the opportunity. The completion of every text is an invitation to unity and wholeness. The reader will not be able to reach it with every text, but the invitation is there each time. We can stand back and see the text's created time as a unity. This potential is one of the great gifts of reading.

The wholeness also involves integrity. When a text portrays anachronisms, characters acting completely out of character, illogicalities, and so forth, unity cannot form since the parts refuse to fit together. There are clashes and holes and disjointedness. Only if a text has integrity can it unify for the reader. And only when it has integrity can it fuse into one's life and contribute to the wholeness of understanding for which one strives.

Wholeness has implicit in it connotations of completeness and healing. Partialness (incompleteness) leads to partiality (bias). Half-truths are not whole or truthful. Wholeness comes when the times are right, or ripe. Wholeness, like time, cannot be rushed, but can flower in the fullness of time. Only in the willingness to let time pass can we escape the segmentation of it and approach wholeness and timelessness.

NOT-TIME

One of our great desires as human beings is to make time stop occasionally, to escape its inexorable pressure. But so bound up are we in time that we really do not even have the language for not-time. Our statements tend to emerge in such absurdities as "I want to stop, if only for a moment." We can, if we are fortunate, experience occasional moments of stillness in which time and world seem at rest. Jeff speaks of reading a particular text that gives "a marvelous feeling of stillness. Time stands still. You get this remarkable feeling that you're standing outside of time. Outside of time, and outside of all the concerns that bother us day to day." Two qualities of time are suggested here: stillness and a freedom from daily concerns. Both are virtually impossible to achieve. Occasionally we manage a few moments of stillness—almost no motion or sound. It is necessary to say "almost," since life seems to involve sound and motion. But the stillness may be intense enough to make an impact—to echo loudly—even if it is brief and not quite total. Freedom from daily concerns is also experienced in short intervals when the attention is wholly absorbed by some experience, such as being lost in a text. Our steps outside of time are brief. ("Brief"—a time word. Is there really any step outside?) The common phrase "time out" is another manifestation of this desire. In sports talk, a time out allows the players to step outside the game; it "stops the clock" and thereby gives respite. We each have our own private pictures of idyllic moments that provide a brief escape, perhaps doing nothing—lying on the grass watching the clouds go by, sitting on the shore listening to the waves roll in. But these moments are made bittersweet by the knowledge that no matter how perfect they may be, they will soon end. Perhaps daydreams and images are so precious to us because they are time-free. We can call them up at will; we can shape them to please ourselves. In them we can be whatever age we wish to be in whatever era or condition. In them we can rearrange time.

Frye suggests a force, perhaps the only force, strong enough to take on time and make a stand. "If even time, the enemy of all living things, and to poets, at least, the most hated and feared of all tyrants, can be broken down by the imagination, anything can be" (1963, p. 33)—very good reason to examine the power and influence of the imagination in human life. Reading is an area of life that provides excellent ground for the imagination to challenge time or any other practical constraint.

If the present is structured by the past, it is also pressured by the future. We always have the awareness that the present, however idyllic, is bound to give way to the future. And the future brings an ending. Only if awareness of the future and endings can be escaped can the present have a vestige of timelessness. Is that possible? "The knowledge is inherent in human awareness that our existence stretches along from birth to death. We cannot step out of time or keep the future from becoming the past. We are radically temporal" (Polkinghorne, 1988, p. 129).

A rich understanding of time requires a grasp of the idea of not-time as well. Finiteness exists within infinity, time within eternity. Each must be understood against its absence, which is something much greater than itself.

> Wild geese, suspended
> Float in mid-air stillness, thus
> Time rests in not-time.
> (Heider, 1965, p. 28)

These geese are mere specks in the broad reach of the sky. Is our time an equally small part of not-time? Reading gives an opportunity to experience time in various ways, to start difficult but significant thinking, to glimpse not-time, and to stretch our imaginative limits.

REFERENCES

Austen, J. (1972). *Pride and prejudice*. Harmondsworth, England: Penguin. (Original work published 1813)

Berger, E., & Luckmann, T. (1966). *The social construction of reality*. Garden City, NY: Doubleday.

Cameron, E. (1968). *The court of the stone children*. New York: Dutton.

Davies, R. (1961). *The personal art*. London: Secker & Warburg.

Frye, N. (1963). *The educated imagination*. Toronto: CBC Publications.

Frye, N. (1969). Sign and significance. *Claremont Reading Conference, 33rd Yearbook*. Claremont, CA: Claremont Graduate School.

Gwyn, R. (1980). *The northern magus*. Toronto: McClelland & Stewart.

Heap, J. (1977). Toward a phenomenology of reading. *Journal of Phenomenological Psychology, 8,* 103–114.

Heider, W. (1965). Not time. In P. Dover (Ed.), *Poetry—An anthology for high schools*. Toronto: Holt, Rinehart & Winston.

Ingarden, R. (1973). *Cognition of the literary work of art*. Evanston, IL: Northwestern University Press.

Iser, W. (1978). *The act of reading*. Baltimore: Johns Hopkins University Press.

James, W. (1890). *The principles of psychology*. New York: Henry Holt.

Nureyev, R. (1963). *Nureyev*. New York: Dutton.

Polkinghorne, D. (1988). *Narrative knowing and the human sciences*. Albany, NY: State University of New York Press.

Spurling, L. (1977). *Phenomenology and the social world*. London: Routledge & Kegan Paul.

Toynbee, A., & Toynbee, P. (1963). *Comparing notes: A dialogue across a generation*. London: Weidenfeld & Nicolson.

Vanauken, S. (1977). *A severe mercy*. New York: Harper & Row.

CHAPTER 5

Cries and Whispers

WILLIAM F. PINAR

I wish to write about death, our deaths. Death which can seem so distant, but which can be so close at hand. Indeed, death here and now, in the midst of lights and life. Death and life.

As students of curriculum, we live and work in the aftermath of the death of our predecessors. Charters and Bobbitt and Rugg were flesh, of course, and sat in rooms like these, speaking to contemporaries about what struck them as germane, just as we do today and will do the remainder of our professional lives. Tyler and Miel live still, testifying to the living presence of the past.

In a poem entitled "The Fathers," Ann Stanford (1970) expresses this sense of past being present, how death is both a disappearance and a presence, how death speaks to and through us now.

The Fathers

I am beset by spirits, layer on layer
they hover over our sleep in the quilted air.
The owl calls and the spirits hang and listen.
Over our breaths, over our hearts they press.
They are wings and eyes, and they come surely to bless
There is hardly room for the crowd of them under the ceiling.

Remember me, remember me, they whisper.

The dark rustles, their faces all are dim.
They know me well, I represent them here.
I keep their lands, their good and fruiting orchards,
I keep their books, their rings, their testaments.

I am their blood of life made visible
I whole their part of life that vanishes.

This paper is written in honor of my father, Frederick E. Pinar, who died June 19, 1988. It was presented to the Bergamo Conference, October 26, 1988.

They whisper to me, names and messages,
Lost in the world, a sifting down of shadows.

I am myself, I say, it is my blood
It is my time of sun and lifting of green,
Nothing is here, but what I touch and see.
They cry out, *we are here in the root and tree.*
It is my night, I say—and yours for sleeping.
They move their wings, I think I hear them weeping.
Blest spirits, let me be.

A thought, a field, a relationship is never ours alone; it is theirs as well. (Rugg is here, in imagination.) To "let me be" can mean to permit me some space of separation, of solitariness, of freedom, but they will not let us be completely. Nor do or should we wish to be free of them, for they are our origins; their flesh is our flesh, and to be truly free of them, is to lose them, and to lose ourselves. Let me be, blessed spirits, but do not leave me.

We have written of autobiography as a way of returning to ourselves. Lost to others, past and present, lost in fantasy, or alternately, in the chimera created by the culture industry, autobiography means being still, slipping back inside, being in this body, in this world, intact, whole. Alive, in time, death at hand.

To be whole means to experience the presence of those who have died. (My father died June 19th.) It is also to experience our own dying. (I will die.)

I am dying.

Heidegger tells us that we work to evade the reality of our dying. "Everybody dies!" "Don't be morbid!" Heidegger tells us that meditation on the fact of death brings this life into focus. When I know, as a bodyreader (Grumet, 1988), bodyknower, that I am dying, I know I am living; I am living in time. Each moment; each decade. My death brings my life into focus, Heidegger says.

Heidegger spirit, Heidegger presence. You and Rugg, together with us, here. You were together in time, not place. Heidegger understanding much of life while understanding not at all the Nazis; Rugg searching for life while fighting American versions of Nazis.

Just as we evade the fact of our deaths, we look the other way at the dying among us. We hide them in nursing homes, hospitals, even on the streets, where we look the other way as outstretched arms and voices beg for life.

We evade death, we try to give it away. We export it to Canada as acid rain, to Louisiana in the petrochemical industries, to the Third World generally, to the working classes, and to African-Americans whom we deprive (more subtly now than then) of work, food, and dignity. There are African-Americans accustomed to deprivation and death, and while being "accustomed to" can bring defeat it can also bring triumph. Lucille Clifton (1987) tells us, in her poem entitled "For DeLawd," that death brings determination, just pushing on.

For DeLawd

people say they have a hard time
understanding how I
go on about my business
playing my Ray Charles
hollering at the kids—
seems like my Afro
cut off in some old image
would show I got a long memory
and I come from a line
of black and going on women
who got used to making it through murdered sons
and who grief kept on pushing
who fried chicken
ironed
swept off back steps
who grief kept
for their still alive sons
for their sons coming for their sons gone
just pushing

Just pushing. Just living. There is life amid death, life in death, life from death.

BERGMAN'S *CRIES AND WHISPERS*

We European-Americans are old hands at exporting death to others. Or so we think. Exporting death to others hides from us the fact that with privilege comes death, unless we give it away constantly, through teaching and other forms of redistribution and caring. Ingmar Bergman's 1972 film *Cries and Whispers* portrays the death of and the death in the privileged classes of Sweden. It also portrays the possibility of life.

If you have seen the film, you recall that it opens in the autumn dawn light, in the twilight of the nineteenth century. We are in the gardens of a country estate, in the mist of morning, chill hovering over warm green grass. Inside the house the clocks tick the "hour of the wolf," and Agnes, in her thirty-seventh year dying of cancer, lies stricken, struggling, in white. She rises to write in her journal: "It is early on Monday morning and I'm in pain. My sisters and Anna are taking it in turns to sit up. Kind of them. I needn't feel so alone with the dark . . ."

Not only Agnes is in pain. Her sisters—Liv Ullmann plays the young flirtatious Maria, Ingrid Thulim plays the elder, anguished Karin—are caught in respective—in the film's phrase—"tissues of lies." Karin is formal, proud of her class and her loyalty to a marriage that is a mistake. As Bergman himself says of this character: "Deep down, under a surface of self-control, she hides an impotent hatred of her husband and a permanent rage against life." The beautiful Maria is also married, but indifferent to her husband. Bergman comments: "She is very much taken up with her own beauty and her body's potentialities for pleasure. . . . She is sufficient unto herself and is never worried by her own or other people's morals" (Bergman, 1972, p. 39). Anna, the servant and the dying Agnes's friend, is full, quietly vibrant, constrained by her status as servant, spiritualized by the death of her daughter. Agnes, the helpless dying one, becomes Anna's dead daughter.

The death in each character's life is portrayed by the full-face shots for which Bergman is famous, which begin in half-face shots, fading to red. There is much white and red in the film; the women often wear white, the rooms red. Bergman comments: "I picture[d] the inside of the soul as a . . . membrane in shades of red" (Bergman, 1972, p. 38). I think of the white flesh of the characters and the red of blood signifying death. There are flashbacks throughout the film, to the sisters' childhood, and in particular to an evening in which Karin and her husband (twenty years her senior, and repulsive to her, physically and mentally) brittlely eat dinner. Afterward, preparing for bed, Anna peels layer after layer of Karin's clothing, laying bare her soul underneath. Exposed to herself in the mirror, she takes a bit of broken wine glass and mutilates her genitals. Crawling into bed, as her husband's lust awakens, she smears her face with blood, smiling and glaring at him all the while. "It's nothing but lies," she tells him. In cold disgust he observes: "You're bleeding" (p. 43).

Joan Mellen criticizes Bergman for portraying women as trapped in their biology, destined to behave in crippled and crippling ways. Mellen suggests that Bergman's men fail primarily because their cries go unanswered. She suggests that the women in Bergman's movies are trapped at a much more primitive level of human development" (Mellen, 1977). While I would agree that Bergman's characterization of women in *Cries and Whispers* reveals a prefeminist awareness of gender politics, I would suggest that his treatment of men is much harsher. Essentially they are absent, only tangentially important. They are adjuncts to the women, and in sadomasochistic ways. Karin's husband is empty and cold; Maria's is self-pitying and ineffective. If Bergman is guilty of misogyny, he is guilty of misanthropy as well.

I take his harshness to be criticism of class more than gender, although that is partly due to his gender blindness. These are privileged, self-involved characters. Even the sweet Agnes, whom one commentator has suggested is dying of cancer of the soul as well as that of the body, is self-deluded. Despite the superficiality and distance characterizing the sisters' affiliation with Agnes, she maintains that they are indeed intimate. Only Anna is capable of suspending self-involvement to serve another.

There is a woman-affirmative moment in the film, I would say a life-affirmative moment. After Agnes has died, has been laid out, after the minister has blessed her by beseeching her to intervene with God on behalf of those remaining under grim and empty skies, the household waits for burial. During the night before burial, Anna is awakened by the sound of a child weeping. Distressed but self-possessed, Anna moves toward the sound; it comes from the room in which the corpse reposes. Outside the door she finds the two sisters standing stunned and silent. Anna enters the room, and sees that it is Agnes who has been crying. Agnes speaks to her: "Are you afraid of me now?" Anna shakes her head no. "I can't get to sleep," Agnes continues, "I can't leave all of you. [She moans softly and the tears are squeezed out from under the closed eyelids.] Can't anyone help me? [She moans.] I'm so tired."

Agnes then asks for Karin, whom Anna brings to the deathbed. Agnes softly asks Karin to hold her hands, to warm her, to kiss her. Karin refuses: "I can't. There isn't a soul who'd do what you ask. I'm alive and I don't want anything to do with your death. Perhaps if I loved you. But I don't. What you ask of me is repulsive. I'll leave you now. In a few days, I'm going away." She leaves the room; Anna returns, and is asked to bring Maria. Maria walks toward the bed, but stops, frightened. Agnes tells her not to be afraid, but to touch her, to warm her. Hesitantly, Maria takes her dead sister's hands. "I'll gladly stay with you as long as you need me," Maria says. "You are my sister and I don't want to leave you alone. I feel so terribly sorry for you. Do you remember when we were little and played together in the twilight? Suddenly, and at the same moment, we felt afraid and cuddled together and held each other tight. It's the same now, isn't it?"

"I can't hear what you're saying," Agnes replies. "You must speak louder and you must lean closer." Maria does lean closer, shaking with terror and nausea. Agnes lifts her hand and removes the combs from Maria's hair. It tumbles down over their faces. Then Agnes moves her hands behind Maria's neck and pulls her violently to her, pressing her lips against Maria's mouth. Maria screams and wrenches herself away, wiping her mouth with her hand; she staggers backwards and spits. Then she runs to the next room. Agnes begins to weep. Anna stands in the doorway. Anna tells Maria: "Agnes wants me to stay with her. You needn't be afraid anymore. I'll look after her." Maria responds: "I have my daughter to think of. She must realize that. I have my husband who needs me." "It's revolting," Karin says. "It's disgusting and meaningless. She has already started to decay. She has great spots on her hands." "I'll go to her," says Anna. "I'll stay with her."

Bergman (1972) describes what happens next: "Anna closes the door. . . . Agnes' lament can still be heard. The daylight fades against the panes. The trees of the garden stand motionless and black. The women's faces can be vaguely seen in the gathering darkness. All colors are obliterated. The red walls fade in the indefinite changing light. Agnes' lament becomes fainter and fainter (a child crying itself to sleep, but still wailing a little). The weeping ceases. There is silence" (p. 66). Anna has climbed into bed with Agnes, and half-clad, holds the dead woman, now comforted, now silent. The pietà.

The next day, after burying Agnes, the sisters return to the house with their husbands. They speak about Anna coldly, despite her twelve years of service to Agnes. When Karin reports she has already offered Anna something of Agnes's, her husband snaps: "How I detest that kind of spontaneity!" Maria's husband, Joakim, informs Anna that she may choose something. Anna declines their "generosity." They permit her to stay until the end of the month. After the others have departed, Maria presses a piece of currency into Anna's hand; she accepts.

The final scene of the film portrays an entry from Agnes's diary. Because the scene expresses what I take to be Bergman's affirmation of human life in the midst of death, I will quote it in its entirety. "A summer's day. It's cool, with almost a tang of autumn in the air, yet so nice and soft. My sisters, Karin and Maria, have come to see me. It's wonderful to be together again as we were in the old days—as we were in our childhood. I'm feeling much better, too. We can even go for a little walk together—such an event for me, especially as I haven't been out-of-doors for so long. We strolled down to the old swinging seat in the oak tree. Then the four of us (Anna came, too) sat in the swing and let it rock to and fro, slowly and gently.

"I closed my eyes and felt the breeze and the sun on my face. All my aches and pains were gone. The people I'm most fond of in the world were with me. I could hear them chatting round about me, I felt the presence of their bodies, the warmth of their hands. I closed my eyes tightly, trying to cling to the moment and thinking, come what may, this is happiness. I can't wish for anything better. Now, for a few minutes, I can experience perfection. And I feel a great gratitude to my life, which gives me so much."

There is beauty and ugliness in this film, life and death, illusion and clarity. There is the beauty of the manor house, with its deep red rooms contrasting with the white of the women's dresses. There is the ugliness of their marriages, the ugliness of the contradictions of the *haute bourgeoisie* in *fin de siècle* Europe. There is the horror of Agnes's suffering, the beauty of her affirmation of both her dying and living. There is the stunning presence of life in death as the corpse cries, begs for warmth from the living, and then is held by the noble Anna. There is the emptiness of patriarchy, in Karin's Frederic—arrogant, cold, pointness; in Maria's Joakim—self-pitying, helpless; in the physician—insight without sympathy. Finally, there is the minister, whose prayer for the dead Agnes and the living family quickly collapses into begging for himself and others.

The minister is the one interesting man in the film. He is shaken by Agnes's death, by her faith, which he tells the sisters is greater than his own. In his testimony of doubt, faith appeals. His prayer is most remarkable, and I repeat it now. It begins conventionally enough. Standing by the deathbed, he clasps his hands: "God, our Father, in His infinite wisdom and mercy, has decided to call you home in the flower of your youth. Prior to that, He found you worthy to bear a heavy and prolonged suffering. You submitted to it patiently and uncomplainingly, in the certain knowledge that your sins would be forgiven through the death on the cross of your Lord Jesus Christ. May your Father in Heaven have mercy on your soul when you step into His presence. May He and His angels disrobe you of the memory of your earthly pain."

The chaplain falls silent, his eyes shut. He kneels; the others mirror his movement. He leans toward the corpse. He begins to beg. "If it is so that you have gathered our suffering in your poor body, if it is so that you have borne it with you through death, if it is so that you meet God over there in the other land, if it is so that He turns His face toward you, if it is so that you can then speak the language that this God understands, if it is so that you can then speak to this God. If it is so, pray for us. Agnes, my dear little child, listen to what I am now telling you. Pray for us who are left here on the dark, dirty earth under an empty and cruel Heaven. Lay your burden of suffering at the God's feet and ask Him to pardon us. Ask Him to free us at last from our anxiety, our weariness, and our deep doubt. Ask Him for a meaning to our lives. Agnes, you who have suffered so unimaginably and so long, you must be worthy to plead our cause."

A dead woman resurrects our hope (Manvell, 1980). Through suffering and dying and witnessing, Agnes—even in her self-delusion—comes to express hope and life. There is death and then there is resurrection. In life there are thousands of deaths and rebirths, as the embodied intellect seeks transcendence of its past and entries into its future. We can take courage and comfort in Agnes's story as it portrays life from death.

TEMPORALITY

For many children who have not yet lost parents and whose grandparents remain alive or who have died at a distance, for many of these children the cries and whispers provoked by death are not real. Blessedly, for these children life seems to go on uninterrupedly, without end. Even in such protected lives there is death in life and life from death, and these are matters for parents and teachers to mention and explain. My own view is that the concepts and realities of death need to be integrated in everyday conversation, in everyday curriculum, not treated as exotic topics of extreme anxiety. I think it is when death is treated as distant that it becomes terrible and provokes fear. Life leads to death. And while one ought not to tempt death, perhaps one ought to make friends with it. Until we parents and teachers have confronted the fact of our impending deaths, we cannot aspire to impart a sense of the presence of death in life to our children.

Death brings time into focus. It makes this moment we share together precious, worthy of caring, worthy of presence. The concept of time might well be developed, in phenomenological fashion, as a key theme in curriculum theory and pedagogy. There is precedent for doing so. Nearly twenty years ago Dwayne Huebner sensed the importance of time in our lives as teachers and students.

After rejecting "learning" as the key concept for curriculum, Huebner reconceives the field's interest in "purposes," "goals," and "objectives" as a concern for temporality (Huebner, 1975). To explicate temporality, Huebner goes to Heidegger's *Being and Time*. For Heidegger time is a fundamental aspect of *Dasein*. "*Dasein's* totality of being as care means: ahead-of-itself-already-being-in [a world] as being-alongside [entities encountered within-the-world]. . . . The 'ahead-of-itself' is grounded in the future. In the 'Being-already-in . . .' the character of 'having been' is made known. 'Being-alongside . . .' becomes possible in making present" (Heidegger, quoted in Huebner, 1975). Huebner comments:

> [The person] does not simply await a future and look back upon a past. The very notion of time arises out of man's [*sic*] existence, which is an emergent. The future is man facing himself in anticipation of his own potentiality for being. The past is finding himself already thrown into a world. It is the having-been which makes possible the projection of his potentiality. The present is the moment of vision when *Dasein,* finding himself thrown into a situation (the past), projects his own potentiality for being. Human life is . . . a present made up of a past and future brought into the moment. . . . Human life is never fixed but is always emergent as the past and future become horizons of present. Education recognizes, assumes responsibility for, and maximizes the consequences of this awareness of man's temporality. (Huebner, 1975, p. 244).

For Huebner this responsibility or concern must take curricular forms that "make possible those moments of vision when the student, and/or those responsible for him, project his potentiality for being into the present, thus tying together the future and the past into the present" (Huebner, 1975).

Just as a discipline is taught to disclose its historicity, its fluidity, the student's responses can be taught to him or her to make explicit his or her own embodiment of time. He or she can observe the past present in his or her learnings. For Norman Holland the past solidifies, takes thematic form, and repeats itself. For Jacques Derrida whatever is present has traces of what is absent. What is solid fragments and turns to liquid; the sense of definitiveness that characterizes curriculum is a "tissue of lies." The relation of the knower to the known is that of an answer to a question: provisional, temporal, requiring faith and skepticism. It is a relation expressed in time, molded by death, expressed as a mode of life.

CONCLUSION

Just as those who have died before us whisper and cry as we speak, our time, our place, ourselves, those who have not yet appeared and those who are appearing—our children—speak in our voices. Our children provoke our parenting, permitting us to reexperience our own childhood, and, as Grumet has explained, our parenting and teaching often contradict what we experienced in our lives as children. Finally, the very fact of children testifies to our dying and to their birthing and gives urgency and immediacy to our pedagogic relationships to them. What is decadent about Karin and Frederic and Maria and Joakim is their (attempted) evasion of time. They have children but we do not see them. We see them as children arrested in time, and so caught, lost to themselves. In the midst of life, these characters have lost their way.

They think they have come to bury their sister, but it is their own deaths to which their presence testifies. Agnes dies but speaks from her death, asking them for the intimacy and companionship the forms of their lives kept from her. Even in her death Agnes's sisters cannot give themselves to her, as they are lost to themselves. Only Anna, servant of God, servant of Agnes, can lend her care and her body to the weeping corpse. Only the corpse is comforted in this film, as the others, trapped in class and social convention, squirm underneath their smiles, each having performed the self-mutilation only Karin has the courage to stage. Only the corpse is alive in this film.

Cries and whispers of the dead who live; cries and whispers of she who dies, who is resurrected, whose death testifies to life. A phenomenology of death might trace these moods and metaphors of death and life, enabling us to affirm those who have gone before us, those who, like us, are dying now, and those children born and unborn who bring life to our dyings, all of us, past, present, future, blessed by death, blessed by life.

REFERENCES

Bergman, I. (1972, October 21). Cries and whispers. *The New Yorker,* pp. 38–74.

Clifton, L. (1987). For DeLawd. In *Good woman: Poems and a memoir 1969–1980.* New York: BOA Editions.

Grumet, M. R. (1988). Bodyreading. In W. F. Pinar (Ed.), *Contemporary curriculum discourses* (pp. 453–473). Scottsdale, AZ: Gorsuch, Scarisbrick.

Huebner, D. (1975). Curriculum as concern for man's temporality. In. W. F. Pinar (Ed.), *Curriculum theorizing: The reconceptualists* (pp. 237–250). Berkeley: McCutchan.

Manvell, R. (1980). *Ingmar Bergman: An appreciation.* New York: Arno.

Mellen, J. (1977). *Big bad wolves.* New York: Pantheon.

Stanford, A. (1970). The fathers. In *The descent.* New York: Viking Penguin.

CHAPTER 6

Remembering Forward

Reflections on Educating for Peace

TERRANCE CARSON

Peace education intends both to educate and to reform. Educating for peace begins with a critical observation on the state of the present global situation, convinced that we need to make some fundamental changes in the ways that we live with one another and with the Earth. But an understanding of peace itself remains elusive. It is known primarily by its absence, and it is this absence that gives meaning to the project of educating for peace. Thus it is through the activity that we come to understand—in the words of the Fellowship of Reconciliation—"there is no way to peace, peace is the way." The claim that we may develop our understandings while bringing about changes in concrete situations makes action research interesting for peace education.

Action research has again become attractive to those who are critical of administratively inspired reform efforts. For some time now there has been a growing sense that teachers are being bypassed in the efforts to improve schools. Rather than being active participants in school change, teachers have found themselves on the receiving end of criticism, new regulations, implementation efforts, external evaluations, and more layers of bureaucratic management. Action research has been seen as a way of giving teaching back to the teachers. But the appealing premise of action research also hides some real differences among projects so labeled. The name "action research" has been applied to questions ranging from individual teachers trying to solve very specific classroom management problems (Hustler, Cassidy, & Cuff, 1986) to research on fundamental pedagogical issues (van Manen, 1984). These reflect a multiplicity of intentions, yielding different insights and different kinds of knowledge. Despite the different forms it takes, there are at least two commonalities. First, all action research subscribes to the belief that we may simultaneously inform and change ourselves. In fact, it is the action that allows deeper understanding. Second, because action research intends to draw together theory and practice, it runs counter to conventional wisdom in educational research, which views these as separate activities.

Given that these are its intentions, action research needs to be critically assessed as to whether or not it creates fresh insights for participants. An analysis of differences among the forms of action research is crucial to such an assessment. This is the main focus of my paper. I want to suggest that radically new ways of knowing and doing may come from action research. This suggestion is supported by our experience of collaboratively working through an education for peace. Whether or not these possibilities are realized depends very much on the kinds of questions addressed by the participants and the way that these are subsequently pursued through a reflective practice. A brief discussion of the historical project of action research will serve to contextualize the understandings contributed by peace education.

THE HISTORICAL PROJECT OF ACTION RESEARCH

The term "action research" was coined by the social psychologist Kurt Lewin during the closing years of World War II. Lewin was concerned about the gap that existed between theories about society and the dynamics of social practice. In his view, we could learn the "general laws of group life" through a careful observation and reflection of the processes of community social change (Lewin, 1946).

Early on, action research was taken up by educators in the "teacher as researcher" movement (Corey, 1953). Advocates such as Stephen Corey, dean of Columbia University Teachers College, suggested that by becoming researchers in their own classrooms, teachers could improve their practices. Action research projects flowered, but soon wilted in the face of criticisms from an increasingly professionalized education research community. Criticisms stuck because Corey and his followers encouraged individual action research efforts without changing institutional assumptions about the respective roles of schools and academia. Failure to affect institutional attitudes toward research ultimately meant that action research was not taken seriously by the academics.

As the division of labor separating teachers from researchers developed and hardened during the 1960s and 1970s, action research remained largely dormant in North America. Here educational research began to follow the conventional assumptions about the relationship between research and practice borrowed from empirical-analytical science. According to this model, theories about curriculum and teaching are derived and validated through observation and analysis. These are then applied as solutions to problems to practice. For example, in the realm of curriculum implementation, theories of educational change are produced by observing what happened as teachers encountered new curricula in order to locate factors that seem to either block or encourage adoption. The results of this research are then made generally available to be applied in new situations in such a way as to improve the likelihood of future adoptions. This now-familiar RD&D (research, development, and diffusion) model appears to serve administrative and organizational needs, but it also brings a host of difficulties. Generalized solutions are often not appropriate to particular circumstances. The application of these measures increasingly changes the nature of teachers' work from pedagogical responsibility to managerial accountability (Carson, 1987).

The regeneration of action research began in Europe in the late 1960s and 1970s partly as a resistance to technical theories of curriculum and teaching that had, by then, become increasingly separated from practice. In Britain, the Ford Teaching Project (1973–1976) involved teachers in collaborative action research in their own classrooms (Elliott, 1977). The thinking behind this project was influenced by Joseph Schwab's (1969) paper which suggested that the arts of the practical are eclectic and situational. Schwab argued that the traditional curriculum field had become moribund because it presented a rationalized picture of the curriculum rather than reflecting its true nature as a deliberative, practical activity. Lawrence Stenhouse (1975) was probably a more direct influence on the Ford Teaching Project in his support for the teacher as a curriculum researcher and developer.

In Germany, the resistance took a less pragmatic direction than it had in Britain. Like those in the Ford Teaching Project, Wolfgang Klafki (1975) held the view that local curriculum development and school improvement could take place through the action research of practitioners. But Klafki also made links between this and Habermas's emerging critical social theory, arguing that action research was an example of a democratic alternative to empirical analytical research.

A renewed interest in action research in the 1980s was strongly influenced by the same critical social theory. Critical social theory attempts to do two things; (1) provide a more comprehensive and systematic critique of technical theories of curriculum and (2) propose an alternative approach based upon a collaborative and critically reflective practice of educators working together to transform schools. This new movement in action research has been centered at Deakin University in Australia. Its program is outlined by Wilfred Carr and Stephen Kemmis in *Becoming Critical: Education, Knowledge and Action Research* (1986).

Carr and Kemmis see action research as a means for developing a "critical educational science." Beginning with the question posed by Faraganis (1975)—"How does one move from theoretical critique to the necessary action that will bring about the desired end?" (Carr & Kemmis, 1986, p. 155)—they show how this might be achieved by using the principles and procedures laid out by Lewin for action research. The desired end of critical theory is the creation of socially just and democratic communities. While traditional critical theory has been strong on analysis, its practice has proven elusive. Carr and Kemmis suggest that Lewin's emphasis on democratic and participatory social change now provides the means by which critical theory may become a concrete practice, at least among educators.

I became aware of action research through the writings of Carr and Kemmis. For me, the strength of their work was the critical rethinking of the theory and practice problem. They seemed to provide a comprehensive analysis of earlier formulations of action research and educational research in general, as well as a promising set of procedures for implementing a new version of action research. Because the peace education action research project in which I was involved was strongly influenced by Carr and Kemmis, I further outline their approach to action research in some detail.

A critical educational science is rooted in what Carr and Kemmis term research *for* education rather than research *about* education (their emphasis). In making this distinction they acknowledge their debt to Jürgen Habermas's *Knowledge and Human Interests* (1972). Habermas indicates that knowledge is produced by the ways that people orient themselves to the world. He outlines three basic orientations, each of which is governed by a particular interest. One is an orientation to material well-being, governed by a technical interest in acting on the world. This produces empirical knowledge in the form of facts and generalizations. A second orientation, toward communication, is governed by a practical interest in understanding others. The form of knowledge that this produces is situational and interpretive, rather than generalizable and empirical. The third orientation is toward freedom, and it is governed by an emancipatory interest in liberating persons from oppressive situations. This produces a critically reflective knowledge.

According to Habermas, each of these forms of knowledge is appropriate in its proper sphere. However, there has been a historical and cultural tendency for a technical interest to extend into the social sciences and into social life generally. This has helped to produce relations of domination and control where people are treated as objects instead of individuals in control of their own destinies. While interpretive knowing is essential for human relationships in order to understand the meaning that participants give to situations, it is inadequate for the task of liberation. People's understandings are deformed by the habits and routines created by the relations of domination. A continuing critical reflective discourse is necessary to root this out in the process of creating communities based upon reason and democratic decision making instead of the authority of unequal power.

The critical theory embodied in Habermas's formulation has provided Carr and Kemmis with an explanation for the failure of what they term "positive research" in education. By positivism they mean the assumption of a

unitary model of research based upon a technical interest that views education as an object of inquiry. For them, Habermas's theory also points out the
inadequacy of interpretive research, which they say "is relatively passive" (p.
183) because of its interest in the subjective understandings of the participants. They argue for the superiority of a critical action research that encompasses both subjectivity and objectivity in dialectical fashion. It recognizes
that the understandings of participants are the basis for social action, but
appreciates that these understandings are constrained by the objective limits
that, after all, are changeable because they are socially constructed. By being
deliberately activist, the participants can alter these limits, thus creating new
understandings. This is what Carr and Kemmis mean by a committed research that is *for* education.

The process of critical action research is collaborative and follows a cycle
consisting of moments of reflection, planning, acting, observing, reflecting,
replanning, and so forth that take place in a spiral fashion. These become
focused on a project that aims at the transformation of practices, understandings, and the situations in which the participants work. The spiral of planning, acting, observing, and reflecting is significant, because it is what sets
critically reflective action research apart from ordinary problem solving,
which Carr and Kemmis disdain as an "arrested action research" (p. 185).
True critically reflective action research is characterized by a continuing program of reform. The eventual hoped-for result would be a new kind of school
and a new society. The main feature of this new rational society is the "organization of enlightenment."

CRITICALLY REFLECTIVE ACTION RESEARCH AND
EDUCATION FOR PEACE

The promise of transformation and a clear process for achieving it lead
to the formation of a collaborative action research group with which I was
involved during the winter and spring of 1988. The experience of belonging
to this group causes me to want to consider again the question of critical
theory and practice. More specifically, it leads me to ask how theories direct
us and what we learn from practice.

We were a group of eight. Each of us had participated in an international
institute on peace education, which I had helped to organize and which had
been held for several summers. Our interest was to begin to work together
to implement education for peace in our respective work settings. The conception of peace that each of us held varied, of course, but it had been evolv-
ing through conversation among ourselves and with others at the summer
institutes. A definition that we accepted as a comprehensive guide for the

purposes of action research was provided by Toh and Cawagas (1987). They identify a broad framework that includes a rejection of militarization, a concern for structural violence (those structures creating and preserving inequalities), the promotion of human rights, development of intercultural trust, and attention to questions of personal peace (alienation, substance abuse, family violence, etc.). This framework provides a guide rather than a prescription for peace education. It implies that educating for peace involves critical reflection and action on teaching approaches and on the school and the wider community beyond. "Think globally and act locally" has been a popular slogan among peace educators. It was up to each of us to decide what form of concrete practice we would take, depending upon the concerns of our own institutions.

Critically reflective action research seemed to be very much in harmony with our intention. As Carr and Kemmis suggest, action research aims to improve practice, improve an understanding of the practice, and improve the situation in which the practice takes place. Thus we interpreted the goals of our group to be:

1. To better understand the meaning of peace education
2. To develop the practice of peace education in our respective teaching situations
3. To help transform the places in which we teach into places that reflect peaceful structures (i.e., places where human rights are attended to, conflicts are resolved nonviolently, etc.)

We named the group CARPE (Collaborative Action Research in Peace Education). Once every three weeks we met at one of our homes, spending the evening in conversation about our projects. We each spoke about the concerns and intentions for peace education in our particular situations, and in general. From time to time people would talk about their specific action research projects that were already in progress or just beginning to emerge. These conversations were all tape recorded. Prior to the next meeting I undertook to analyze the previous conversation for the purposes of identifying the topics we covered. Of particular interest were the questions that seemed to direct our conversation. In my interpretive report back to the group I attempted to highlight these questions.

Question One: How Can We Discover Hope After All?

Les teaches junior high social studies in an upper-middle-class neighborhood. The school prides itself on high standards of academic excellence. During our first meeting, Les described an innovative way that his students designed to raise money to support the school's foster child from India. Others in the CARPE group questioned the wisdom of aid in the form of charity to individuals in Third World nations. Les understood these arguments and was sympathetic to this view, but he remarked that his main concern was that students have something positive to do. He says, "I find my students show a sadness at the legacy that has been left them—last year they made peace posters and wrote letters, but after that there wasn't much more they could do." So Les continued to encourage the students in their fundraising ideas for the foster-parents plan, believing that taking positive action would help to sustain their interest and hope.

We felt rightfully critical of the underlying view of economic development as charity. A critical consciousness understands that this creates a relationship of dependence between the giver and the receiver, deflecting attention away from the real problem of global economic justice. But the critical argument is an abstract one. Les's choice was governed by a concrete situation that required a pedagogical sensitivity to his students' need to have confidence and hope for the future.

Question Two: What to Do When the Global Encounters the Local?

Elaine, a social studies teacher at a large suburban Catholic high school, recounted the following experience. To counteract incipient racist attitudes among some of the students in this middle-class school, one part of her action research project involved twinning her class with one in Indonesia. The first package arrived from Indonesia. For some unknown reason it came addressed to a boy in her class who had been forced to withdraw for lack of attendance (a school rule). She knew where the boy was, in the school smoking lounge known as "the pit." The boy was found there and invited to come back to the classroom to pick up his package. Handing it to him, Elaine asked if he would like to stay and open it. He agreed. Inside there were photos of students in the Indonesian partner class, letters and cards of greeting, and some gifts.

Elaine said of this experience, "As the boy opened the cheap wrapping paper of the package you could see the class begin to understand that Indonesia was not a well-off country. I noticed also how stereotypes began to melt away as they saw the photographs of the Indonesian students. In fact, they were surprised to see many of them wearing jeans similar to theirs (but they should not have been surprised, as many of them are made in Southeast Asia)." Elaine also commented about the odd circumstance for the boy who had received this package addressed to him. "He was tickled pink, and he stayed for the rest of the class. He hasn't been back since, but for that brief time he was part of the class community again, sharing what he had received."

Elaine's prior understanding of peace education allowed her to see how the twinning project achieved its anticipated results. In addition, the temporary annoyance of the misdirected parcel developed a consideration of her own school's alienating administrative practices, which routinely excluded students from class for infractions of school rules. Conversation in the CARPE group highlighted this as a contradiction, reversing the favorite peace education slogan by asking us to think locally while acting globally.

Question Three: What Is a Project Anyway?

In the beginning, the CARPE group was quite task oriented. Concerned about following the protocols of collaborative, critically reflective action research, most of us felt compelled to identify a project early on. Hans, however, indicated that he was having some difficulty moving from his overall intention to educate for peace to the identification of a concrete project that he could begin to implement in the prescribed action research spiral. He was teaching social studies and counseling part time in a school that had been experiencing a number of difficulties. Many of his students lived in a mobile home park that had been badly damaged the previous summer by a tornado. According to Hans, there had been a sense of homelessness and family dislocations before the tornado, too. At the second meeting Hans talked about this situation, asking, "Is there any possibility for educating for a more peaceful world when there is so little personal peace within the family and the lives of these children?" At the third meeting he told of the progress of his thinking: "I'm interested in a project that would get the students' lives back into the curriculum, perhaps something dealing with changes in their own lives as a beginning." Subsequently, he planned an integrated language arts and social studies unit with the school librarian.

At the last meeting (our seventh) he reflected on the relationship between his "project" and the conversations in the CARPE group. He reported then: "I feel a little frustrated, because I wanted to be more task oriented. That's the thing about peace education, you have a certain awareness, you can see the problem and you feel like you should be doing something. Yet you can't do it as an individual. I'm saying that I feel a frustration about making connections between what I do and what we talk about."

Peace education as it relates to Hans's situation is so large that it really cannot be contained within an identifiable plan upon which to act. Through the lens of educating for peace, Hans saw too much crying out for his attention. Although he could not yet discern a specific project in the prescribed form, in his reflections there was a pedagogical orientation to the children and the community in which they live. This is a project of a different kind. It is a longer-range, more indeterminate matter that has been described by Alfred Schutz as a life project (Wagner, 1983).

Question Four: What Is a Community?

Colleen had been engaged in several high-profile peace education projects in her capacity as coordinator of religious education, as well social studies teacher, at a large Catholic junior high school. The summer peace education institutes at the university and the CARPE group provided the impetus to take on still more. While we met she confessed that she was becoming tired and beginning to feel isolated from her colleagues at school. At the fifth CARPE meeting in late March, she described her situation like this: "For me there is the problem of being involved with too many projects. I get time off, coverage from the media, but I'm concerned about overloading the school, and I think that is rather resented by other teachers. I'm not sure how to handle that."

Gloria, a high school English teacher, was having a similar experience. She had formed a youth group in her school. This group achieved wide recognition in the province for producing effective dramatic presentations on contemporary problems of peace. But she also began to notice a growing isolation in her school, saying "there is a funny erosion going on, I no longer care to go into the staffroom."

These observations shook me. I began to question the rhetoric of community in action research. What kind of community are we building through collaborative action research in peace education? Colleen was beginning to feel more isolated. As her sense of belonging to the community slipped away, she said of her peace education work: "It's not just projects, projects help to focus on some issue. It's more to do with what you're doing within yourself and the effect you're having on the person you are having coffee with in the morning."

As Colleen and Gloria worked with their students planning events and activities educating for peace, they had become increasingly different from their colleagues. They also raised uncomfortable questions with their co-workers, drawing attention to matters many may have preferred to ignore. In one particularly poignant moment, Gloria described a confrontation with another teacher over his seeming indifference to a talk on human rights violations given by some visiting Third World students. Later, when Gloria confronted this teacher in the staffroom, he responded, "Look, I have two young children of my own, I deal with as much as I can."

This conversation caused our group to ask what a school is as a community. Gloria's and Colleen's accounts of their experiences allowed us to see that the school community as a lived-in place is filled with contradictions. On one level it is a comfortable place of good-natured chitchat and camaraderie. On another level it may become a place where comfortable assumptions are questioned and where change can take place (this is the sense that

Carr and Kemmis speak about). But it is more than these two definitions. There are different interests, different levels of commitment, and different views about what the community is among staff members. To speak in lofty terms about *community* hides these variations and the contradictions that they can bring about. Colleen and Gloria showed how we live these contradictions, needing the support of colleagues, but also wishing to influence change.

RETHINKING CRITICALLY REFLECTIVE ACTION RESEARCH

On the one hand, critically reflective action research urges us to reject the fiction that we can detach ourselves and become merely objective observers of educational situations. On the other hand, it also mistrusts practitioners' "subjective" interpretations of their own situations and attempts to go beyond these to reach a critical understanding through transformative action. As participants in a collaborative action research, the CARPE group did, in fact, move toward a deeper appreciation of various dimensions of peace education in practice. In the process we also developed some critical insight into our previously held views of peace. But our view did not become as clearly and unequivocally critical as Carr and Kemmis would wish it to be. In fact, what emerged more forcibly was the ambiguity and difficulty of peace education concepts in practice. A case in point is the decision to support Les in his efforts to have his class raise money for an individual child in the Third World. A critical theory of development had been a helpful peace education concept, because it showed how the relations of power and dependence are perpetuated through individualized charity work that fails to address the problems of structural violence. If we were to accept this and proceed with critical practice informed by this theoretical insight, then we would have used the students' solution as an occasion to question that charitable impulse, thus raising consciousness of their complicity in oppression. This would have been the politically correct action. But there was more at stake here than politics. As educators we are also concerned with what is pedagogically appropriate. I think our gentle treatment of Les's project implicitly recognized his tactful decision to encourage his students' hope rather than heighten their critical sensibilities. No doubt with adults our choice might have been different.

Peace education casts politics, pedagogy, and what it means to be a teacher in a different light. Carr and Kemmis's version of critically reflective action research aims at a clarity through cycles of strategic action; the purpose of such research is to implement a plan that has been worked out on the basis of reconnaissance and reflections derived from problems of practice.

This kind of clarity was difficult for the CARPE group to achieve, and it is not really the point of peace education. The point of peace education is learning to relate to one another and to the world differently. At present, peace is better known to us as the insistent question of our time, not as a potentially clear course to be followed through an unfolding spiral of action and reflection such as that suggested by Carr and Kemmis. All around us there is evidence that we must learn to cooperate and live in harmony with one another. But there are few prescriptions. Educating for peace is done with cognizance of the human security problem in an age of transformation. The security problem has many dimensions—physical, environmental, social, economic, and cultural—all within the shadow of weapons of immense power in an increasingly interdependent world.

Despite our slogans, the way to a more peaceful world is far from clear for global politics, or for the more constrained space of the classroom and the school. Teachers of peace education encounter ambiguity and difficulty on a daily basis as they attempt to develop the ideals and understandings of peace. The dimensions of school peace concerns extend through many aspects of school life. This makes it necessary to talk and to regularly engage in thoughtful reflection. My worry with Carr and Kemmis's version of action research is that their enthusiasm for applying Habermas inhibits the very dialogue that is most crucial: acknowledging the value of participants' reflections and interpretations. This dialogue for them is only a means to an end. The end is the creation of the critical educational science they have already defined. The features of a critical educational science constitute the test that distinguishes an emancipatory consciousness. Because they feel they must define this as the measure of truth outside of participants' practice, Carr and Kemmis betray their own preference for theory over practice in action research.

Action Research as Interpretive Knowing

Peace education returns practice and participants' reflections on practice. This is what has distinguished action research from other forms of knowing. While this has been a consistent first principle of action research, the character of the argument for action research has altered as understandings of the relationship between theory and practice have changed. What is new in the debate today is the importance being placed on interpretation. In many fields of social science, including education, there is the sense that we have fragmented and abstracted the human experience in such a way that we no longer understand it as it is embedded in life itself. In other words, we have been witnessing a deep and fundamental split between theory and practice. Thus in education, for example, we have curriculum theories, theories of instruction, learning theories, and so forth; each of these illuminate some aspects of teaching, but at the cost of removing them from their meanings in the lives of teachers and children. The turn toward interpretation is now an effort to reground our understandings in practice.

Hermeneutics is the name given to the art and science of interpretation. Paul Ricoeur (1973) remarks that hermeneutics is a humble gesture beginning not with a theoretical explanation but with the frank acknowledgment that we do not understand. In retrospect, the peace education project is an example of hermeneutically oriented action research. Interpretation is necessary with a topic such as education for peace, where many of the old assurances and certainties of direction begin to break down. As I have suggested above, in peace education we realize that we really do not have the answers, only the insistent question of the survival of humanity. What collaborative action research in peace education does is begin to enlarge the public space, allowing the many voices of teachers and students to speak about this question. Voices outside the classroom enter, too, because the problem of peace and security is global. We are enjoined by the content of peace education to hear the people of the Third World, and at the same time to hear the silent people in our midst.

When we ask hermeneutically what kind of knowing action research is, we cast the theory and practice problem into a new light. Admitting that we do not understand, we learn to "read" everyday life more carefully and attentively. This requires an openness to our own experience and to the experience of others that causes us to put aside dogmatic arguments and preconceived opinions. The participants in the CARPE group found theories about peace (drawn from the work of Toh and Cawagas) and theories about action research (drawn from Carr and Kemmis) to be useful guides for their practice. Both of these theories critique positivistic formulations of the theory and practice relationship. But the implementation of these ideas in our respective teaching situations awakened us to a deeper layer of experience—how we live authentically with our colleagues and students.

Peace education is the exploration of a possible life together. As such, it acts, in the words of Kierkegaard, as a kind of "remembering forward." We begin with an understanding of peace as absence. In this sense we are not trying to implement some-thing, but to unfold a possibility. And because we are concerned about life together, we need to consider the other people we work with truly as others and not merely as instruments on the way to producing preformed conclusions about what is good for them.

The experiences described in this article focus on difficulty. As John Caputo suggests, this is the object of a radicalized hermeneutics—to restore life to its original difficulty, but not to make it impossible (Caputo, 1987, p. 7). In this sense the difficulty we encountered in implementing peace education should be seen not as an irritation but as a positive experience awakening us to meaning and to the complexity of life. For us as members of the CARPE group, the four questions about action research described here are examples of new insights into the meaning of developing a peace practice in the everyday lifeworld of our work. Action and reflection have made these new understandings possible. In this way, action research as a way of knowing becomes a *hermeneutics of practice*. A hermeneutics of practice tries to attend most carefully to interpreting the way we are with our colleagues and students in schools. It does not neglect the desire to make specific improvements, but it tempers this with the realization that, because of our deeply ingrained habits of prescription and totalization, we will easily be convinced to impose these improvements willy-nilly on everyone. An emphasis on interpretation attempts to resist and reform this habit, urging us to better develop our abilities to hear others. In the end, probably the most fundamental improvement that action research as a hermeneutics of practice attempts to make is the improvement of the quality of our life together.

REFERENCES

Caputo, J. (1986). Hermeneutics as the recovery of man. In B. R. Wachterhauser (Ed.), *Hermeneutics and modern philosophy* (pp. 416–445). Albany: State University of New York Press.

Caputo, J. (1987). *Radical hermeneutics: Repetition, deconstruction, and the hermeneutic project*. Bloomington: Indiana University Press.

Carr, W., & Kemmis, S. (1986). *Becoming critical: Education, knowledge and action research*. London: Falmer.

Carson, T. (1986). Closing the gap between research and practice: Conversation as a mode of research." *Phenomenology and Pedagogy* 4(2), 73–85.

Carson, T. (1987). Understanding curriculum and implementation. In T. Aoki, D. Franks, & K. Jacknicke (Eds.), *Understanding curriculum as lived: Curriculum Canada VII*. Vancouver: University of British Columbia.

Corey, S. (1953). *Action research to improve school practices*. New York: Columbia University.

Elliott, J. (1977). Developing hypotheses about classrooms from teachers' practical constructs: An account of the Ford Teaching Project. *Interchange, 7*(2), 2–20.

Faraganis, J. (1975). A preface to critical theory. *Theory and Society, 2*(4), 483–508.

Habermas, J. (1972). *Knowledge and human interests* (J. Shapiro, Trans.). Boston: Beacon.

Hustler, D., Cassidy, A., & Cuff, E. (1986). *Action research in classrooms*. London: Allen & Unwin.

Klafki, W. (1975). Decentralized curriculum development in the form of action research. *Council of Europe Information Bulletin*, No. 1, 13–22.

Lewin, K. (1946). Action research and minority problems. *Journal of Social Issues,* *1*(2), 34–36.

Ricoeur, P. (1973). The task of hermeneutics. *Philosophy Today, 17*(2/4), 112–128.

Schwab, J. (1969). The practical: A language for curriculum. *School Review, 78,* 1–24.

Stenhouse, L. (1975). *Introduction to curriculum research and development.* London: Heinemann.

Toh, S-H., & Cawagas, V. (1987). *Peace education: A framework for the Philippines.* Manila: Phoenix.

van Manen, M. (1984). Action research as a theory of the unique. (Department of Secondary Education Curriculum Praxis Occasional Papers Series, No. 31). Edmonton: University of Alberta.

Wagner, H. (1983). *Phenomenology of consciousness and sociology of the life-world: An introductory study.* Edmonton: University of Alberta Press.

CHAPTER 7

Reflections on Education, Hermeneutics, and Ambiguity

Hermeneutics as a Restoring of Life to Its Original Difficulty

DAVID W. JARDINE

Education is concerned with the "bringing forth" (*educare*) of human life. It is thus essentially a "generative" discipline, concerned with the emergence of new life in our midst, and what it is we might hope for this new life, what it is we might wish to engender. Ideally, each new child embodies the possibility that things can become other than what they have already become. What could be called a "conservative" reading of this ideal would be one that finds this ideal precisely the *problem* of education: How are we to educe new life in a way that conserves what already is? The opposite extreme is one that finds this ideal to be precisely the *hope* of education: How are we to educe the new? Underlying both of these readings is a more fundamental question: How are we to respond to new life in our midst in such a way that life together can go on, in a way that does not foreclose on the future? (Smith, 1988a)

Hermeneutics, "radically" interpreted, is concerned with precisely this issue. It distinguishes itself from other forms of inquiry by its essentially educational nature. That is to say, hermeneutic inquiry has as its goal to educe understanding, to bring forth the presuppositions in which we already live. Its task, therefore, is not to methodically achieve a relationship to some matter and to secure understanding in such a method. Rather, its task is to re-collect the contours and textures of the life we are already living, a life that is not secured by the methods we can wield to render such a life our object. The title of Hans-Georg Gadamer's seminal text, *Truth and Method* (1975), is thus essentially ironic: "Truth," hermeneutically conceived, has little to do with "method." "The hermeneutic phenomenon is basically not a problem of method at all" (p. xi).

Methodical, technically based approaches to inquiry in education offer themselves as essentially *informative*. They are designed to pass on information that is already understood, *given* a certain method or research design and a specific history of inquiry. In such approaches, understanding begins and ends with method and operates in service to such a method. Understanding is thus educationally neutered: It is not designed to educe the possibility of understanding, but *assumes* such a possibility of its ground. This is why Heidegger (1927/1972) maintained that we have come upon an age where the *matters* of inquiry have become matters of method. If we play the original meaning of the word "data," what is most fundamentally granted or given in inquiry is not *the matters themselves,* but rather the *method* whereby what is given is rendered objectively presentable. Such inquiries thereby speak on behalf of themselves and their own methodological self-security. It is to method that such inquiries are obedient; it is method that they most fundamentally heed (*ab audire,* to listen, to attend, the roots of the term "obedience").

In the area of education, technical images of inquiry have come to hold sway, and we have become inundated with research that is aimed at pinning down the life of the developing child in such a way that, in the end, nothing more will need to be said.

> Ideally, research orients to the first articulation of what it means to be a child or an adult about which nothing more needs to be said, about which no further specification is needed or possible, in relation to which every variable has been controlled such that, in the end, research would dispel the need or the possibility of saying more. Being a child or being an adult would, ideally, become exhausted issues, in need of no further consideration. The impetus of such research seems to be the as-yet-unfixed variable, the discovery of which warrants further research. The goal of such research seems to be silence—the end of the need to address such issues. (Misgeld & Jardine, 1989, p. 263)

In the face of such a prospect—the hoped-for end of the Word—I would like to offer an analogy.

This analogy responds to Caputo's (1987) provocative formulation of hermeneutics as entailing a "restoring of life to its original difficulty" (p. 1). Technical-scientific discourse offers itself up as a *remedy* to the difficulties of life. The analogy developed below implicitly raises the question as to whether technical-scientific discourse, rather than simply being a remedy to life's difficulties, has rather come to recast the nature of life's difficulties into precisely the sort of thing for which a technical solution is appropriate; that is, life's difficulties are technical problems requiring a "technical fix." The hermeneutic critique of technical-scientific images of inquiry and discourse is not an attempt to say that such approaches should proceed otherwise. As Gadamer (1977) maintains, "such pronouncements have always had something comical about them" since such approaches "will continue along (their) own path with an inner necessity beyond (their) control, and . . . will produce more and more breathtaking *knowledge* and controlling power. It can be no other way" (p. 10). Rather, hermeneutics wants to recover the original difficulties of life, difficulties that are concealed in technical-scientific reconstructions, concealed in the attempt to render human life objectively presentable. "Original" in this usage does not mean a longing for some unspecifiable past "before" technology (a sort of nostalgia) or a longing for one's own past, one's childhood (echoing in some forms of phenomenological pedagogy), but it is nevertheless a longing. It is a longing for fundamental questions of how life together can go on in such a way that new life is possible in our midst (Smith, 1988a).

The problem with technical-scientific discourse is not some indigenous evil or surreptitious intent; rather it is found in the way in which such discourse has come to pervade the possibility of raising questions about our lives and the lives of children. The language it offers is *already foreclosed* (or, at least, it longs for such foreclosure). It longs for the last word; it longs for a world in which the Word no longer lives, a world in which the droning silence of objective presentability finally holds sway over human life. The difficult nature of human life will be solved. We will finally have the curriculum "right" once and for all. We will have turned children inside-out and searched out every nook and cranny. Nothing more will need to be said. Obviously, no educational theorist or practitioner would actually claim to want this. But the hesitancy to make such a claim occurs in the same breath that we hear about "having solved just one piece of the puzzle, just one part of the picture. Further research always needs to be done." Such talk, even in its admirable hesitancy, already operates with an implicit image of the life of the developing child as an objective picture with specifiable component parts. Our exact specifications may be incorrect and further specification is always possible, but such openness does not disrupt the fundamental belief that human life *is* an objective picture that, however complex, is objectively "there" (Jardine, 1988) to be rendered presentable, piece by relentless piece (Heidegger, 1954/1977). As an "object" of technical-scientific discourse, the possibility of the last Word is what makes that discourse possible, howling as it does, even in its hesitancy. It is *here,* perhaps, that the hermeneutic critique sits most squarely. For it is not the actual procedures, methods, concepts, and orientations of technical-scientific discourse that are at issue, but rather the deep *denial of desire* found in that discourse. What hermeneutics unearths— and it is not alone or exclusive in such a project—is the desire for finality, the desire for control, the relentless human lust to render the world a harmless picture for our indifferent and disinterested perusal. This is why the work of Nietzsche is of such interest to those in the hermeneutic tradition. It was Nietzsche's work that rescued the *will to power* from its various objectifications (God, sense data, substance, mathematics, scientific method). It was this cue that disrupted the desire for foundations, for finality—no longer was it easy to simply point with convincing argument to a *fundamentum* without facing up to our lusty fundamentalism and the dogmatism it entails. Once the difficult play (*lude*) of life is denied or objectified into some dispassionate *fundamentum* (e.g., statistically documentable results that provide the basis for claims about the life of the developing child), inquiry becomes deluded, unable to face its own liveliness, its own life, its own desire.

Hermeneutics does not wish to enter into the fray with an alternate foundation. The returning of life to its original difficulty is a returning of the possibility of the living Word. It is a return to the essential generativity of human life, a sense of life in which there is always something left to say, with all the difficulty, risk, and ambiguity that such generativity entails. Hermeneutic inquiry is thus concerned with the ambiguous nature of life itself. It does not desire to render such ambiguity objectively presentable (as if the ambiguity of life were something to dispel, some "error in the system" that needed correction) but rather to attend to it, to give it a voice. And it does this while recognizing its own embeddedness in the very life of which it is the expression. Its manner of speaking is therefore not "informative," standing outside of the ambiguity of life as a voyeur demanding a good show, demanding presentability. It is, rather, provocative, a "calling forth," a voice crying out from within the midst of things. It is, therefore, not "disinterested" but profoundly interested (*inter ease*—right in the midst of things). But even in such interest, hermeneutics involves a recognition that it is not placidly "at home" in the midst of things. One might have to excuse the implicit conservativism of Gadamer's hermeneutics to say this, where *Bildung,* becoming cultured, edification, the well-informed, experienced, and wise edifices of the scholarly academic German tradition underlie the movement of experience, leaving a vague sense of nostalgia in *Truth and Method.* And, of course, this must be coupled with Heidegger's contention that Being speaks Greek, and if not Greek, German, a contention that is in fact true— there are our resources in giving a voice to what is—but might perhaps be the *problem* of inquiry, rather than its nostalgic homeland.

If we are able to sidestep the implicit convervativism in hermeneutics, we see that it persistently asks anew the question of the place of inquiry; it persistently asks anew after what needs to be said. Hermeneutics is thus an analogue for human life, conceived not as an objectively renderable picture, but as a "horizon of future . . . , still undecided possibilities" (Gadamer, 1975, p. 101). It involves a recognition that the Word is essentially homeless, with no prescribed method in which it might rest assured of the eventual foreclosure of the question of one's place; it involves a recognition that the Word cannot be pinned down, for when we attempt to do so, the Word will rise again. Such rising anew means that hermeneutics deeply recognizes the place of language, culture, and history in human life and discourse and the propelling ways in which life is conditioned and contextualized by such phenomena. But it also holds open a place for renewal, for the rebirth of the spirit, for new life. Although hermeneutics may begin here, human life cannot be deeply understood through a thorough historical, linguistic, and cultural interpretation. In the midst of such potentially dusty and deadened talk, new life interrupts, causing a rupture right in the middle of things. It comes asking for room, hoping for the reenlivenment of human life, needing a place of its own to be born. So again, hermeneutics links up essentially rather than accidentally with education, with the emergence or bringing forth of human life. But let us play out the paradoxical biblical image here and not ignore it. At its birth, the living Word was told that *there was no room.* The living Word had to be born right out in the middle of things, and it was such a birth that made it not only part of what already was but also a heralding of the new, of renewal, the possibility of life.

What, then, is the proper hermeneutic response in education? Is the denial of room in order that the Word might live? Perhaps renewal requires our denial, our unwillingness to provide a foundation. But there is the paradox: Perhaps renewal requires our providing room, providing a foundation that is denied in renewal. Perhaps the antifoundationalism of later hermeneutics and deconstructionism is an attempt to take over renewal for ourselves. Perhaps it is a childish attempt to be the child ourselves and deny childhood to our children. Children become nothing more than interruptions of our own playfulness, needing us to be more sure, more "grounded," more authoritative than we desire to be. Yet perhaps it is an attempt to understand the precious child in us all, the precious possibility of renewal that constitutes human life. Perhaps it is an attempt to bring forth the living Word in which we *all* dwell, to show that, *even in our authoritativeness as adults,* the Word can live both for us and for children, that child and adult deeply require each other. Perhaps it is an affirmation that none of us need be de-luded, that the precious play of the world is open to all. This paradox will not sit still and resolve itself. It will not finally and definitively touch one axis or another—it is parabolic, a parable that we cannot solve, fix, or ignore. We must simply learn to live with it, and perhaps a properly hermeneutic response is one that savors its ambiguity and is willing to face the difficulty it evokes without withdrawing into either mute, declarative authoritarianism or involving ourselves in the pretense that we are not adults.

> The old unilateral options of *gericentrism* (appealing to the authority of age, convention, tradition, nostalgia) and *pedocentrism* (child-centered pedagogy) only produce monstrous states of siege which are irresponsible to the matters at hand, that is, to the question of how life is mediated through relations between old and young. (Smith, 1988a, p. 28)

To bring out the possibility of this provocative return to the living Word that hermeneutics seems to long for—the possibility, one might say, of a true *conversation* between young and old which is not foreclosed by either extreme of reverence for the old *or* titillation with the new—I offer the following analogy.

Animals under various forms of threat—the continuous presence of predators, lack of adequate food, drought, and the like—tend to play less and less. They tend, quite naturally, to revert to those kinds of activities that will aid them in gaining comparative control over their environment, activities that involve little or no risk. They revert, so to speak, to what is tried and true, what is most familiar. Although, in times of leisure (paradoxically, the original meaning of *schola,* the root of "school"), play may aid in the development of new and more adaptive ways to gain control over the environment, play *itself* does not offer such control, but is rather risk-laden.

As an analogue to this, one could say that a predatory job market and adverse economic conditions have turned education more and more toward the development of "marketable skills" and away from a "liberal" education, which has come to be rather vaguely equated with not knowing how to *do* anything. Education has turned away from the risks of self-transcendence involved in the exploration of many possibilities of understanding, self understanding and mutual understanding—an exploration in which one is engaged in confronting that which is "other," involving a "moment of loss of self" (Gadamer, 1977, p. 51). It has turned toward the comparative security of self-possession (involved in the accumulation and securing of specific technical skills, intended to give one comparative control over one's place in the world, ways of "having command," not only over the world, but over one's self-understanding, e.g., "I can do this; I have these skills; I have mastered these techniques").

I would like to push this analogy one step further, since there is a point at which it fundamentally breaks down.

The increasing specialization of technical knowledge seems to bring with it the perception that one does not really understand the world, oneself, or others without such knowledge. One could witness how, for example, the relentless proliferation of research data on every conceivable feature of the child's life seems to engender the feeling of knowing less and less, of being more and more unable in the face of such proliferation, so that the only way to survive is to diligently attempt to "get on top of things" and try to "pin them down." Because an overwhelming technical knowledge of every conceivable phenomenon is *possible*, this possibility begins to harbor the perception that one is increasingly out of control if one does not *pursue* this possibility. One is increasingly in danger of no longer understanding. Understanding begins to appear possible only to the extent that we have methodically guarded ourselves against the possibility of misunderstanding (Gadamer, 1977). And this perception of being out of control without technical knowledge, of being "left behind," leads precisely to the anxiety that drives us to relentlessly pursue it, since it is precisely technical knowledge that offers us the promise of relative control. Minuscule obedience to the letter of the law seems to ensure salvation, dividing and subdividing human life into the smallest possible manipulable and controllable bits.

In this way, the mere existence of technical knowledge as a possibility creates the need for the possibility by engendering the anxiety for which it sets itself up as the remedy, not the cause. Once human life becomes the object of technical-scientific reconceptualization, the difficulties of that life become understandable only as technical problems requiring technical solutions. Being alive becomes something to *solve*, and finding one's life difficult, ambiguous, or uncertain is a *mistake* to be corrected. In education, once our understanding of being human becomes estranged from the ongoing, interpretive narrative of everyday life (a narrative rife with possibilities, ambiguity, and risk) and is reconstructed into an object ripe for technical manipulation—once the difficulty of human life comes to be seen as a mistake to be corrected—we begin the horrifying task of chasing our own tails with the hope of eventually closing down the risk-laden conversation that such a narrative involves and requires. We begin to be caught up in the exhausting and consumptive pursuit of "mastery" and "excellence" as something that can be achieved solely as a function of individual methodical diligence and effort, and we begin to engender such exhaustion in our children. If such mastery is not achieved, the only recourse we have available is accusation and guilt— one failed to apply oneself, proper instruction was not given, the rules were not made clear. Thus emerges in education the grand reversal where *not* achieving "excellence" must be accounted for against the background of the assumption that everyone can, and should, be excellent. Education becomes a matter of technical specification and manipulation. Nothing is truly *difficult* and *risky;* it is simply effortful, simply a matter of finding out the trick and applying the correct techniques appropriately. Appropriateness, however, becomes a matter of application. The possibility of failure, of error, must be reduced to technical matters that can be fixed by technical means open to everyone and anyone. In the face of this, there is no real *difference* left, no need for conversation, no interplay.

With all of this, there is no "play" left in life, not only in the sense of "recreational time" (although even this has become an occasion for vicious and relentless "self-improvement"—a form of "getting ahead") but in the sense that life becomes reduced to its actualities, bereft of the possibility of lateral movement into something new or different, and bereft of any sense that there is *time* for such movement. If we "waste time" dwelling in the ambiguous interplays of life, joining in on the conversation with the texts and textures of human life, we are not "getting ahead" in any securable and specifiable way.

Life becomes haunted by an unnamed grieving for what is lost. It is a grieving for the loss of the ability to actually *face* the troublesome character of life in such a way that life together might itself have a chance (Smith, 1988a), in such a way that new life, liveliness, some "movement" might be possible. In the very midst of the breathtaking advance of technology—an advance aimed at *solving* the difficulty of life—private space, the isolation of the Walkman and the computer, television and videogame screens, narcissistic self-improvement (from aerobics to channelling), and a peculiar loneliness ensue. Reduced to its actualities, life becomes degenerative, longing for the last word, longing for foreclosure, longing for death. Under the deluge of research reports and more and more detailed objectively presentable specifications of our lives, one longs for it to be over, to be finally fixed once and for all. Or, in the face of such a deluge, we simply withdraw into self-indulgence, handing over questions of the possibility of life to those "in the know" and understanding ourselves in that withdrawal as peculiarly helpless in the face of such questions. We become banished to a debilitating and immobilizing form of episodic "individualism" as the last vestige of the Word. ("This is my opinion, this is my experience, but then, who is to say who is right? Each of us has our own perspective.") This is clearly witnessed by the recent proliferation of talk shows on which everyone has an opinion, the increasing popularity of the titillating and bizarre (a recent issue of the *National Enquirer* maintained that statues of Elvis were found on Mars), and the disturbing reliance of news media on opinion polls in political reporting, *as if* political issues are equivalent to anyone's or everyone's opinion about those issues).

These have become the grand alternatives: the immobility of technical foreclosure or the immobility of impotent "subjectivity." The only alternative left to a technological foreclosure and the death of the living Word is the tyranny of subjectivity, which leads us to titillation by bizarre phenomena. It does not help us live *out* our lives together. We simply become attached to televised spectacles that we watch with a sort of immobile, pornographic vicariousness.

In education, we have begun to provoke our children to "keep up," haunted as we are with vague cultural specters of "falling behind" and images of human life as sequentially achieved mastery. Technical-scientific understanding, as a response/cause/correlate of this haunting state begins, as Heidegger (1927/1962) put it, to "take over guidance for Being-in-the-world" (p. 90) by offering itself as that form of understanding that will remedy the anxiety produced by such original estrangement. For example, the experimental method in educational research becomes attractive because of its methodological trustworthiness, providing as it does the feeling that we are actually "getting somewhere" in inquiry. If human life really is something to be mastered, we must place our trust in those methods that offer ways of mastering. In light of this, hermeneutics is often viewed with a deep and understandable suspicion—it seems to be "up to something" that it refuses to specify or make explicit, operating perhaps with some hidden agenda. Whatever it is up to, it seems to be against what "we" take as fundamental. It *claims* to not want to change a letter of the law, but it seems to be persistently negative. In light of a view of human life as something to be mastered, inquiry can be nothing other than a form of fundamentalism, and the difference of hermeneutics can only be a matter of a different foundation, different basic concepts or a different method of operation. So the question comes up, over and over again, as to what hermeneutic method really is (*even though* it aggravatingly claims that it is not a matter of method). Hermeneutics becomes something impotent and ignorable by being turned into "one more damn thing" (Smith, 1988b), and a rather peevish thing at that, because it refuses to say where it stands. It becomes as impotent and ignorable as children become when we can master and control their difference by being able to fix and locate them on a universal developmental sequence. Hermeneutics, in adamantly refusing to be fixed, becomes nothing more than an undisciplined child (Misgeld & Jardine, 1989).

But if life dwells in an original difficulty, an original ambiguity that cannot be mastered but only lived with well, the pursuit of such mastery can only lead to immobility or exhaustion—it does not lead to *understanding* human life-as-lived in a deep way. Life as something to be mastered seems to deny what we already know about being alive. A hermeneutic notion of understanding is centered on the dispossession of understanding from its methodical, prepared self-security. It returns inquiry in education to the original, serious, and difficult interpretive play in which we live our lives together with children; it returns inquiry to the need and possibility of true conversation.

It is here that the voice of so-called qualitative research in education emerges—in the rich and ambiguous moments of actually living our lives with children, moments in which we cannot proceed with the brazen confidence and clarity of other forms of research—not because of a failure to be precise, but because of the nature of the matters at hand. One begins to attend to the "data" of human life as they are actually given or granted. It is an attentive, and, one might say, appreciative response to that which is given, to this "gift." It is for this reason that Heidegger (1954/1968) rather playfully links up *Denken* and *Danken*—thinking, inquiry, becomes a form of thanks for what is given:

> The things for which we owe thanks are not things we have from ourselves. They are given to us. We receive many gifts, of many kinds. But the highest and really most lasting gift given to us is always our essential nature, with which we are gifted in such a way that we are what we are only through it. That is why we owe thanks for this endowment, first and unceasingly. (p. 142)

Inquiry in hermeneutics is therefore a form of recollecting what is granted, a way of "gathering" that recognizes how inquiry itself already belongs to the very life for which it gives thanks, that very life which it "thinks." Inquiry so conceived cannot lay out a methodical agenda of pre-given concepts and methods *as if* the epistemic conditions of inquiry take some sort of precedence over the conversation of life itself. A pre-secured method already comes too late in its attempts to render what is already given, prior to such securing. More to the point, such securing is "unthankful" and "unthinking," since it cannot take up this gift as something freely given. Taking up this gift as freely given means recognizing that it does not emanate from us; it does not fall within the purview of that which can be mastered and enslaved to a method of our own making that makes methodical demands on the given, requiring repeatability, presentability, and the like. Taking up this gift requires a peculiar dispossession of understanding, a "self-transcendence" of which technical-scientific discourse is not capable. Perhaps, then, such approaches should be understood as forms of suspicion and refusal, a wanting to methodically foreclose on the elusive, ambiguous, and tenuous character of what is given, suspiciously seeking motive, cause, or agenda. "The method of modern science is characterized from the start by a refusal: namely, to exclude all that which actually eludes its own methodology and procedures. Precisely in this way it would prove to itself that it is without limits and never wanting for self-justification" (Gadamer, 1977, p. 93). Perhaps this is why Heidegger abrasively says that the sciences do not *think*. In light of this:

> One has to ask oneself whether the dynamic law of human life can be conceived adequately in terms of progress, of a continual advance from the unknown into the known, and whether the course of human culture is actually a linear progression from mythology to enlightenment. One should entertain a completely different notion: whether the movement of human existence does not issue in a

relentless inner tension between illumination and concealment. Might it not just be a prejudice of modern times that the notion of progress that is in fact constitutive for the spirit of scientific research should be transferable to the whole of human living and human culture? One has to ask whether progress, as it is at home in the special field of scientific research, is at all consonant with the conditions of human existence in general. Is the notion of an ever-mounting and self-perfecting enlightenment finally ambiguous? (Gadamer, 1983, p. 104–105)

This notion of an "ever-mounting and self-perfecting enlightenment" must especially be questioned in the field of education, for it portends an image of being human in which generativity—the gift of new life, not only the lives of children, but also in the sense that our lives, as adults, can become something other than we might have methodically anticipated—can, in principle, be foreclosed. It portends an image of education as accidental. Even if only understood in principle, once such enlightenment is reached, education is no longer needed. Understanding will not need to be educed; knowledge will simply have to be reproduced in children, information will simply have to be handed over. But in this reproduction, in this handing over, children will have nothing to say, and what we have to say will have already been said. In fact, their *being* children will simply be a result of the accident of birth; becoming an adult will be a technical repairing of the accident of natality. So this image of enlightenment that underlies progress reveals itself as little more than an eventual hatred of children, a hatred of the difference they bring, the difference they make in our lives. If human lives are to culminate in a foreclosing self-perfection, progress and mastery must eventually turn on the young who long to speak, to get in on the conversation, when we as adults already know that there is nothing left to say.

In the inner tension between illumination and concealment, the elusive Word can live. Hermeneutically conceived, the task of inquiry is not to dispel this tension, but to live and speak from within it. It is this tension that propels the generativity of the Word—that makes education hopeful, that makes it possible. It is its love of this generativity and its longing to open up inquiry to such generativity that makes hermeneutics appear so negative in regard to certain forms of inquiry and discourse. It is this love that undergirds hermeneutics' intolerance of those who would traffic in the business of education as if it were as meaningless, as deadened, as unthankful and unthinking as they propose it to be. It is unimaginable to bring new life into a world in which there is nothing left to say, in which the Word no lnger lives. Detached from this original, vibrant difficulty, the original ambiguity, inquiry, and discourse become degenerative, wanting to have the last Word. How can we want this and be educators as well?

REFERENCES

Caputo, J. (1987). *Radical hermeneutics: Repetition deconstruction and the hermeneutic project*. Bloomington: Indiana University Press.

Gadamer, H. G. (1975). *Truth and method*. New York: Seabury.

Gadamer, H. G. (1977). *Philosophical hermeneutics*. Berkeley: University of California Press.

Gadamer, H. G. (1983). *Reason in the age of science*. Cambridge, MA: MIT Press.

Heidegger, M. (1962). *Being and time*. New York: Harper & Row. (Original work published 1927)

Heidegger, M. (1968). *What is called thinking?* New York: Harper & Row.

Heidegger, M. (1972). The end of philosophy and the task of thinking. In *On time and being* (pp. 55–73). New York: Harper & Row.

Heidegger, M. (1977). The age of the world-picture. In *The question concerning technology* (pp. 115–154). New York: Harper & Row. (Original work published 1954)

Jardine, D. W. (1988). There are children all around us. *Journal of Educational Thought, 22*(2A), 178–186.

Misgeld, D., & Jardine, D. (1989). Hermeneutics as the undisciplined child: Hermeneutic and technical images of education. In M. Packer & R. Addison (Eds.), *Entering the circle: Hermeneutic inquiry in psychology* (pp. 259–274). Albany: State University of New York Press.

Smith, D. G. (1988a). Children and the gods of war. *Phenomenology and Pedagogy, 6*(1), 25–29.

Smith, D. G. (1988b, October). *From logocentrism to rhysomatics: Braking through the boundary police to a new love*. Paper presented at the Bergamo Conference on Curriculum Theory and Classroom Practice, Dayton, OH.

Part II

UNDERSTANDING CURRICULUM AS DECONSTRUCTED TEXT

CHAPTER 8

Mapping the Terrain of the Post-Modern Subject
Post-Structuralism and the Educated Woman

REBECCA A. MARTUSEWICZ

What does it mean to be an educated woman, a woman who knows? This question is multidimensional because it involves asking about the meaning of woman, the meaning of knowing, and probably even more fundamentally the relations of power within which such meanings circulate. Questions involving knowledge and women are beginning to be considered by feminist scholars across academic disciplines as necessarily caught in a hierarchized set of meanings that constitute culture. Moreover, the conditions of social and economic life are beginning to be understood as struggled over within a complex symbolic matrix where relations of discourse and power produce men's and women's social and personal identities. "Woman" is being analyzed as a social construct within Western cultures, an active category within a hierarchized system of meaning that operates upon the material conditions of women's lives. On the other hand, "women" refers to the actual historical beings who are defined within those cultures and have not yet escaped those social formations (de Lauretis 1984, 1986).

We can begin to understand women's relation to education by analyzing the sociosymbolic order within which control over the meaning of gender and knowledge is fought for and won. This essay explores the theories that make this kind of analysis possible, a major stream of thought that is pushing out the perimeters of feminist thinking and research in education.

A historic shift in the way we think about being in the world is slowly altering the landscape of the social sciences. Referred to by some as revolutionary, this shift is embodied in what has been called by Jean Francois Lyotard (1984) *The Post-Modern Condition*. Post-modernism, alternatively called modernity, is characterized by a crisis in legitimation, specifically of knowledge, in which an attitude of suspicion or lack of belief with regard to "the master narratives" prevails. That is, our assumptions about what constitutes everyday knowledge as well as academic knowledge, indeed the very possibility of knowing, have been placed deeply into question, causing a major upheaval among Western philosophers of science in how we think about the human relation to the world.

Contemporary French thought—philosophical, theoretical, and methodological—has its roots in the multifaceted movement that we have come to refer to loosely as structuralism, and it is of major importance for postmodernism. Broadly speaking, this movement is represented in the works of Ferdinand de Saussure, Claude Levi-Strauss, and Roland Barthes through Jacques Lacan, Jacques Derrida, and Michel Foucault—to name only the most popularized and well known of the "founding fathers." Spanning a wide range of disciplines, including linguistics, literary criticism, anthropology, history, and psychoanalysis, the work of these men represents very diverse interests. Despite this diversity, however, their works harbor a common theme that is at the heart of their importance for social research: the rejection of the unified knowing subject and the adoption of a notion of knowledge and of subjectivity as inscribed in culture through language.

This interest is also found in the writing of French women, such as Julia Kristeva, Helene Cixous, and Luce Irigaray, but is increasingly demonstrated in American and British feminist work as well. Drawing on the insights and work of their French male colleagues, these women have begun to challenge the "truth" of the traditional, naturalized representation and subjective positions assigned to women by a male-dominated symbolic order. This chapter will lay out the intersection of these budding feminist critiques within the multidimensional post-modern movement, especially as it is impacting the scholarship on women in education.

BANNING THE CARTESIAN SUBJECT: THE STRUCTURALIST REVOLUTION

Frederic Jameson has noted that structuralism in its broadest definition seeks to study "the unconscious value system or system of representation which *orders* social life at any of its levels, and against which . . . individual, conscious social acts and events take place and become comprehensible" (1972, p. 13). In other words, structuralism is based on the assumption that social and cultural phenomena are more than simply material phenomena. Human actions and events have meaning and, moreover, are dependent upon an underlying system of relations and distinctions that make meaning possible and define the form that such actions and events may take. This focus upon an underlying system of relations or representations challenges the humanist notion that meaning is essential, that it arises from individual experience. This challenge, as the following review will demonstrate, is precisely what may be considered structuralism's "revolutionary" contribution, a contribution whose foundation is often attributed to the insights of Swiss linguist Ferdinand de Saussure.

Dissatisfied by the preoccupations of his turn-of-the-century colleagues and their predecessors with studying the evolution and etymologies of particular languages, Saussure insisted that language should be studied and understood synchronically, as a system of signs functioning at a particular moment in time, structurally specific to the moment. This emphasis on *synchronic* rather than *diachronic* analysis introduced an important shift into linguistics and eventually into the social sciences. As Saussure suggested, it made language the object of a science, or, as he called it, semiology, which could be expanded beyond linguistics to encompass the study of a plethora of cultural and social phenomena (Saussure, 1959).

To accomplish such a scientific analysis, Saussure proposed another fundamental distinction in the study of language between *langue,* the system of set rules in a particular language, and *parole,* the use of that system, or actual speech. Rather than study what people actually said, or historically had said, Saussure made linguistics the object of a synchronic analysis of *langue* and studied general principles and conventions on which language was organized. Specifically, *langue* was seen to be a nonsubstantive, unconscious system of relations between signs, each sign being made up of the associative relationship between a *signifier* (or mental acoustical image) and a *signified* (the concept or meaning).

According to Saussure, this tridimensional pattern, extended into a system of differential relations between signs, constitutes the production of meaning within the organization of language. As stated in *Course in General Linguistics* (1916/1959):

> in language there are only differences. Even more important: a difference generally implies positive terms between which the difference is set up; *but in language there are only differences without positive terms.* Whether we take the signified or the signifier, language has neither ideas nor sounds that existed before the linguistic system, but only conceptual and phonic differences that have issued from the system. (p. 120; emphasis added)

Meaning is thus not inherent to the sign but is made possible only within a relation between two or more signs, only insofar as one sign is *different* from another. Thus the identity of a particular sign or entity is not an identity of substance but only of form, defined by its relation to other entities. As Jonathan Culler puts it: "Language is a system of unrelated items and the value and identity of these items is defined by their place in the system rather than by their history" (Culler, 1975, p. 12).

This concept of relational identity is crucial to structural analyses of all kinds. Following Saussure's suggestion that aside from language social and cultural phenomenon could be analyzed as sign systems, French anthropologist Claude Levi-Strauss affirmed that Saussure's linguistic model could be utilized in the analysis of the meaning structures underlying kinship systems or myths in so-called primitive societies. For Levi-Strauss the relation between functional oppositions produces meaning in a particular society. Used in the analysis of primitive myths, Levi-Strauss's method looks for binary oppositions, for example, a man and a jaguar, which, he explains, come to represent conceptual differences, for example, culture and nature. These images do not have meaning because of anything inherent to themselves, but rather because of the differences manifested between them and because of the society's ability to assign meaning to a particular combination based on its own system of oppositions. Such combinations, according to Levi-Strauss, are governed by a set of rules or relations beneath the surface of the mythological narrative that, as with language, are inherent in the human mind itself as mental operations that classify and organize society (Levi-Strauss, 1972).

Similarly, Roland Barthes utilized the theories developed by Saussure to analyze the "collective representations" that make up mass culture. Reflecting on what he refers to as "some of the myths of French daily life" through a variety of forms—professional wrestling, cinema and literary images and personalities, the French holiday, culinary art—Barthes's work is a critique of ideology, an effort to "account for the mystification which transforms petit bourgeois culture into a universal nature" (Barthes, 1972, p. 11) by treating these forms as sign systems. Thus the world of wresting is taken apart to show an underlying system of signs that produce specific shared categories of meaning—suffering, justice, defeat—functioning to create a spectacle, to capture the attentions of and elicit a particular response from the audience. In this sense, according to Barthes, myth functions like a language to classify and organize our daily lives, to represent ideology as natural (Barthes, 1972).

In addition to social analyses like those of Barthes and Levi-Strauss, other fields, particular literary criticism, have been greatly influenced by Saussurian linguistics. Meaning within a text began to be seen as independent of any external influence or authorial intention, constituted instead by the system or structure of relations inherent in the text itself. Thus structuralist criticism bracketed out content to focus upon form, a practice reflecting the important shift in perspectives that all these analyses, as contributors to the structuralist movement, express: specifically, as described by Vincent Descombes, that "the origin of meaning can no longer be located where the phenomenologists had thought to find it, in the author of discourse, the individual who believes he is expressing himself, but rather . . . it lies in language itself" (Descombes, 1980, p. 17).

This brings us to one of the most important consequences of structuralist analysis: the disappearance of the traditional notion of the subject. While Descartes argued, with theological overtones, that "I think therefore I am" and the phenomenologists sought to make the self a subject that would endow the world with meaning, the structuralists deprived the conscious subject of its role as source of meaning, locating the production of meaning, instead, within the relations of an *unconscious* conventional system of differences, language (Culler, 1975). This intellectual shift represents the rejection of the notion of man as the center of truth. As Michel Foucault states in *The Order of Things*, "man is only a recent invention, a figure not yet two centuries old, a simple fold in our knowledge and he will disappear as soon as that knowledge has found a new form" (1970, p. 15).

The relation between human beings and the world depends on the particular configuration of knowledge at a particular moment in history. Meaning is not the expressed result of a "lived experience," as the phenomenologists would insist, but rather the result of a symbolic system into which we are born. In this sense, language is more than a tool for communication. We are not simply the creators of language; on the contrary, language creates us.

Thus structuralism "bracketed out" the subject at best and, at worst, tossed the subject out all together in favor of a system or structure within which meaning, or "reality," was produced. But human subjectivity cannot be dispensed with so easily, for as Jonathan Culler points out, the individual subject:

> may no longer be the origin of meaning, but meaning must move through him. Structures and relations are not objective properties of external objects; they emerge only in a structuring process. And though the individual may not originate or even control this process—he assimilates it as part of his culture—it takes place through him. (1975, p. 30)

Saussure's insistence upon *langue,* or the system of rules in language, as the proper object of linguistic study had far-reaching and important effects, as I have outlined above, but his exclusion of *parole,* or the individual use of language, denied the inseparability and interdependence of the two categories. His insight that value or differences between signs motivated the production of meaning was fundamental to the revolutionary shift in perspective within the social sciences, but he did not acknowledge that it is the human ability to differentiate and discriminate between signs that motivates the structuring process. By avoiding questions of the relation between structure and use of language, Saussure avoided questioning the relation between the individual and culture. He reduced culture and the collective to a linguistic system that was encapsulated within the unconscious, but he did not include the individual within that collective.

Moreover, Saussure's emphasis on synchronic rather than diachronic analysis prioritized structure in a closed system over function, a position that again disregarded the individual's interaction with or performance in the structure and that ultimately invalidated history, change, and movement in the system and society itself. Together, these shortcomings resulted in structuralism's failure to follow its insights through to their important social implications, to account for the historical relation between the individual and larger social system as it is mediated by language.

It is precisely with these implications that contemporary French thought is concerned and that the issues of post-modern feminism become most embroiled. Without dismissing the contributions that structuralism has made but rather pushing at the boundaries of its assumptions, opening it up, a new mode of thinking, often referred to in the United States as post-stucturalism, is reinserting the subject into the questions of language and the production of meaning. For women writers in France and those in the United States who have begun to wander into the labyrinth of French post-modern thought, these questions have had a very important impact. They have opened up a whole new terrain upon which to ask what it means to be a woman and to challenge the traditional answer to that question.

The following pages will explore the varied and uncertain landscape of this new terrain by sketching the work of these major French men theorists and the corresponding women's intersections and responses. The first two men, Jacques Lacan and Jacques Derrida, have attracted the attention of three leading women scholars in France, Julia Kristeva, Luce Irigaray, and Helene Cixous, far more than the third, Michel Foucault, whose theories are the point of focus for several Americans and British women whose work will be reviewed.

THEORIZING THE POST-MODERN SUBJECT: LACAN AND DERRIDA

The most controversial theorist in France for women is Jacques Lacan. His importance to women does not stem from any pro-feminism on his part; on the contrary, he was contemptuous of women's movements in France. Rather, it is his original treatment of the human subject in relation to society and to language that has caught the attention of women writers. Lacan's work is the reading of Freud and the reinterpretation of psychoanalysis through the linguistic principles developed in structuralism. He returns to what he sees as Freud's most important discovery—the unconscious and its relation to human sexuality—to pursue the question of how men and women come to be sexually differentiated beings.

Writing from within this question in a style that is purposely obscure and often impenetrable, Lacan mounts his attack on a wide range of other psychoanalytic interpretations that he claims misunderstand and therefore undercut Freud's most important insights. For Lacan, theories such as those developed in America since Freud—ego psychology and object relations, for example—are caught in the ideological trap of humanism by implying that the human subject or ego is present, that it exists from the beginning as a center point from which the normal person or nonpatient then exercises choice and control over his or her life. From this perspective, the task of the analyst is to restore a sense of self, of identity and control, to the patient (Mitchell & Rose, 1982).

But Lacan challenges all humanistic interpretations by denying that the human unconscious and sexuality are predetermined facts. These are, according to his reading of Freud, historically and socially constructed, and it is the task of psychoanalysis to uncover how this construction occurs, how the human subject comes into being. From this perspective it is possible to understand the interest that some feminists have developed in Lacan; woman is no longer a naturally given object, but a socially constructed one. The whole question of female sexuality and identity is put into an entirely new light. To understand this further and to lay the grounds upon which this feminist writing is based, we must consider some of the basic tenets of Lacan's work.

Drawing upon and extending the work of Saussure, Lacan asserts that human beings are born into language and that the human subject is created from within the relations and laws of language. Language does not exist as a natural resource or talent within the individual but rather waits as an external law through which all humans must pass to become sexually differentiated subjects. As Juliet Mitchell explains in an introduction to Lacan's work: "Language always 'belongs' to another person. The human subject is created from a general law that comes to it from outside itself and through the speech of other people, though this speech in its turn must relate to a general law" (Mitchell & Rose, 1982, p. 13).

Following Freud, Lacan sees this process of subjection as occurring through a number of stages or states of being, beginning with what he terms the "imaginary." The imaginary refers to a state in which there is no clear distinction between subject and object, between the infant and mother or external world, a state corresponding with Freud's pre-Oedipal state in which the child is in symbiotic relation to the mother's body. In this state there is no clear definition of self, but as the child enters into what Lacan calls the "mirror stage" there begins a process of identity construction as the child sees reflected from the place of the other an image that it takes to be itself. The child develops a sense of the unified "I" by internalizing this image, an image that, like an image in a mirror, both is and is not itself (Lacan, 1977).

In this sense, the image with which the child identifies is always an alienated one, and the sense of unity that the child experiences is a fiction. Thus the imaginary is precisely that state in which we perceive for ourselves, throughout our lives, an identity that is never precisely ourselves. There is a split. It is the state in which the ego functions and which enables the subject to function as "I." As Lacan indicates, however, following the linguistic theory of Benveniste, the pronoun "I" is never a stable entity of meaning, for it shifts and moves depending upon who happens to be using it at the moment of utterance. Jacqueline Rose points out that "the mirror image represents the moment when the subject is located in an order outside itself to which it will henceforth refer" (Mitchell & Rose, 1982, p. 31).

That order is what Lacan refers to as the symbolic, and its importance becomes most evident in his serious consideration of what Freud described as the bedrock of psychoanalysis, the castration complex. As we have seen, the pre-Oedipal stage of the infant's development is characterized by a "dyadic structure": the child and the mother's body. As the child enters into what Freud called the Oedipus complex, a third term, the father, is introduced into the structure, disrupting the duality of the mother-child relation. The father, signifying the social taboo on incest, intrudes upon the libidinal relation of the child to the mother, splitting it apart and forcing the repression of the child's desire for the mother. In this way the child is forced to recognize its place in a wider social relation. The father's entrance upon the scene marks the first moment in the process of sexual differentiation and the constitution of the subject. It is in this moment that a key element for psychoanalysis is introduced. That element, much debated and the target of feminist attacks on psychoanalysis, is the phallus (Freud, 1955).

According to Freud, the presence or the absence of the phallus marks the difference between the sexes. Before the Oedipus complex the little boy and little girl share the same sexual history, a masculine history. With the entrance of the father, the little girl realizes that she lacks the phallus (she is "castrated") and so transfers her object love from her mother to her father, whom she recognizes as having what she does not—a phallus. In hatred she identifies with her mother. The boy, fearing castration, is forced to deny his love for the mother and identify with the father. For both Freud and his disciple Lacan, the concept of castration is the foundation for the determination of sexual identity.

But Lacan's interpretation is unique. For him, the phallus represents the first moment of symbolization; that is, the moment when the child realizes that something could be missing, the moment of desire. Standing before the mirror, the child encounters an imaginary fullness of self, where no gaps in meaning or differences are yet apparent. With the introduction of the phallus, however, that fullness is shattered and the realization that one's identity depends upon a relation of difference and similarity occurs. Similarly, the child begins to symbolize or use language when he or she realizes that a sign or word stands in place of that which is missing, the object of desire. Moreover,

Lacan argues, these signs have meanings only in relation to other signs (Lacan, 1977). Terry Eagleton explains that:

> just as the child is unconsciously learning these lessons in the sphere of language, it is also learning them in the sphere of sexuality. The presence of the father, symbolized by the phallus, teaches the child that it must take a place in the family which is defined by sexual difference, by exclusion (it cannot be its parents' lover), and by absence (it must relinquish its earlier bonds to the mother's body). (1983, p. 1967)

Indeed, the lessons of sexuality are lessons of *langue,* since for Lacan the unconscious is an effect of language. Upon entering the Oedipal stage, the child has entered into the realm of the symbolic, the pre-given set of rules and relations—the Law of the Father—that makes possible human subjectivity. The phallus *stands for* the moment of rupture, the moment when difference is introduced into the structure, the moment when desire for the lost object (the phallus itself) begins to circulate in an endless system of substitution—language. Thus sexual identity, according to Lacan, is accomplished at a price, the subjection to a law in which the phallus is the primary signifier (Lacan, 1977).

It is precisely on this point, the privileging of the phallus as the primary signifier of sexual identity, that another post-modern thinker, Jacques Derrida, has criticized Lacan and, indeed, allied himself to women theorists in France (Derrida, 1975). In fact, as women writers have picked up and reinterpreted the work of both Lacan and Derrida according to their own interests, an important connection between these two men has been established. Although women have attacked Lacan's focus on the phallus as signifier of signifiers, his focus on the subject as implicated in language has had great impact on the development of new understandings of the construction of the female subject. At the same time, Derrida's very different approach to the problem of the subject's relation to language has also enabled women to push at the boundaries of their own writing, to develop important critiques of dominating discourse that they describe, following Derrida, as "phallogocentric" (Derrida, 1975, p. 98).

"Phallogocentrism" is the term Derrida uses to describe what he sees as Lacan's privileging of the male over the female in his conception of the construction of the sexually differentiated human subject. According to Derrida, such valorization of one term over another is characteristic of the metaphysical tradition of Western thought, which is organized by the desire for and belief in one truth, one transcendental signifier, which will provide the unquestionable origin of meaning for all others. Historically, we have seen this desire manifested in such concepts as God, Man, Knowledge, the Self, and so on. Out of this general search for the foundation of truth, which Derrida

calls "logocentrism" (Derrida, 1970), has come the construction of a hierarchy of meaning governing our thought. So, for example, since Plato, language has taken a subservient position in relation to the idea in Western
philosophy. Contrary to Saussure's principle that language produces meaning, language has been traditionally conceived as the mere vehicle or medium
of meaning.

Accordingly, we divide our world into a series of culturally determined
hierarchized oppositions: Thought takes precedence over language, speech
over writing, culture over nature, reason over emotion, strength over weak-
ness, male over female. For Derrida, this kind of thinking assumes an implicit
belief in a center or presence of meaning around which all other meanings
turn (Derrida, 1970). With the advent of Saussarian linguistics, however,
such thinking must ultimately be seen as a fiction because, as we have seen,
for any meaning to be possible other signs must already exist. That is, originary meaning is impossible, for meaning only comes about from within the
differential relation of a least two signs. Thus, Derrida argues, Saussure's
notion that in language there are only differences between positive terms
authorizes a powerful critique of logocentrism and therefore must be taken
very seriously (Derrida, 1982).

In addition, the assumption of a teleology of meaning that would ultimately reach the final truth or goal as implied in the hierarchical organization
of the *logos* is made problematic by Derrida in a Nietzschean affirmation of
the play of difference. Referring to what he calls "differance," a deliberately
ambiguous term meaning both to defer and to differ from, Derrida strives to
undermine the notion that meaning, knowledge, and therefore subjectivity
are stable, predictable entities. For him meaning is constituted of the infinite
play or relation between signifiers; "differance" is designated as that which
denies the distinction between or separation of signifier and signified. As
soon as a signified appears, it immediately becomes a signifier for another
signified, which will move on to become a signifier with another signified
and so on in an endlessly multiplying chain (Derrida, 1982).

In other words, meaning is never immediately present in a sign. It is
always what the sign is *not* and so in a way is absent from the sign, dependent
upon its relation to other signs. In the same way, the present is never really
present but exists only in its relation to the past and the future. Constantly
deferred, the present is present only in its absence.

In this same sense, the subject can never be fully present to itself or to
anyone else, since as an effect of language it is constantly shifting, flickering
in absence and presence like the constant movement along the signifying
chain. And it is precisely this shifting unpredictability that Derrida sees as
the power of "differance."

It is the domination of beings that difference everywhere comes to solicit, in the sense that *sollicitare,* in old Latin, means to shake as a whole, to make tremble in entirety. Therefore, it is the determination of Being as presence or as beingness that is interrogated by the thought of differance. . . . It is not present being, however excellent, principal, or transcendent. . . . Not only is there no kingdom of differance, but differance instigates the subversion of every kingdom. Which makes it so obviously threatening and infallibly dreaded by everything within us that desires a kingdom. (Derrida, 1982, pp. 21–22)

If Being as presence is a fiction, then it follows that a stable natural human identity is also a fiction, that identity is only the production of a particular set of relations, a representation within the symbolic order, or, to blur the terminology of Lacan and Derrida, an imaginary moment of presence.

Woman, then, must be seen as a category of thought, a product of that set of relations, of a male-dominated symbolic order. In fact, for a growing body of women's writing, woman is the subordinate term within an oppositional hierarchy organizing the whole of Western metaphysics.

THE FEMININE SUBJECT(S): CIXOUS, IRIGARARY, AND KRISTEVA

The complete set of symbolic systems—everything said, everything organized as discourse—art, religion, family, language—everything that seizes us, everything that forms us—everything is organized on the basis of hierarchical oppositions which come back to the opposition man/woman. (Cixous, quoted in Stanton, 1980, p. 73).

For a number of French women scholars, most notably Helene Cixous, Julia Kristeva, and Luce Irigaray, this latter pair provides the basis for all others. In fact, they argue, the symbolic order, that order to which all consciousness is subjected and through which it becomes possible, is an order constituted and imposed by men. Phallogocentrism naturalizes the phallus as master signifier and assigns woman to the passive, silent side of the binary, defining and identifying her as man's opposite. But for these women the phallus is a fraud. Their work represents an attempt to dismantle the powerful discourses that valorize the masculine voice as it represses the female.

In so doing they have entered into a critical engagement with psychoanalysis, specifically with Lacan's rereading of Freud, embracing the tenuous, moving subject appearing at the intersection of language and social relations, while rejecting both Freud's and Lacan's conservative acceptance and theoretical perpetuation of the sexual status quo. This is particularly at issue for

Kristeva and Irigaray. Both are psychoanalysts, yet they approach the problem of female identity from different positions and styles.

For Irigaray, Western philosophical discourse from Plato and Hegel through Freud and Lacan is founded upon a masculine model of sexuality presented as unified and neutral. It is thus founded as well upon the exclusion of woman or, more specifically, upon the repression of feminine desire in favor of what Irigaray (1985a) calls "the old dream of symmetry." Irigaray argues that women are defined in male discourse as man's opposite, as his inverse, as the "other" in an economy of sameness.

> The "feminine" is always described in terms of deficiency or atrophy, as the other side of the sex that alone holds a monopoly on value: the male sex. . . . How can we accept the idea that woman's entire sexual development is governed by her lack of, and thus by her longing for, jealousy of, and demand for, the male organ? . . . All Freud's statements describing feminine sexuality overlook the fact that the female sex might possibly have its own "specificity." (Irigaray, 1985a, p. 69)

Irigaray seeks not to elaborate a new theory of woman but to "jam the theoretical machinery itself" by exposing how the feminine finds itself defined as the negative image in male discourse and by reclaiming the female body as the celebrated location of woman's unique pleasure, her desire and her difference. She seeks escape both from the simple reversal of the masculine position, from asserting the "feminine" as the new standard for sexual difference, and from asking for equality with men, responses that only perpetuate the "economy of sameness" (Irigaray, 1985b). Her concern is with denying the phallic principle of identity and setting free the multiple, indeterminate female subject in writing. Her writing is an attempt to break from semantic authority with laughter and movement, an attempt to articulate woman's nonhierarchical difference in language.

> a woman touches herself by and within herself directly, without mediation and before any distinction between activity and passivity is possible . . . for her sex is composed of two lips which embrace continually. . . . She is neither one nor two. She cannot, strictly speaking, be defined as one person or as two. She renders any definition inadequate. Moreover, she has no "proper" name. And her sex organ which is not *a* sex organ, is counted as *no* sex organ. (Irigaray, quoted in Marks & de Courtivron, 1981, p. 100)

The influence of Lacan is evident in Irigaray's interest in the unconscious and her constant reference to the inseparable relation among sexuality, subjectivity, and the symbolic. But her style, her serious effort in writing to push at the constraining boundaries of language, her attempts to be at once inside and outside, present and absent is obviously influenced by Derrida. Moreover, it is clear that in her critique of Lacanian psychoanalysis she finds an ally in Derrida, who writes:

> Woman (truth) will not be pinned down. In truth woman, truth will not be pinned down. That which will not be pinned down by truth is, in truth feminine. This should not, however, be hastily mistaken for a woman's femininity, for female sexuality, or for any other of those essentializing fetishes which might still tantalize the dogmatic philosopher, the impotent artist or the inexperienced seducer who has not yet escaped his foolish hopes of capture. (1979, p. 55)

Irigaray's writing is consciously poetic, illusory, open-ended. She wants to defy and discredit the old repressive representations by writing the unpredictable, undefinable subject that slips happily away, forever missing from its place.

Less poetic in style, though highly interested in the importance of poetic language, is the work of Julia Kristeva. As in Irigaray's writing, the Lacanian precept that identity is linguistic, that it is demarcated in language, is very much present in Kristeva's work. Like Irigaray, she too pursues important questions and issues excluded by Lacan and Freud. Specifically, what are the "female" forms and operations within language and what is the relation of the maternal, of motherhood, to language and identity?

Kristeva situates these issues within a complex analysis of the processes of signification, which she sees as divided between two general functions or modalities—the symbolic and the semiotic. She describes the relation between these two sides of language as not unlike a master-slave relation, with the symbolic function as the dominating discourse, the *logos,* while the semiotic, remaining primarily repressed, appears in the child's nonsense or the madman's babble (Kristeva, 1984).

The symbolic function can be understood as the system or law into which we enter in order to represent what is absent to us; that is, it corresponds to the system of language as sign and syntax, that which we take for granted as language itself. Carolyn Burke describes this function in a discussion of Kristeva's theory.

> Although the symbolic functions never entirely displaced the semiotic, they come to dominate in speech, as in writing. When we learn what we call sentence structure, we absorb a concept of identity as defined by syntax, which posits as a given the subject and its objects. (Gallop & Burke, 1980, p. 43)

The semiotic function, on the other hand, is presymbolic; it is founded upon, derives its energy from the fetus's experience of the womb and the infant's attachment to the mother's body. It is made manifest through the rhythms and intonations that are anterior to the first phonemes, sentences, and so forth that the child enters into as he or she learns to speak. Kristeva posits the semiotic as the realm of instinctual drives "anterior to naming, to the One, to the father, and consequently maternally connoted" (1980, p. 133). This insightful assertion has obviously important implications for feminism, since it clearly points to an operation in the production of meaning that is dependent upon the relation to the maternal body. Indeed, it is at this level of signification that Kristeva finds the important possibility of breaking through, rupturing the rigid, oppressive, paternal function of language represented by the symbolic.

The semiotic pushes to the surface, "introducing wandering, or fuzziness" into poetic language. There, in the works of Mallarmé, Lautréamont, Artaud, and Sade, Kristeva discovers the subject-in-process:

> The unsettled and questionable subject of poetic language . . . maintains itself at the cost of reactivating this repressed instinctual, maternal element . . . it is within the economy of signification itself that the questionable subject-in-process appropriated to itself this archaic, instinctual, and maternal territory; thus it simultaneously prevents the word from becoming mere sign and the mother from becoming an object like any other. (1980, p. 136)

In an important contribution to feminism, as well as to linguistics and psychoanalysis, Kristeva asserts a bisexuality within the speaking subject. Against the phallocentrism of the dominant discourses, she recognizes the multiple possibilities of signification by posing sexual difference as a metaphor for plurality within the creation of meaning. Moreover, from within the creative spaces of poetic language Kristeva welcomes the appearance of the "aimless" subject, a subject that challenges the constraints of the symbolic order and the oppressive hierarchical binary implicit to the *logos*.

This is precisely what she sees as the women's movement's most urgent task, "to fight against social and cultural archaisms" by exposing what is repressed in the dominant discourses, by creating gaps in meaning through writing that subverts the patriarchal tradition and allows the forbidden subject(s) to be spoken (Marks & de Courtivron, 1981). Yet, for Kristeva, women's writing and the female impulse (*le feminin*) cannot be distinguished from other subversive, dissident forms that arise from the repressed semiotic modality of language. This difference sets her apart from Cixous and Irigaray, who seek to inscribe the excluded female in language.

Like Irigaray, however, she is deeply concerned about and critical of forms of feminism that identify with and seek only to reverse the very forms of power that women are fighting.

> Woman is here to shake up, to disturb, to deflate masculine values, and not to espouse them. Her role is to maintain differences by pointing to them, by giving

them life, by putting them into play against one another. (Kristeva, quoted in Feral, 1980, p. 92)

The interest in this work by the French women writers is to "forge the antilogos weapon," to take apart the dominant male discourses that define woman according to man's image of himself, and to articulate woman's difference in and through language. In Helene Cixous's words, "woman must put herself into the text—as into the world and into history—by her own movement." Indeed, for Cixous it is writing as a female, "ecriture feminine," which will provide the necessary space, "will knock the wind out of the codes" with its attention to the female body, and will be the springboard for the transformation of social cultural structures (1976, pp. 875–880).

This critical women's writing has not gone without criticism from within the ranks of either French feminist scholarship or American feminist writing. The most common complaint, voiced in large part by Marxist feminist theorists, is that the focus on language as the foundation of women's oppression and as the potential site of our liberation is not sufficiently grounded in material reality. Material reality is associated with the forces and relations of production constituting capitalism, a view that accounts for behaviors and psychic makeup in terms of ideological distortions or a "false consciousness" produced within class relations of a capitalist economy.

Within this criticism, the analysis of language is seen as replacing one totalizing category for another. There is the fear that assertion of "ecriture feminine," as a means of articulating repressed female sexuality and subjectivity, implies the presence of an essential female eroticism. As such, it is argued the French women's work does not transcend the limits of the discourse that it attacks (Stanton, 1980, pp. 78–79).

Although such criticism indeed points out the possibility of contradictions and binds within their writing, dissatisfaction with the French women's writing is often a result of misinterpretation due in part to the poor availability of translations. To accuse their work of disregard for material reality is to overlook their concern for the fundamental materiality of language itself; that is, their work asserts that the practices and relations which constitute our daily lives are produced within a complex system of signs and signification in which we are inscribed as subjects.

This focus on woman's relation to the unconscious is coupled with a corresponding interest in woman's sexuality and body. The body is recognized as the historical site of the objectifications of woman, but, in the refusal to repeat the denial of the female, woman's body is reclaimed as a source of metaphor for multiplicity and difference. Their interest in language does not deny the existence of injustices in concrete economic, political, and social structures; rather it sees these injustices as manifestations of a phallocentric constitution of meaning within the symbolic order.

Further, the demand that feminist theory be grounded in "material reality" reveals an important gap between French and American women's scholarship. Alice Jardine has discussed this gap in her book *Gynesis: Configurations of Woman and Modernity*. She points to the French women's immersion in rather abstract discussions of the subject's relation to language typical of contemporary thought in France. American feminists, on the other hand, favor a more concrete analysis of the constraints of social context, a perspective criticized in France as "the famous American 'refusal of the unconscious,' insistence on 'self,' and emphasis on language as only a natural, communicative function" (Jardine, 1985, p. 42).

Although this critique may be a fair estimation of a general trend in American theory, not all American feminism is hostile to the ideas asserted in the French post-modern perspective, as Biddy Martin clearly demonstrates when she writes:

> Feminist criticism must be engaged in elaborating the extent to which the phal-
> locentric meanings and truths of our culture have necessarily repressed multiplic-
> ity and the possibility of actual difference by appropriating difference, naming it
> opposition and subsuming it under the Identity of Man. Feminism shares with
> post-structuralist criticism a critique of the hegemony of the identical and the
> desire for other forms of discourse. (1988, p. 13)

But Martin does not take the same path as the French women in exploring these issues. In part, her work exemplifies Jardine's observation of the social-contextual orientation of American feminist interests. But, more importantly, it also reflects the influence of another important French theorist.

POWER/KNOWLEDGE/SUBJECT: MICHEL FOUCAULT

While the works of Derrida and Lacan provide the "primary texts" for the women discussed, Martin, joining other British and American feminists, turns her attention to Michel Foucault. Foucault's work is grounded in the contextual social analysis of the production of meaning and the subject as it occurs within a growing technology and institutionalization of knowledge.

Foucault's work differs in many ways from both Derrida's and Lacan's. In general, his focus is more social and historical; that is, he is concerned with meaning not only as it is made within language but as it is made within and structures social practices and institutions. This different focus is helpful in understanding women's historical relation to knowledge and education.

Sharing the characteristic post-modern denunciation of humanism's dream of a totalizing central truth, Foucault exposes the moment and the processes by which "man" became the object of scientific knowledge. His work is a careful excavation of the recent historical relations through which an image of humanity has been produced and crystallized as truth in the so-called human sciences. As an inquiry into how and why Western thought has shaped a particular representation of human forms, Foucault's work is influencing the development of important questions within feminist social analysis.

For example, zeroing in on a central issue in Foucault's work, the relation between power and knowledge, Martin asks, "how are discipline and power constituted at the moment at which woman is made the object of knowledge?" (Martin, 1988, p. 14). Her question brings to light a different dimension in the analysis of woman's relation to the symbolic order by locating it within the production of knowledge, that is, within relations of discourse rather than within relations between signs. An important shift in the analysis of the subject is made possible by Foucault's break with traditional theories of representation and power.

For Foucault, the constitution of the subject is inseparable from the complex relations between knowledge and power. Power, in Foucault's terms, should be understood as more than negative, repressive force; rather, it is a productive "multiplicity of force relations." It resides everywhere, in every relation, as "the process which, through ceaseless struggles and confrontations, transforms, strengthens, or reverses" these relations. "Power, insofar as it is permanent, repetitious, inert and self-reproducing, is simply the over-all effect of these mobilities, the concatenation that rests on each of them and seeks in turn to arrest their movement . . . it is the name that one attributes to a complex strategical situation in a particular society" (Foucault, 1980, pp. 92–93).

In this sense, Foucault seeks to uncover the ways that power functions positively in production, the ways that it is involved in making us who we are within social fields of force. Discourses, and the institutions and practices that support them, are for Foucault social forces that motivate and guarantee the production of knowledge—a function that cannot be separated from his conception of power. For it is precisely the function and circulation of knowledge and the creation of shifting conditions of truth that make power possible. And it is precisely the effects of power that can run counter to or resist particular conditions of truth.

> It is in discourse that power and knowledge are joined together. And for this very reason, we must conceive discourse as a series of discontinuous segments whose tactical function is neither uniform nor stable. To be more precise, we must not imagine a world of discourse divided between accepted discourse and excluded discourse, . . . but as a multiplicity of discursive elements that can come into play in various strategies. . . . Discourse can be both an instrument and an effect of power, but also a hindrance, a stumbling block, a point of resistance and a starting point for an opposing strategy. (Foucault, 1980, pp. 100–101).

Within these shifting relations of knowledge and power, of opposing discursive strategies, human subjects are constituted. Foucault asserts power as a system of relations and oppositions that mark, categorize, and identify individuals. It "imposes a law of truth on him which he must recognize and others have to recognize in him" (Foucault, 1982, p. 212). And yet it is not simply a repressive force; it entails struggle and contradiction, discursive elements that both engage certain social forms and oppose them, that produce certain subjective positions and struggle against them.

> It is a form of power which makes individuals subjects. There are two meanings to the word subject: subject to someone else by control and dependence, and tied to his own identity by a conscience or self-knowledge. Both meanings suggest a form of power which subjects and makes subject to.
>   . . . nowadays, the struggle against the forms of subjection—against the submission of subjectivity—is becoming more and more important, even though the struggles against forms of domination and exploitation have not disappeared. Quite the contrary. (Foucault, 1982, pp. 212–213)

In this later work, Foucault traces a transformation in the organization and mechanism of power that affected the production of particular representations of the "normal" and "abnormal" individual. During the seventeenth century a shift was effected from overt forms of control and repression emanating from a sovereign center—the king and his law—to a less visible system of social regulation produced through a network of knowledge practices. With this shift to what Foucault has called positive technologies of power, the body became the object of the scientific gaze around which discourses of "truth" produced a complex system of regulation and discipline, a biopolitics of the population. Here the concept of technology is redefined as a set of procedures, techniques, and mechanisms deployed within relations of power to produce subjects, practice, and knowledges (Foucault, 1977).

Power became organized over and centered upon the body, upon life; its function was no longer

> a matter of bringing death into play in the field of sovereignty, but of distributing the living in the domain of value and utility. Such a power has to qualify, measure, appraise and hierarchize. . . . It effects distributions around the norm. . . . A normalizing society is the historical outcome of a technology of power centered on life. (Foucault, 1980, p. 144)

Knowledge and power, then, are two sides of the same process. As Alan Sheridan explains, "knowledge derives not from some subject of knowledge, but from the power relations that invest it. Knowledge does not 'reflect' power relations; . . . it is immanent in them." (1980, p. 220)

In *The History of Sexuality,* Foucault (1980) takes apart the traditional conception that sex in Western capitalist societies is repressed. He exposes how, in fact, it has been *deployed* discursively. His analysis reveals that the rising bourgeois classes, in the interest of staking out a place for themselves against the aristocracy, produced a complex technology of sex, a surveillance of its *own* body. Strength, health, and vigor—indeed, the capacity for life and the avoidance of death through knowledge of the body—became extremely important to the bourgeoisie in establishing their hegemony. Out of this desire grew a complicated web of discourse that made bodies—especially those of women and children—the objects of knowledge invested with power. An apparatus of knowledge and technology was supported by institutional discourses and practices within medicine, psychiatry, economics, and education. As an object of science, knowledge of the sexual body was deployed throughout society as an interest of every individual, household, and institution.

Far from being repressed, the sexual body became an intense object of social and personal concern. As the bourgeoisie struggled to confirm and safeguard its hegemony, it produced a hegemony of identity. The discourse on the individual and social body produced new social forms and subject positions. Though the hysteric, the pervert, and the sexualized child became privileged fictions of scientific knowledge, virtually every individual in society was required to place themselves under surveillance. A new social subject was produced, a subject injected with sexuality, a subject intensely interested in the control of its own body. (Foucault, 1980).

Foucault's work advances the theory that categories of normality and abnormality are produced socially rather than reflected naturally from the body or individual mind. His analysis shows us how these categories, validated as properties of knowledge and truth, function to control and to discipline. Martin writes of Foucault's work that, "his methodological deconstructions explode the self-evidence of constituted meanings, defy the acceptance of received categories as exhaustive, and expose the cost at which such coherence and solidity are effected" (1988, p. 11).

Foucault questions the "truth" of the human condition as it has been provided in religion, literature, and the scientific disciplines. He sets out to trace the history of "the games of truth and error" as they have been effected within these disciplines (Foucault, 1985, p. 6). His work does not consider closely enough, however, the issue of gender in relation to these truths and errors, as several feminists influenced by his work have pointed out. Teresa de Lauretis, for example, has pointed out that sexuality in Foucault "is not understood as gendered, as having a male form and a female form, but is taken to be the same for all—and consequently male" (1987, p. 14).

Still, given this important limitation in Foucault's work, the powerful influence it has had on feminist social analysis cannot be denied. It provides a new way of reading "the woman question," encouraging the close examination of the question of sexual difference and female identity as it has been inscribed in the major discourses throughout history, as exemplified in Martin's work.

> Having created sex and gender as problems of a particular kind, the experts must necessarily intervene in our lives to provide solutions and to bind us within a particular identity, a subjectivity. Woman, as a category of meaning, and women have been subject to the psychoanalytic and aesthetic experts who do the work of limiting and regulating what it means to be a woman in line with exigencies of their own discursive fields and legitimating truths. (Martin, 1988, p. 14)

Foucault has broken down many of the barriers to social research inherent to the French post-modern perspective. Feminist research drawing upon these insights is increasingly making its mark on the intellectual scene. Feminist historian Joan Scott, for example, has challenged historians of women to scrutinize traditional methods of analysis and to reformulate questions organizing their work. She calls upon feminist historical analysis to

> disrupt the notion of fixity, to discover the nature of the debate or repression that leads to the appearance of timeless permanence in binary gender representation. This kind of analysis must include a notion of politics as well as reference to social institutions and organizations. (1986, p. 1068)

Feminist social analyses, which at once use and push beyond Foucault's concept, form a multifaceted exploration of the relation of such categories as "woman" and "femininity" in textually mediated discourses to the real historical actors, including women who participate in their production. In the words of Dorothy Smith:

> To explore "femininity" as discourse means a shift away form viewing it as a normative order, reproduced through socialization, to which women are somehow subordinated. Rather, femininity is addressed as a complex of actual relations vested in texts. . . . To address femininity is to address a textual discourse vested in women's magazines and television, advertisements, the appearance of cosmetic counters, fashion displays and to a lesser extent books.
> . . . Discourse also involves the talk women do in relation to such texts, the work of producing oneself to realize the textual images. . . . It locates the social relations of a "symbolic" terrain and the material practices which bring it into being and sustain it. (1988, p. 41)

With popular cultural forms—film, magazines, romance novels, fashion, punk slam dance, rock and roll—as well as academic discursive forms—psychology, anorexia nervosa, teenage pregnancy, historiography, mathematics, philosophy—as objects of critique, feminist scholars are beginning to create a rich and full body of research on the construction of gender, of the female, feminized subject (Henriques et al., 1984; de Lauretis, 1984, 1986, 1987; Lesko, 1988, 1989; Roman & Christian-Smith, 1988; Scott, 1986). Film critic de Lauretis has argued that "the representation of gender is its construction," which is to say that we are created as man or as woman, or as educated man or educated woman, within a complex discursive apparatus:

> The construction of gender goes on today through the various technologies of gender (e.g., cinema) and institutional discourses (e.g., theory) with power to control the field of social meaning and thus produce, promote, and "implant" representations of gender. (de Lauretis, 1987, p. 19)

Schools and educational discourses form a part of the technology constructing gender. A number of feminist educational scholars are beginning to use the work started by Foucault to examine the power/knowledge relations associated with education and educational institutions. The following section returns to the question of women's relation to education with the work of a feminist scholar who makes important and original use of Foucault's contributions to social and historical analysis.

EDUCATION AND THE FEMALE SUBJECT: VALERIE WALKERDINE

Focusing in particular on forms of curriculum in British primary schools, Valerie Walkerdine, a British scholar of education, seeks to uncover how modern concepts of woman and the child have been constructed. Demonstrating the value of Foucault's theory of the subject to a feminist analysis, her work studies the ways that children, particularly girls, are constituted as subjects within so-called child-centered curricula and pedagogy, forms that she sees as "fictions functioning in truth" (Walkerdine, 1985b).

Invested with the hope for a better world, the child has become the object of the scientific gaze. A powerful set of discourses organized by categorical oppositions—such as normality and abnormality, natural and unnatural—has produced a set of pedagogical practices that the child is subjected to and through which he or she is produced as learner. Within these discursive practices the child is defined as active, while the environment (the teacher) is passive; the child who reasons is the child with mastery over the environment.

But, according to Walkerdine, this set of definitions of the natural child presents a dilemma for the education of girls. Children are active; girls are passive. Walkerdine's analysis asks the question, can girls become "the child" as defined by the powerful truth conditions for the natural development of children. In brief, her research exposes a number of conflicting, contradictory categories that position girls as subordinate learners (Walkerdine, 1984, 1985a, 1988).

In a different but related study Walkerdine examines girls' relations to the study of mathematics in an attempt to uncover how relations of power/ knowledge are set up to prove girls' inability to perform as well as boys due to an inferior capacity for reason—an elaborate fantasy of man's capacity for total control over nature. These relations and the positioning of woman as inferior can be traced in discourse historically to the Enlightenment. For Walkerdine, a historical analysis is indispensable to understanding the production of this "fact":

> ideas about reason and reasoning cannot be understood outside of considerations of gender. Since the Enlightenment . . . reason, or the Cogito, has been deeply embroiled with attempts to control nature. The rationality of the Cogito was taken to be a kind of re-birth of the rational self, in this case without the intervention of woman. The rational self, was in this sense a profoundly masculine one from which the woman was excluded, her powers not only inferior but also subservient. The "thinking" subject was male; the female provided both the biological prop to procreation and to servicing the possibility of "man." (1985c, p. 6)

By the nineteenth century the female body had become the object of the scientific gaze and the "truth" of woman's nature was asserted, backed up with hard evidence. Woman's relation to knowledge was restricted to her naturalized capacity for nurturance; she was assigned the place of the facilitator of knowledge as mother and as teacher, servicing the knower but distinct from and incapable of becoming the knower herself.

Following the work of Foucault, Walkerdine asks: How is this truth of woman constituted and what are its effects? Her question and her research bring us back to the problem of woman's subjective relation to education. Woman's relation to knowledge, to education, and to professional life has been manifested within the bounds of a regulating discursive system that insists on defining her as the inverse, the opposite of man. What is more, women's attempts to disprove the evidence against them, to assert legitimate claims to knowledge, are caught up in the same terms to the discourse, the same conditions of truth. Women have entered the battle on the grounds laid out by male science and remain "the other of reason."

For Walkerdine, this is the fundamental problem. She argues forcefully that women need not accept the terms of the debate provided by men but must

> question their very foundation. We are not duty bound to accept the existing truth conditions. . . . Showing the truth about girls to be a production in which there are not simple matters of fact is a central and strategic part of our struggle. (1985c, p. 9)

In this sense, we can see important connections between Walkerdine's research and the work of the other women outlined above that lead us toward understanding the implications of these post-modern perspectives. In addition, other feminist educational scholars have taken the trail broken by Walkerdine and are beginning to forge ahead, crossing new intellectual ground in pursuit of a clearer understanding of the educated woman. In a historical analysis of women's relation to higher education, for example, I examine the use of the category "reason" in the discourse of middle-class women. This study uncovers a discursive double-bind that trapped turn-of-the-century educated women within a representation of woman as man's inferior other. Thus, in spite of their strategies to escape oppressive social and personal identities, middle-class women participated in a regime of truth that ultimately positions woman as less capable in relation to the standard of rationality: man (Martusewicz, 1988).

This location of feminist practice and discourse on education within a larger sociosymbolic matrix of knowledge and power is also the concern of feminists who choose contemporary academic discourse and institutions as their focus. Jennifer Gore analyzes the ways in which current radical discourses in education, including feminist pedagogy, operate as regimes of truth. Gore uncovers the specific techniques and practices within feminist discourse about pedagogy that function in effect to discipline and define both the teacher and theorist and, hence, reconstitute authoritarian and patriarchal structures of meaning via the will to knowledge (Gore, 1989).

While Gore's work directs our attention to the reassertion of authority and power within educational discourses that claim to work against such regimes of truth, other feminist work focuses more directly upon the issue of identity construction within educational institutions and in the organization of curricula. Nancy Lesko draws upon both semiotics and a Foucauldian framework to analyze the construction of female identities within the symbolic relations of a Catholic high school (Lesko, 1988). More recently, her work focuses on the popular discourses around teenage pregnancy and the curricula designed for school-aged mothers. In this work, Lesko argues for a critical perspective on curriculum as part of a wider social discourse, part of an interrelated discursive network between institutions-such as the family, the legal system, the media, schools, language, general social practices—and conceptions of the self. Lesko argues that the curricular thrust of a school for teenage mothers must be located within the established themes of the media's construction of the problem, in which pregnant teenagers are represented as deviant or sinful. In an alternative school setting, such girls are offered social redemption and forgiveness through a curriculum that defines for them what it means to be "good mothers" (Lesko, 1989).

These examples of scholarship demonstrate the impact that poststructuralism and, specifically, the work of Michel Foucault is having on the study of education and gender and our understanding of what it means to be a woman in relation to knowledge. They express a crisis in the old master narratives and self-reflective, critical search for possibilities.

NEW BEGINNINGS

While it would be wrong to collapse the differences between these scholars into each other, they clearly concur in the object of their criticism. The "truth" of woman as provided us by science, philosophy, religion, and literature, indeed by culture itself, is an elaborate fiction, and, though their methodologies vary, these writers share the goal to shake loose, to untangle the knots of discourse that have tied us to such powerful truth. It is the "hegemony of identity," the everyday commonsense truths about who we are, that they seek to explode in the struggle against subordination and subjection.

The Foucauldian attention to the categorization and subjection of the individual within relations of power/knowledge, combined with the specific interest in identification/subordination of woman within symbolic systems that the French women's work offers, provides a firm and important theoretical foundation from which to understand women's positions in social life and, more importantly, to begin to change that position. While a Foucauldian analysis exposes the relations of power and the categories of knowledge produced through language that subject the individual and produce specific limited subjective positions, the French women writers, influenced by Derrida, are interested in producing a new discourse on language, disrupting the old oppressive categories of thought and setting free this "present" subject in the infinitely shifting relation of "differance."

This intellectual intersection implies a necessary (performative and reformative) relation. The activity that Foucault refers to as archaeology exposes relations of control embedded in Western knowledge forms and practices, but it also embodies an important, disruptive shift in the relation between categories of meaning, in the way that we think about knowledge and our relation to it. It is, as described by Peggy Kamuf, the beginning of a process of ending a shift in our discursive history. Offering what turns out to be an uncannily accurate description of the post-modern landscape itself in this explanation of Foucault's theoretical position, she writes:

> This process of ending has begun when thought moves beyond the limits of what has made it possible to think "man" as an autonomous whole, a circum-scribable object, and into those regions surrounding the humanistic homeland, what one might call the no-man's land of the unconscious, the autonomous structures of language and the dynamics of history. (Kamuf, 1982, p. 43)

To push beyond the process of ending and into new beginnings is the function of research that is intent on challenging the bounds of a restrictive humanist tradition, even while understanding our immersion in that tradition. This requires a challenge to old representations and categories that have shaped the contours or our thinking about the world.

From within this post-modern no-man's land the terms of women's historical oppression are unearthed. This is the place from which feminist scholars begin to dig into women's historical, culturally mediated relation to knowledge and to education. This work is an attempt to expose the discursive conditions of that relation and the resulting subjection of women. This is the space within which the subject of feminism is being created. As de Lauretis points out:

> The construction of gender is also affected by its deconstruction, . . . for gender like the real, is not only the effect of representation but also its excess, what remains outside discourse as a potential trauma which can rupture or destabilize, if not contained, any representation.
> . . . The terms of a different construction of gender . . . exist, in the margins of hegemonic discourses. Posed from outside the heterosexual social contract, and inscribed in micropolitical practices, these terms can also have a part in the construction of gender, and their effects are rather at the "local" level of resist-ances, in subjectivity and self-representation. (1987, pp. 3, 18)

The critique that these women scholars practice is about creating spaces. What does it mean to be a woman who knows? Post-modern feminist critique, long relegated to the margins of academic discourse and popular cultural life, is pushing the limits of possible answers to that question. Thus, while the educated woman is historically born of the master narratives, she also embodies a tension of resistance and possibility. As de Lauretis, Walkerdine, and others are teaching us, to live as feminist educators is to live a tension between a critical theoretical space and an affirmative political space. It is within this in-between, this "elsewhere," that we must seek the educated woman.

REFERENCES

Barthes, R. (1972). *Mythologies.* New York: Hill & Wang.

Burke, C. G. (1978). Report from Paris: Women's writing and the women's movement. *Signs: Journal of Women in Culture and Society, 3* (4), 843–855.

Cixous, H. (1976). The laugh of the Medusa. *Signs: Journal of Women in Culture and Society, 1* (4), 875–893.

Culler, J. (1975). *Structuralist poetic: Structuralism, linguistics, and the study of literature.* London: Routledge & Kegan Paul.

Derrida, J. (1970). Structure, sign and play in the discourse of the human sciences. In R. Macksey & E. Donato (Eds.), *The language of criticism and the sciences of man: The structuralist controversy* (pp. 247–272). Baltimore, MD: Johns Hopkins University Press.

Derrida, J. (1975). The purveyor of truth. *Graphesis* (Yale French Studies No. 52).

Derrida, J. (1979). *Spurs* (B. Harlow, Trans.). Chicago: University of Chicago Press.

Derrida, J. (1982). *Margins of philosophy* (A. Bass, Trans.). Chicago: University of Chicago Press.

Descombes, V. (1980). *Modern French philosophy* (L. S. Fox & J. M. Harding, Trans.). London: Cambridge University Press.

Eagleton, T. (1983). *Literary theory: An introduction.* Minneapolis: University of Minnesota Press.

Feral, J. (1980). The powers of difference. In H. Eisenstein & A. Jardine (Eds.), *The future of difference* (pp. 88–94). Boston: G. K. Hall.

Foucault, M. (1970). *The order of things: An archaeology of the human sciences* (A. Sheridan, Trans.). London: Random House.

Foucault, M. (1972). *The archaeology of knowledge and the discourse of language* (A. M. Sheridan Smith, Trans.). New York: Pantheon.

Foucault, M. (1977). *Language, counter-memory and practice* (D. F. Bouchard, Ed. & Trans.). Ithaca, NY: Cornell University Press.

Foucault, M. (1979). *Discipline and punish: The birth of the prison* (A. Sheridan, Trans.). New York: Allen Lane.

Foucault, M. (1980). *The history of sexuality: Vol. I. An introduction* (R. Hurley, Trans.). New York: Vintage.

Foucault, M. (1982). Afterword: The subject and power. In H. L. Dreyfus & P. Rabinow (Eds.), *Michel Foucault: Beyond structuralism and hermeneutics* (pp. 208–226). Chicago: University of Chicago Press.

Foucault, M. (1985). *The use of pleasure: The history of sexuality, Vol. II* (R. Hurley, Trans.). New York: Vintage.

Freud, S. (1955). *The interpretation of dreams.* New York: Basic Books.

Gallop, J., & Burke, C. (1980). Psychoanalysis and feminism in France. In H. Eisenstein & A. Jardine (Eds.), *The future of difference* (pp. 106–120). Boston: G. K. Hall.

Garner, S. N., Kahane, C., & Sprenghether, M. (Eds.). (1985). *The (m)other tongue: Essays in feminist psychoanalytic interpretation.* Ithaca, NY: Cornell University Press.

Gore, J. (1989, October). *The struggle for pedagogies: Critical and feminist discourses as "regimes of truth."* Paper presented at the Conference on Curriculum Theory and Classroom Practice, Dayton, OH.

Henriques, J., Hollway, W., Urwin, C., Venn, C., & Walkerdine, V. (1984). *Changing the subject: Psychology, social regulation and subjectivity.* London: Methuen.

Irigaray, L. (1985a). *Speculum of the other woman* (G. C. Gill, Trans.). Ithaca, NY: Cornell University Press.

Irigaray, L. (1985b). *This sex which is not one* (C. Porter, Trans.). Ithaca, NY: Cornell University Press.

Jameson, F. (1972). *The prison house of language: A critical account of structuralism and Russian formalism.* Princeton, NJ: Princeton University Press.

Jardine, A. (1985). *Gynesis: Configurations of woman and modernity.* Ithaca, NY: Cornell University Press.

Kamuf, P. (1982, Summer). Replacing feminist criticism. In *Cherchez la femme: Feminist critique/feminine text* [special issue]. *Diacritics: A Review of Contemporary Criticism, 12,* 42–47.

Kristeva, J. (1980). *Desire in language: A semiotic approach to literature and art* (T. Gora, A. Jardine, & L. S. Roudiez, Trans.). New York: Columbia University Press.

Kristeva, J. (1984). *Revolution in poetic language* (M. Waller, Trans.). New York: Columbia University Press.

Lacan, J. (1977). *Ecrits: A selection* (A. Sheridan, Trans.). New York: Norton.

Lauretis, T. de. (1984). *Alice doesn't: Feminism, semiotics, cinema.* Bloomington: Indiana University Press.

Lauretis, T. de. (1986). *Feminist studies/critical studies.* Bloomington: Indiana University Press.

Lauretis, T. de. (1987). *Technologies of gender: Essays on theory, film and fiction.* Bloomington: Indiana University Press.

Lesko, N. (1988). *Symbolizing society: Stories, rites and structure in a Catholic high school.* Lewes, England: Falmer.

Lesko, N. (1989). *Curriculum differentiation as social redemption.* Unpublished manuscript.

Levi-Strauss, C. (1972). *Structural anthropology* (C. Jacobson & B. Grundefest Schoepf, Trans.). Hammondsworth, England: Penguin.

Lyotard, J. F. (1984). *The post-modern condition: A report on knowledge* (G. Bennington & E. Massumi, Trans.). Minneapolis: University of Minnesota Press.

Marks, E., & de Courtivron, I. (Eds.). (1981). *New French feminisms.* New York: Schocken.

Martin, B. (1988). Feminism, criticism and Foucault. In I. Diamond & L. Quinby (Eds.), *Feminism and Foucault: Reflection and resistance* (pp. 3–19). Boston: Northeastern University Press.

Martusewicz, R. (1988). *The will to know: An archaeology of womanhood and education, 1880–1920.* Unpublished doctoral dissertation, University of Rochester.

Mitchell, J. & Rose, J. (Eds.). (1982). *Feminine sexuality: Jacques Lacan and the école Freudienne.* New York: Pantheon.

Roman, L., & Christian-Smith, L. (Eds.). (1988). *Becoming feminine: The politics of popular culture*. London: Falmer.

Saussure, F. de. (1959). *Course in general linguistics* (W. Baskin, Trans.). New York: Philosophical Library.

Scott, J. W. (1986). Gender: A useful category of historical analysis. *American Historical Review, 91* (5), 1053–1075.

Sheridan, A. (1980). *Michel Foucault: The will to truth*. London: Tavistock.

Smith, D. (1988). Femininity as discourse. In L. Roman & L. Christian-Smith (Eds.), *Becoming feminine: The politics of popular culture* (pp. 37–59). London: Falmer.

Stanton, D. C. (1980). Language and revolution: The Franco-American disconnection. In H. Eisenstein & A. Jardine (Eds.), *The future of difference* (pp. 73–87). Boston: G. K. Hall.

Steedman, C., Urwin, C., & Walkerdine, V. (Eds.). *Language, gender, and childhood*. London: Routledge & Kegan Paul.

Walkerdine, V. (1984). Developmental psychology and the child-centered pedagogy: The insertion of Piaget into early education. In J. Henriques, W. Hollway, C. Urwin, C. Venn, & V. Walkerdine, *Changing the subject: Psychology, social regulation and subjectivity* (pp. 153–202). London: Methuen.

Walkerdine, V. (1985a). On the regulation of speaking and silence: Subjectivity, class and gender in contemporary schooling. In C. Steedman, C. Urwin, & V. Walkerdine (Eds.), *Language, gender, and childhood* (pp. 203–241). London: Routledge & Kegan Paul.

Walkerdine, V. (1985b, March). *Schoolgirl fictions*. Talk given at the University of Rochester.

Walkerdine, V. (1985c). Science and the female mind: The burden of proof. *Psych-Critique, 1* (1), 1–20.

Walkerdine, V. (1988). *The mastery of reason*. London: Routledge & Kegan Paul.

CHAPTER 9

Curriculum as Felt Through Six Layers of an Aesthetically Embodied Skin
The Arch-Writing on the Body

jan jagodzinski

To make the aesthetic dimension meaningful rather than an empty category of experience that is indiscriminately applied to the arts, i propose to outline six ontological dimensions of its appearance. Social existence, as communication with action, is always informed by one of its appearances. The anthropological roots for these layers of aesthetic experience are not provided. These, i would claim, are part of the arch-writing on the body, part of the body's recollection of being (Levin, 1985). Each of these dimensions is informed by a binary opposition, and hence they are consistent with structuralist tenets. These i perceive as being the extreme states of the body that inform experience *(Erlebnis)*. Lived experience, the day-to-dayness, however, occurs between them. This is the space of play, of risk, of creativity. Although i recognize that this position can fall into an essentialism, once historicized and framed by a historicized perception, it becomes an existentialism. Such an existentialism allows the claim of alienation from oneself, from nature, and from exploring nondiscursive dimensions of humane existence that are denied in the experience of a technological curriculum.

Throughout this essay words will occasionally be purposefully "exploded" in order to have a more visual meaning manifest itself, or else the exploded word helps the intended meaning to emerge more fully. For example "wo(man)" is written to visually indicate that man is born within the pregnant brackets of woman. Also, the reader will find that i use the personification of the Earth as "Gaia." This name is used, following the work of Lovelock (1979), to indicate that the whole Earth is a system and possesses consciousness. Since this system interconnects all "things" through forms of consciousness we have yet to (un)cover, it is only fitting that the Earth have a name. Gaia is the Greek name for the Mother Earth. She was the oldest of the divinities. The Olympian gods, under Zeus, took over her ancient shrines, yet they swore oaths by her name, since they knew they were subject to her law (Walker, 1983). In the same vein "oikoumenical" (Greek: *oikos* 'home') replaces the more familiar term "ecumenical" in order to distance myself from the Christian notion of worldwide values. Oikoumenical values would also be worldwide but would go beyond any one identifiable religious tradition. An ecological perspective that treats the Earth as *oikos,* a home, would be more in keeping with the spirit that lies behind this word.

The reader will find the use of yet another visual trope. Throughout the body of the essay, the lowercase "i" has been used purposely to subdue the ego that lies behind authorship as represented by Cartesian thought and modernism in general. In the evolution of consciousness, the birth of the ego, or an "I," occurs during the "age of heros." The word "I" first appears in Homer's *Odyssey.* In order to distance myself from the sense of a heroic sense of the ego (an act that i would coin as "distantiation"), a small "i" is employed throughout. Indeed, the whole notion of a "journey" as developed by a male "I" suggests a striving—a quest for the Holy Grail. The archetypal symbol of the labyrinth, which also requires a journey to discover its inner-most secret, is more representative of the experiences necessary to become attuned to the body aesthetic. The geomancy of hermeneutic circle and the dynamics of the spiral would in(form) such an experience. For a similar reason the word "humane" replaces "human" in order to instill the flavor that our future conscious transcendence will be much softer, more compassionate than the one we are living in. The word "human" also evokes associations of civilization founded by males. There is far too much stress on the second syllable—man.

Lastly, throughout this essay the word "thing" is often used even when there appears to be no distinction between a "thing" as an object or "thing" as a person. This has purposefully been done to try to eliminate the mind/body dichotomy prevalent in positivist thought where *res extensa* is distinguished from *res cognita.* In this essay there is no such "thing" as inert material. All "things" possess a consciousness. Body, in this sense, also includes mind and soul. Sometimes the word "body" appears alone; other times it is written as mind/body.

LINE: LIVED EXPERIENCE OF DIRECTIONALITY— MAKING THE GRADE

To begin, the most fundamental human experience is rhythm followed by movement. The spacial-temporal experience of "line" is continually informed by the body's negotiation between becoming *lost* and finding a *direction.* Such journeys are always packed with ambiguity, paradox, and, above all, surprise. It is the feeling that new vistas, new elevations, new edges are always presenting themselves as each new step is taken. Constructing an argument during a conversation, following a melody in music, creating a path through the dance of the body; all have a ground from which they began, an paradoxical point of origin. The left hand of the piano plays the rhythm, the right the melody. The dancer begins in stillness and leaps away. Each representive instance of creative freedom and intuitive exploration begins with a point *and* a direction (May, 1975). Line is directionality. It is a criss-cross informed by both the feminine and masculine presence, held in binary tension through the interaction of the horizontal and the vertical within the labyrinth of thought.

Rhythm is primordial. It is the up and down of the heart beat, the in and out of our breathing. The dialectical binary tension of this, the first level of aesthetic experience, is maintained between *directionality* and being *lost,* between *intentionality* and *accident,* between that which we can control and that which eludes our scrutiny, blindness, and insight. It is the journey of attention, of a perpetual walk toward an edge. Heightened consciousness is the mediation between life and death; both inform and deform the moment of movement. Only then can new ground be found and life lived. To avoid the monotony of the journey, which happens when teachers predetermine the direction of the body, choreograph its trajectory, keep it on track without deviation, one must take risks; otherwise humane flexibility is lost. Failure replaces tolerance. "Grades" are not lived as plateaus; they become the imprisonment of a letter. This stills the body needlessly. Its life is lost. Educational risk-taking requires that we place the body in a healthy tension. A dichotomous consciousness merely increases anxiety. Desire is perverted so that boundaries are maintained.

Putting one's consciousness "on the line," walking on the edge or on a tightrope, is the aesthetic experience that animates us. Tightrope walkers, downhill racers, mountain climbers, racecar drivers, continually put their life on the line since at any time the humane risk-taking may snap. In conversation, it is only through the question that a "way" may be created, the journey activated, an intentional arc bridged with the Other. In music, the creation of noise indicates that one has become lost. Mistakes, on the other hand, surprise both the player and the listener from the well-defined path. The lived-life between tonality and atonality. The inner song, *inner Klang* as Kandinsky (1912/1947) called it, can become lost. For it is the tone, the tension (Latin: *tonus* 'tension'; Greek: *tonus* 'the act of stretching') of the voice that helps to communicate our inner "soul." It is the "pitch"—as when one throws out a message—which gives a line that must be grasped. The loudness and timber of the message must consciously break into the natural way of hearing. To be heard means to have fused with the horizon of the Other.

For teachers the voice should maintain the oral tradition of leaders, peacemakers, prophets, and visionaries. Their voice should lead us out to dialogue. Since all conversation journeys start from a point, the teacher must make a moral choice as to which line is taken. Such a choice, claimed Fromm (1981), might lead to civil disobedience for the cause of justice. The heretic must expose and unveil. Leadership requires a conscious awareness as to the direction the journey will take. The oikumenical good to be achieved must be informed by the tradition chosen. The ethics of line, of direction, requires an inescapable eschatology, a philosophy of history as *progress* in social relationships.

The experience of line, however, may be monological rather than symbiotic. When one thinks of the energy transfer of the life line, the complementarity that must occur between opposites to generate life, then the telephone wire and the electric chord are analogous to Nature's umbilical cord, the root, the blood vessel; all are instances of the transference of life—the need to exchange a message. When there is no purpose or meaning to life, one's existence becomes directionless, empty, lifeless. Noise sets in. Such are curricular experiences when we do not allow the risk to take place. Students must have maps to see them through. Maps allow the surveillance of the land from a safe distance. To see the "lay of the land" eases student anxiety. They show the student where they have been, where they are going, and how they may get there. Maps freeze time and must be activated by the journey of learning experiences. Curricular outlines as maps are the necessary starting point. It is only when the journey is plotted with precision that they become programs of repression. The computer-instructed program becomes the antithesis of such topological mapmaking. Such programs cannot handle the strayed path. Surprise is reduced to a branching mentality, to predetermined, coded sets of choices. The primacy of straight and clean line in the Western aesthetic tradition (i.e., perspective) is evident from the rationality of mechanical drawing to the straight edges of our carpentered world (Segall, Campbell, & Herskovits, 1966). Aesthetics has become one-dimensional future. Line is required for being minimally rational, but left at this functionalist state it becomes extremely boring and dull. Education as information versus education as communication makes evident the difference. *Educationally, we must recognize that all lines are bridges to new direction.* How should educators throw out their life-lines to students in their care?

COLOR: LIVED EXPERIENCE OF MOOD—THE PERIOD

A jump beyond living a line mentality is to consciously recognize the place of mood in our lives. A mood is like a blanket that covers us when we reflect upon a conversation that has been completed. It is a recalled memory that vivifies life. It is much more than a pause. Silence, as that inward gaze, marks the time of reflection and nonparticipation in action—the listening to oneself. Archetypally, the snake has eaten its tail—the bridge has been crossed. When the totality, pardoxically as a fragment, as a period, can be reflected upon, when the paragraph can be examined, then the centering of the body, between the binary opposites of unity and disunity, between harmony and disharmony, may begin. The felt tension is found in the color of a conversation. It is the line turning to make a shape that conveys a self-contained totality, a thick idea that then presents itself in a certain shade or tint, as bass, baritone, or soprano. This can only happen when the journey has been completed, fulfilled, as when the artist has said "Enough! This stands on its own." This happens when children "round" their dance movements, when rocks are placed in a circle to form a boundary and children call it their place. This also happens when women bleed. It is their time—a period, a time of rest. When any space is bounded, as in a circus ring, a wedding ring, or a bell's ring, a centering of attention presents itself. The classroom should also be perceived as a ring, a pitch, a place to center oneself. And periods should be colored fragments that make the day.

The shape speaks the color it most easily harbors. Gold, yellow, orange, red—the embodiment of a circle—give us warmth. The shape is reflective of the voices that are allowed to speak harmoniously or in conflict. A witch's coven or a knight's round table are bound by consensual vows. The talk goes on until the spell is broken and the conversation has been rounded. Each actor "leans" and accommodates the other. Leadership becomes acephalous, a "leaner-ship." A circle generates intimate friends. It generates warmth and intimate exchange. The conversation becomes more than two people. It evokes voices of an ancestral past that has spoken on similar themes. It demands that color be more musical and fluid, not attached to the rigors of form but *released to form* its own harmonics of exchange. A musical key suggests a relationship between notes. It is an identification. It shows us who we are and how we bound to others occupying the same shape. The music in our schools has a harmony. We feel it in the halls, in our classes, in the lunchrooms. The buzz, the whispers, the shrills tell us the states of our bodies.

Personality is exposed color. The tension of the circle, the tension between the binary oppositions of hot and cold, between laughing and crying, the extremes of our body's psychological and physiological tolerance, can only be maintained by "blanket" spaces. The "blanket" has to be a security force that allows one to speak, to be exposed in a community of friends. The blanket forms a canopy, a temporary space like a tent or igloo so that talk might begin. It prevents the danger of shame and embarrassment that is worn on the surface of the skin. Symbols such as the crown, the hood, the tiara, the helmet suggest privileges in the conversation. The form becomes cephalous. Such are the ethics of color and shape.

Western technocracy has avoided the shape of the circle and the colors of warmth, care, and security. In nature the nurturing colors of green break down and ripen into red, yellow, and blue pigments. They do not remain cool. The shapes of a culture become iconic. Spiked shapes, like stars, speak of highlighting and striking out. Square shapes speak of stasis and inertia. These shapes are experienced as hierarchy and dominance. The rectangle spreads the possibility of teacher-student confrontation.

Organic shapes round the edges. They suggest softness, growth, and pregnancy. They are horizontal in their direction. They open vistas, they allow the head/body to rotate a full 180 degrees. Direction is pregnant with possibility. However, centering oneself within the carpentered world of stars, squares, and rectangles always draws the eye to a POINT. It is a vertical in its intent. It points upwards toward those on top. One's head is always lifting up or looking down. The body is always being stratified within a hierarchy of dominance.

The colors of industry and conservatism suggest the anonymity of cold, calculated pursuit of the good life, the costs and benefits of Bentham's felicific calculus. It has been shown through studies of Western art and literature that our sensitivity to the values of blues and violets, the dark end of the spectrum, has increased since the sixteenth century. Burgundy violets and the *habit noir* of the nineteenth-century businessman linger in the dark business suit and the tuxedo. Religion, too, is in the same habit. Justice is embodied in black, sometimes red to show the gravity of the spilling of blood. Women, who were excluded until recently from the business world, were given the "privilege" to be flighty, frivolous. Color was at their disposal. But the businesswoman must also blend into the picture. Now, when hot colors appear in our culture, they do so to mock the anti-humaneness of our bureaucracies, like hot jazz and the punk look.

What are the ethics of color? Has color lost all sense of spiritual symbolism as it once had among many indigenous peoples? Has it been appropriated only in the name of power and dominance—the colors of gravity denying eros? White, the color of the most powerful racial skin, has come to symbolize the clinical mind, the germ-free, dust-free environment of high technology, the operating room, and, of course, the labor room.

Most of us in any large organization must remain camouflaged. Our true colors are rarely shown; they are repressed. This repression merely recapitulates the separation between private and public spaces, as other feminists have pointed out (Elshtain, 1981). Within intimate spaces and intimate relations we wear what we wish. The ground between lovers is cleared through fights, squabbles, and love-making. In large bureaucracies, what Goffman (1961) called "total institutions," few are high steppers. The majority labor by shuffling around. What colors are our curricula? What colors are the dances of our students? If we claim all knowledge to be neutral and teach in this way, what does that indicate? Does coolness and indifference prevail?

TEXTURE: THE LIVED EXPERIENCE OF HOME ROOM–FAMILIARITY

Texture forms the third level of the aesthetic dimension. Texture is the conversation with "things" to enable one to know them intimately. It is the language of poetry, the adjectives and adverbs that form the ground of distinction. Texture is our personal communication with Nature's dialogue: It is the experience of craft that intimately binds our consciousness with Gaia's material consciousness. It is the potter in conversation with clay, it is the weaver in conversation with fiber, it is the lapidary maker in conversation with leather, it is the crafts tradition that is the very fabric of technology. Texture touches. It is found within the palm of the hand. The grasp of the fingers presents an immediate response. The greatest amount of gray matter in the brain is dedicated to the hands. They play, they sensitize, they touch.

Texture is the exposed history of the "thing" embodied on its patina, worn like our skin. The texture of things harbors the binary opposition of home and alienation. When we know the texture of things we feel comfort, security, and a belonging, as when we see a familiar face. We must touch things in order to make them our own, participate in them to see the surfaces and their responses; otherwise the Other is always alienated. Textures cannot be known without differentiation, without felt similarities and differences throughout the body. To generate such knowledge requires "worn" spaces, a continual coming back to the thing so that we might make it our own—make it familiar within our famil(y)arity. It requires the traveled look. Only then can we make it a part of our biographies, something we can stand for. It gives us our character.

A home away from home suggests a cared-for place. The dialectical tension between the binary opposition requires that we embrace everything we touch to make it a part of ourselves. We must avoid "breaking" or "making" things. Historically these appear to be signs of dominance. Repair embodies the ethics of texture, for in the art of repair there is a mending and a healing, a love to keep a thing's essence alive.

This is also true of ourselves. We must accept the wear marks of our own bodies, the wrinkles on our faces, the writing of our hands as the body takes on a history of experiences as we proceed toward our death. This personal history, this body and this psyche, taking on signs of growth and destruction must be cared for and repaired, not unlike the baseball glove that comes to fit the individual hand or the sweater that fits the body. These too must be restitched and refurbished to give them added meaning and comfort. Old clothes possess a history, a texture of the battles, abuses, victories, and festivals the thing has gone through. Antique furniture, used books, flea markets, heirlooms, handed-down sacred objects of tribal life, old toys—all such things hold a history about them. In short, all tool kits are "re-re-membered" by the body. Former songs bring forth a nostalgia as we are reminded of times when we were younger. A certain style of a bygone era reactivates our memories and revives our youth.

Texture is therefore an understanding of our waste and decay. What we consume and dispose, both physically and mentally, allows us to grow. What we excrete from our minds and our bodies may be reused and placed in new contexts. It is through our failures that we learn who we are. Repair is nurturing and healing. All living things require nurture and healing if their life is to be preserved. Everything new demands that it be approached with a "soft" instrumentalism, gently prodded and closely felt. Van Gogh knew this well. He painted with heavy texture everything he came in contact with.

Western capitalism has denied us this dimension of the aesthetic experience. Western capitalism has generated wants rather than needs, the *simulacra* of the commodity, which is to say that all named things are representations and that the origin or the essence of any one thing can never be found (Baudrillard, 1983). Such reasoning puts to question what is "real" and "true," as the proverbial joke of electronic technology asks: Is it live or is it Memorex? It is the consumerism of things that now drives the market. The corporate sector continues to commit the "sin" of gluttony. Waste is not recycled for further growth; rather a consumer mentality of needless production is propagated. The history of things is eliminated. Repair, as the nurturing back to life of a thing, is being eliminated. Built-in obsolescence is one way; throwing the thing away is another. As Jameson (1983) points out, in a postmodernist society everything is a pastiche of everything else. The self, as reflected by a well-defined artistic style, is gone. Furthermore, the self has become schizophrenic (Deleuze & Guattari, 1983). Because history cannot be totalized (Foucault, 1972), we cannot locate ourselves historically. There is a continual breakdown in the relationship between signifiers. Our language becomes very soft.

Unquestionably, natural material leaves the mark of character. Leather, clay, wood, wool, and organic fibers bear the wrinkles and blemishes left on them. They possess consciousness. Plastics do not. Plastics do not take on a patina, a life. One is merely able to keep them longer and looking like new longer, like a silicone breast. The experience of texture is left for the very rich—those who can afford to buy antiques, vintage cars and wines, and historical houses in need of restoration. The connoisseur, the aesthete, becomes our artistic expert in residence. Art preserves its elite status of "excellence." Rather than recognizing that the dimension of lived aesthetic experience is available for all, we have relinquished our power of discrimination to those who can claim extraordinary refinement. Yet everywhere we may find signs of creative "adhocism" (Jencks, 1973); what has been described as folk, primitive, and naive art is where humane creativity flowers through personal solutions to psychological and physical problems. Rather than *haute cuisine*, home-cooked meals and handed-down recipes provide the identity of a distinctive style—that "little bit extra," much like natural brewed beer or organic food, that family restaurant that provides a distinctive taste.

All this, when compared with consumerism and fast-food takeouts, shows how impoverished this dimension has become. When i slurp from a McDonald's plastic cup, through a straw, it is a very one-dimensional experience. It becomes iconic of Western functionality. i do not examine the color of the liquid i am drinking, nor would i want to from fear of being repulsed. Slurping it through a straw hardly makes the liquid linger in my mouth. Coke and Pepsi have manufactured our loss for the taste of pure water (the ramifications of this for health reasons are just too staggering to contemplate). Nor does grasping a plastic, waxed-paper cup create a pleasant experience. Japanese tea ceremonies, Viennese coffee houses, British pubs are reminiscent of what we have lost. Spaces are now meant to be occupied for a short time. Conversations are kept brief in such garish surroundings. If all this was otherwise, McDonald's and companies like it would be out of business.

Texture speaks to the curriculum in many ways. Much has been written about one-shot implementation procedures (a male metaphor for the quick and dirty business of getting in and out "of another body"). These are quick, irresponsible love-makings that never work, merely objectify the relations between school boards and teachers. Texture, of course, speaks for the need of recognizing the distinctive style that has emerged in any school setting—how the curriculum has been adopted, interpreted, modified, and how children have made knowledge their own. Their personal biographies should be allowed to flourish and be bound in books to become home away from home, rather than simply a functioning space. Its decoration should resonate with their voices. The hallways should house their murals. Like the artist's studio, it must feel as though all is possible. The classroom tells me who the teacher is and who the children are. We put up familiar objects in our homes to remind us who we are and what we are. My child's room tells who he is.

The sense of textural repair suggests more than remedial help for children. It speaks to the human dimension of overcoming personal problems, which strengthens one's character rather than uprooting it. This is the antithesis of a "kit" mentality that aims to help the "individual." But this is a stratified individual, determined by color, class, age, and IQ. The plethora of kits and prepackaged materials on the market were intended to help the teachers cope with the incredible workloads that they must meet. These curricular resources were intended to make teaching more flexible, enabling teachers to free up their time. However, many times the curricular resources available to the teacher determine the curriculum taught. Inadvertently, the opposite of flexibility occurs. Paradoxically, it is precisely the making of tailor-made materials by the teacher for the classroom that preserves the experience of texture. It is the experience of dramatic improvisation, like the playing of jazz. Such thinking is not a step backwards to the Middle Ages but the very recognition that curriculum is experienced at the personal level. It is the negotiated reality of the curricular journey between teacher and student that generates paradox, ambiguity, and surprise—the essence of creative thought. This must be reclaimed in our post-modern period.

INTER(LUDUS)

The first three dimensions of the aesthetic speak mostly to the development of a personal aesthetic. One's personal biography is informed by them. One might think that aesthetic consciousness is continually formed and reformed by movement from a point of rest toward a creative explorative journey, fueled by desire. We might well claim these first three dimensions as the *s(muther)* of the Mother. There is a striving for bliss and harmony; to achieve that state before the split from the mother (Lacan, 1977). Motivation is generated as the body undergoes a ritual that shapes the lived-experience between where the journey has started and where it will eventually finish. The dramatization of that journey builds color and character as the curriculum unfolds. Eventually a style, a character, a texture emerges. Curricular experiences in this sense are enriching, creative, full of mystery and surprise as vistas continually unfold and growth occurs. This question emerges: How much joy and life has been squeezed out of the experience of learning through the continual rationalization of knowledge? In itself, the personal realm is the private realm. In our schools, most of arts education is left at this level. Rarely is the personal made political, that is, made public. In order to move past the private/public dichotomization that exists, it is necessary to recognize three further aesthetic layers that have been primarily within the minds and HANDS of male discourse. They, in contrast, are the rule of the Father. They enter us into the symbolic realm of public discourse (Lacan, 1977).

SIZE: THE LIVED EXPERIENCE OF SCALE

The question of size, of design, of theater, requires that the aesthetic dimension reach out to a wider audience. The question of scale becomes important. The binary oppositions between the mega and the micro, between the megalithic and the miniature, inform the tension of a centered self who tries to mediate the superego through the psychological proportionality of things. This is a standing up to the Father. Both things and people, larger than self, must be accommodated by the individual psyche. Miniatures, for example, allow for the reduction of things to a surveyable scale. Psychologically, they provide the control of structures too large for the body to handle proportionately. Miniaturization allows for the reduction of things to the level of endearment. The impulse to keep a fish tank, to practice the ancient Chinese art of feng shui (Rossbach, 1983) or the ancient Japanese art of bonsai, to collect stamps of countries around the world, to wear medallions, badges, lockets, and wristwatches, to model cars and buildings, to use coins—these are all substitutions, surrogates and reminders of the larger institutional and personal values that they represent. They offer a form of transportable presence to the larger whole. Miniatures are engulfed by the body. Their size, where they appear on the body as ornament, and at what distance they are viewed, determine their relative importance. One might think of cut precious stones as representative of the extreme care and intricacy of miniature production. One has to look at the subtlety of detail to appreciate their worth. All miniaturization is suggestive of fine tooling, fine control, flashes of brilliance and exquisiteness. As teachers, we have all experienced those moments when a lesson mirrors many sides, so that students feel that they have gotten on "top" of the issue. They have mastered the concept.

Staged drama as theater is yet another source of the body negotiating the concerns of society. The scale of this form is larger than the improvisation of *adhocism* found only at the local level. Theater provides the exemplar through which a broader theme may emerge.

In the pre-industrial world, the craftsperson provided the proportionality of things to clients as use value. Inequalities among the classes were perpetuated through such things as shoe length, materials used, and, of course, the time of production required. Customization rather than standardization was the measure of proportionality. Production was limited but quality prevailed. In *Modern Times,* to hark back to Chaplin's delightfully funny satire, we live in a mega society where the standardization of things is based on an ideal individual, a faceless individual. The ideal man, woman, child, family in a particular age cohort become the targets of industrial design (Papanek, 1974). Vast sectors of the physically disabled and the aged are overlooked. Particular ethnic needs are leveled out. Young army recruits become testers for many of the products designed by industry. Again, the best-designed things, such as clothing, housing, and cars, are extremely expensive and out of reach for the broad populace. Rather, overproduced goods that offer variations in cosmetic change of design proliferate. Research becomes advertising, selling the same thing in a different package rather than authentic product redesign for humane use. As the old adage goes, putting the same old wine in new bottles. Designer water, like Perrier, exemplifies the irony of the age. Million-year-old icebergs are next to be "bottled." This mega mentality of post-modernism has dwarfed the individual. We are stuffed full of over-choice.

Perhaps the proliferation of all sorts of course options in our schools is a useful analogy to the production-for-production's-sake mentality of the economy. The substance of education is lost. For the curriculum, size always presents a problem for implementation. Teacher-student ratios are determined as a number, not as a local manifestation. The standardization of curricula and the control of it from a centralized bureaucracy have also dwarfed the teacher and the learner. Schools must close if they cannot provide for the variety of courses demanded. Curricula breadth and differentiation is at stake. Miniaturization becomes a bad thing for the local authorities. There is less likely to be personal involvement, the fine-tooling characteristic of experience that goes beyond the constraints of economy and production. Standardized government competency exams try to evaluate the teacher and student to some predetermined criteria. More likely this will lead to a response of added antagonism and violence, a flight by teachers away from education to medi-ocre teaching in order to meet minimum requirements. The universalization of the curriculum shows us that the mentality to socialize youngsters into the accepted order has grown out of proportion, out of manageable size. Its scale needs reducing. The presence of graffiti on classroom desks and school walls, whose size screams to be heard, should not surprise us. The ego has become pathological.

The ethics of size are particularly important with regard to educational dialogue. The belittlement of the other through sarcasm and ridicule, psy-chologically cutting one down to size, betrays the good faith of conversation. Ironically, this psychological maneuver may work to the advantage of the oppressed when they can name the transgression against them, like calling authoritarian men phallocrats or making a derogatory term, like "nigger," their own. Milder forms of such leveling of size and resistance occurs when students call their teachers by their first names or even their nicknames or when the French and Germans drop their formal pronouns with strangers. Tribal life also indicated that psychological advantage was gained when an evil god's name was repeated over and over, each time shortening the sacred name until the god was psychologically overcome.

As teachers, such redresses of power must be exercised. Difficult concepts and loaded words should be unpacked by exposing the experience that sup-ports them. As teachers, we need to exercise the virtues of humility, empow-ering children so that they feel like equals in a conversation. Humility is lost when things are blown out of proportion. Disguises are then taken on, mystification promoted, jargon presented. Teachers become pompous and proud in their display of knowledge. Historical instances are readily available. One need only think of the differences between Linear A and Linear B writing in the Egyptian context, the continued use of Latin in Catholic tradition, and the continued esoteric wording of jurisprudence as examples of discourse that separate groups rather than enabling them to understand each other. This is the scaling of a stratified society. Each of these instances preserves the conversation in the hands of the few. Size and design are therefore important questions for classroom justice. Understanding at this lived aesthetic dimension means that *an* institution is under investigation. The art of satire and dystopia is able to present the truth of its perversion through an exaggeration of its disabling characteristics in contrast to fantasy and utopian visions, which are able to present the perversion from its enabling characteristics.

Western capitalism, with its bureaucratic mindset, continues to maintain borders between disciplines. This is successfully maintained through the language games that are generated by each discipline's professionals. This is also true of the arts. Their role, as university subjects competing with other "more important" academic disciplines, has forced them to become equally esoteric, to claim their territory of expertise. Currently, the deconstructive and semiological movements in the arts have made literature and fine arts hermetic. Post-modernism presents us with two faces: one nihilistic and the other critical. The first leaves us with artworks that are allegorical, often obscure, alienating the general public and catering to those few who are in the know (Krauss, 1985; Rosler, 1984). Art becomes a quotation that is in danger of becoming another secret society. A neo-medievalism is emerging. The second has been referred to as a site/sight/cite of a denaturalizing critique. Such artworks are often parodic in their attempt to "de-doxify" cultural representation (Hutcheon, 1989).

MASS: THE LIVED EXPERIENCE OF GRAVITY

Mass, as the fifth aesthetic dimension, is informed through the binary oppositions between gravity (permanence) and lightness (moveability). Our minds quiver from the pull of tradition and the hope of utopia. These are out-of-body experiences that we try to comprehend. At this level we recall archetypes that lie between heaven and hell, between good and evil. Gravity means denseness and compactness. It means weighty concerns—the lure of well-trod traditions. We are creatures of permanence. Our *raison d'être* is left in things that endure through time. Perhaps it is our way to push back death, to leave something of ourselves behind. It is perhaps the impulse of the funereal arts. We preserve the traces of ourselves through mummification, embalming, statues and images built in effigy, yet paradoxically, there is a mindfulness that we ultimately belong to Gaia.

"Things" of mass embody the meanings, the summation of the history of a people and a culture. They can, as in autobiography, also embody the summation of one person, a leader. Together, they represent the sculpture, the music, the great epics, great literature of any period. They are our civilizational archetypes. Such symbols possess power over us and are encrusted with the weight of their sacredness; they are holy. They push on our backs and propel us forward on well-worn paths already traveled by our predecessors. Turned into orthodoxy, the wisdom within these "texts" becomes stultified.

The "body's" re-memberance of mass may be extended through the corridors of time—to a moment when birth and development are continuous and nondivisible, where gravity, which informs Gaia, embodies the memory of our planet (Lovelock, 1979). Punctuated evolution occurs. New species come into existence only when that link with their past is broken and a dissipation of the structure occurs (Prigogine, 1980). The "tradition" or archetype that informs that species no longer serves its creation, its evolvement. Today, we as a species, *Homo sapiens sapiens,* are undergoing a similar dissipation. Feminists have raised the issue as to whether our current archetypes are one-sided—heroic and male. Could and should other archetypes inform our species if we are to continue to live on the skin of Gaia?

Such traditions are heavy. Gravity, Gaia's consciousness, pulls at them with all her might. Yet they are difficult to move, for their composition is interwoven with many voices and countless generations. And unlike the insects' world, where new species are discovered daily, wo(man) is unique to the Earth. History as myth, as the conscious experiences of men and women, has been one-sided. Its "underside," its belly is missing (Boulding, 1976). As male experience, the history of civilization endures and is difficult to deconstruct. Like a WHiTE dwarf its gravitational pull is greater that that of the earth. Gaia is slowly dying. Perhaps only through disequilibrium can the tension of gravity be met. Certain texts, like the Bible, the Torah, the Koran, are conversations that stand as monuments to the accomplishments of a male culture's history. They are the dolmens of the Axial Age (Jaspers, 1957). *Yet such dolmens require constant reinterpretation, misreading to produce a reading that speaks to today's age.* Their gravity must speak to a myriad of transcendental concerns about justice, love, and freedom. Their music must be uplifting and transvaluative. Is it time that such dolmens be stood on their heads? But, to do so, one must first learn their structures to make them light enough to lift.

Works of gravity move masses: Men and women go into battle for a cause; a nation mourns the loss of a treasured leader; requiems are staged for the dead during disasters. Spiritual "masses" celebrate collective events. Pageants, festivals, potlatches, rituals require orchestration and duration to take place. Similarly oracles, pow wows, summit meetings, require build up and deliberation before major gravities can be dealt with. The collective tension that a group feels between the pull of permanence and the freedom of ephemerality requires that balance always be asymmetrical. Such an enigma requires that permanence be continually challenged by the guidance of the "god."

RE, a pre-fix which stands with diligence in our syntax. The tradition must be (re)read, (re)searched, (re)thought, (re)experienced, to make understanding of a tradition lighter, more parsimonious. Through this eternal return, the old is (mis)read, (mis)understood into the new. *The introduction of the prefix, the "goddess" MiS, as the dialectical counterpoint to the prefix RE, (re)cognizes the "harmony" of (dis)equilibrium and (de)construction.* This, in itself, is a paradox since the act generates the prefixes DiS and DE, which, in the English language, are (prefixes) that anticipate (de)struction rather than (re)construction of the new. Whatever appears permanent, orthodox, enduring, everlasting, parading as the gospel of the many, must be (de)institutionalized, (re)duced, its structures made threadbare, the useless timbers discarded so that new meanings might emerge. Such a task requires "spiritual" guidance. The Muses must be (re)called and (re)examined, especially Clio (history), Calliope (heroic poetry), and their mother, Mnemosyne (memory). In this way no cults can be preserved. No one lives off the spirit of another's reputation. Such experiences of translation embody the very essence of economy. Mnemonics of the mind, body, and soul are required, for it is the soul that harbors the collective dreams of a people. Since the Enlightenment, the soul has disappeared from metaphysical discourse. It needs to be (re)called (Hillman, 1975) within the aesthetics of mass.

The struggle among giants and titans, heroes and heretics, David and Goliath, legends of the Amazons, gods and goddesses, are among the archetypal symbols of cultural belief. These are the instances that embody the narratives of mass experience. In these legends are the lessons of wisdom (*sophia*), which are meant to be (re)vealed. Within myths and fairy tales lie the mores of the culture (Von Franz, 1978). To understand their structure is to be able to animate an entire body, to lighten any load. Such knowledge, converted to the level of practical knowledge (*phronesis*), provides the new turn in the path for the tradition to walk on. Phronesis has a long and rich history (Gadamer, 1975). A more colloquial term might be "political savvy," as displayed by such world leaders such as Gorbachev and Czechoslovakia's Vaclav Havel. The wise person understands the structure of things. The wise person, the crone, the wizard, the witch, the scholar, the prophet, and the author (Foucault, 1984) are able to manipulate the tradition effortlessly, move large bodies of knowledge subtly. They are like the sculptors who always work with material of the age. This material, too, is manipulated effort-lessly, be it steel, glass, iron, stone, or ferrocement. Like sculpture displayed in the midst of our cities as well as all alone in the deserts, such people coexist in both places, perhaps once more (re)capitulating the private/public dichot-omization. Physical summations of mass are presented in the forms of math-ematical systems; perhaps these need to be sup(planted) with musical sum-mations, a new coven of Muses found. Humane summations have been presented as epics, philosophies, religions, which claim a path to truth, righ-teousness, heaven, nirvana, (re)working the "hell" its creators felt born into. Today science, the latest Western summation of mass, needs to be sup(planted) by a new myth.

The ethics of the aesthetics of mass suggest that sacred spaces, special places are needed to harbor such traditions if their dialogues are to be kept alive. Historically, the paleolithic caves, the delphic oracles, the academies, the universities, the mosques, the churches have provided for the word to be read and interpreted. Characteristically, the re(interpretation) of traditions has taken place within times of crisis and only when a *critical* mass was achieved did humane consciousness change (Jaynes, 1976). What should the responsibility of educators be if they hold such power to shape a tradition? What should be the role of our organic intellectuals? Einstein and Oppen-heimer struggled with such questions, as did Joan of Arc. How should power be delegated? Who should conduct the new orchestration? Should the tradi-tional of leadership itself be questioned? Perhaps the new orchestration is to be found within each autobiography, the entire tradition improvised through anarchy?

Psychologically, the Western technological imagination treats the manip-ulation of mass clinically, that is, ideologically. The mass is well orchestrated, manipulated through the communications media and propaganda. The power of the state comes under question. To what extent has the state given the public a voice? How has the public forum been maintained? What space has been cleared for the discussion of the "sacred" knowledge, as developed above, that affects our very Being? Is the space created by representative de-mocracy enough? Could other forms of participatory democracy (Stravri-anos, 1976) be developed?

Physically, the myth of Icarus has been realized and exemplified by the technological ability to literally "move mountains" and "touch the heavens." When we push a heavy vault door with ease, see a jumbo jet or the *Challenger* leave the earth, we feel a sense of magic and awe. However, the world econ-omy is out of balance. The market price overrides any sense of use value. The stockpiling of foodstuffs, nuclear bombs, nuclear waste, the placement of our aged into nursing homes, the hording and cornering of the stock market, the perpetuation of unemployment so that supply and demand of labor may be controlled—all indicate that technological rationality maintains that the hording of mass provides MAN with the greatest of pleasure.

Mass raises interesting problems for curricular theorizing. The structure of the disciplines has come and gone, but perhaps the questioning of traditions in our schools has only begun to be initiated. Bodies of knowledge, Foucault's articulation of "discourse" (Dreyfus & Rabinow, 1982) as traditions that answer questions of profoundly enigmatic human concerns, are the achievement of the humanities, which are underdeveloped in our schools. Currently, curricula that speak to such matters appear under the auspices of orthodox religious practices, where questions concerning the practical (ethical) life have been fashioned by a male discourse. Parochial schools have taken on the task of filling the spiritual vacuum created by the Enlightenment. That religion is also deeply patriarchal in our schools is an issue that has hardly been touched (Daly, 1973; Fiorenza, 1985). It requires the examination of cross-cultural solutions to the universals of power, equality, peace, and death if alternatives are to be found. The ethics and politics of a mass aesthetics have been stripped of this transcendent potential. Current attempts to view knowledge as a hermeneutic enterprise (Gadamer, 1975) require that educators face the question that all knowledge stands within a historical conversation that shapes our collective myth, and women of all persuasions are trying to take part in that conversation, to add to its gravity by lightening its current structure.

SPACE: THE LIVED EXPERIENCE OF THE COSMOS

The final frontier? The aesthetic dimension of space as embodied in the architecture of a culture forms the final analysis. More than a canopy or shelter, it is, rather, an envelope that symbolizes the mythology of a culture. It forms the highest and most spiritual creative dimension. Topple the Tower of Babel and you deconstruct the sacred ground it rests on. Unearth the deified archetypes and you expose the soul of a tradition. Destroy the gods and goddesses and you destroy the very core of beliefs that both blind and bind a culture. Architecture provides the (re)newing experience for a people. It is the place for spiritual bathing. In them one experiences the sublime, the awe and the mystery of the universe. Stonehenge, the pyramids, mastabas, churches, synagogues, temples, and, today, our space science centers are such (re)newing baths through which one becomes baptized into a culture's cosmology. The architect, as the composer of unearthly music, must capture the highest aspirations, the collective unconscious imagination, and give it spiritual form. Today the global envelope, Gaia, is emerging to compete against the current cosmology (Whitmont, 1982). Opposing this are the post-modern multicorporation buildings with their pastiche of styles that allude to the greatness of the past.

All of the previous aesthetic dimensions are subsumed under this collective vision. It is informed through binary oppositions of an envelope and the open air, between participation and ostracism, between the Earth and the Cosmos. Exile, both physical and psychological, is perhaps the most difficult CROSS to bear because it demands that we struggle with the paradox of having to reject an entire tradition that bore us but also realize that a new space needs to be created. Perhaps such feelings inform the explorations of the adventurer, the astronaut, the inventor, the stargazer. On their journeys, they take something along with them to remind them of the culture they once knew. If they return, they do so with reluctance. Their Mother culture is now perceived through a new body. The aesthetics of space requires coming back full circle, starting the journey of line once more, perhaps hungry, shelterless, and thirsty, yet having full knowledge that such a journey must be taken since the current worldview must be rejected, a new cosmos discovered. Such are the birth pains of an ideology critique. Such are the pains and joys experienced by a Galileo or a Lilith (Phillips, 1984). Perhaps the ecological and feminist movements will provide the new cosmology?

The Western Englightenment has left us only with patriarchal dominance; the lived spaces of functionality speak neither to the sacred nor to the profane. They just are. The clean-line aesthetic (*Sachlikeit*) and the vertical dominance of skyscraper celebrate the male victory of corporate power. It is primarily the male who has perceived the verticality of power. His lens searches the universe for new planets to conquer. His energies are concentrated on a multibillion-dollar weapons industry and the economic exploitation of space, which is out of Gaia's reach. Horizontally, on Gaia's surface, food, shelter, and clothing remain a major problem for her people due to this perversion of power.

For the curriculum, oikoumenical concerns play a very minor role. Spirituality has been confined to a dominating form of religion that occupies the transmittal of dogma and a well-defined catechism. For the most part the separation of church and state has left the spiritual domain empty and void in the curriculum. Parochial schools sometimes stultify it, or reduce it to rules. Perhaps only "peace education" is entertaining worldwide notions of how to live together on Gaia's skin. Under its rubric, educators are finding a (re)newing sense of spirituality. Rather than escaping from her pull via the space shuttle or protecting her from nuclear holocaust through the technology of Star Wars, peace educators have begun a global conversion. In terms of a (re)vivified curriculum, the hope exists that their circumpolar direction can be reintegrated with ecological movements that have similar oikoumenical interests. The potential of a new cosmology rests here.

THE QUESTION OF DICHOTOMY AND GENDER

These, then, are the six dimensions of feeling, of aesthetic experience, written archetypes on the body, manifested through the body. Our metaphorical/holographic mind/body is capable of participating in all six dimensions of experience. We do this when we become conscious of the binary oppositions that (in)form each of these levels of perception. These binary oppositions are complementarities that are intuitively understood by dwelling between them and in them with our bodies. They are not dichotomies. Each level presents a posture, that is, a gesture, a motility against the world and is (in)formed by that world. As such, each level presents the actor-teacher with an ethical and political choice. For example, only well-thought-out ironic works of art can undermine a whole tradition to reveal its falsity. Satire, too, can show us, through exaggeration and distortions, greater truth about lived reality. Performance art is riddled with such attempts. The power of the aesthetic is the ability to defamiliarize everyday life. It does so by playing on one or more of the levels that i have outlined.

Since the fifteenth century, the bourgeois mentality has separated these six forms into well-defined disciplines. In the visual arts drawing and printmaking (line), painting (color), the decorative arts (texture), industrial design (size), sculpture (mass), and architecture (space) follow the ontological aesthetic divisions that have been presented. Each artform, be it music, dance, drama, or literature, has similar stratifications. Analogies are easily found. These arts, whose associations are usually linked to the feminine and the "right" side of the brain, have not only been suppressed in the Western tradition, but a professional divisiveness has left them weak and fragmented. Returning to their ontological roots might be a way to collectively strengthen the power of their story.

The last three aesthetic ways of knowing the world are more public. The arts of design, sculpture, and architecture have been shrunk by the disappearance of the public sphere in bourgeois society. By and large these have become standardized concerns. Design, sculpture, and architecture have been appropriated by the corporate image and are no longer "public" as they once were; that is, they are no longer expressions of a people but rather of corporations. These three areas of aesthetic being do not usually find their way into the school system, although there are exceptions. Personal expression, exemplified by the first three ways of aesthetic being, find their most prolific expression in the schools and are given the highest priority. These are safe and confine the potential power of the arts. Doing so, they preserve the liberalist ideology of free expression, but without the other three they help to promote the myth of capitalist individualism, making the ego ineffective in the real world.

Throughout the "body" of this paper the gender implications have been exposed. Gender, however, is *not* just another level that besets the postmodern age along with class, color, and age. It is foundational and goes to a much deeper level. It is this gendered body that must negotiate these complementarities that have been one-sided since the emergence of patriarchy from 3100 to 600 B.C.E. (Lerner, 1986). Since the time of the Greek *polis,* democracy has been in the hands of a male discourse that has utilized an abstracted logic of technological rationality, developed and refined through the recovery of the Greek frame of mind and perpetuated by a technocratic male elite in all parts of the world. These are strangleholds to creative thought and new solutions. Since the turn of the twentieth century, when the electric age (and now the electronic age) emerged as the new foundation of our economic growth, we have been "watching" a digital, dichotomous logic penetrating all levels of communicative discourse. All discourse is being reduced to an either/or logic, a "0" or "1" binary computer mentality. The intangibility of the aesthetic humane dimension is being lost in this electronization of all communication. Semiology has become the new science of information communication.

We dichotomize male from female, we dichotomize our subject disciplines, we separate cognition from affection, left brain from the right brain, work from play, state from church, those who have artistic talent from those who do not—the list is endless. The problem of the age is to work beyond these dichotomies in each institutional sphere. It is the area of the included middle, where the gendered body must negotiate the reality between these opposites; *the s(muther) of the Mother and the Rule of the Father.* There lies the creative spirit. It is in this area that boundaries are broken, new body choreographs and rhythms of time experienced. To the extent that we, as educators, begin to think dialectically and break free of the dichotomous boundaries that hold us, change toward a new future will begin. One hopes that an ecological consciousness will spread to counteract the tendencies towards objectification.

POSSIBLE SIGNS OF PRAXIS

The radical restructuring of educational disciplines might make possible the (re)working of male dominance and technical rationality through the six aesthetic layers. This possibility is already being realized slowly in physical education, where the dominant male values of competition and a "jock" mentality are under seige through the introduction of *movement* education. The idea of "dance" provides the syncopation between male and female and perhaps sublimates youthful sexuality in a more meaningful way. The psychomotor domain, which has always treated the body as an object of competition, and some say even with a violence that leads to war, is at least being questioned. One might dream of similar attempts to combine mathematics and music in such a way that the rhythms of life would be consonant with a comparable mathematics; a system of "musimatics" which could handle accident, chance, and arhythmic dissipation—perhaps the way atonal music has demonstrated. All "inert" matter possesses consciousness. How can we, *or* do we already, communicate with it? Perhaps such discipline boundary breaking can be extended throughout the school curriculum. Poetry and literature have already fused with visual art (Kostelanetz, 1979). New patternings and visual expressions could be generated through the examination of rational and irrational numbers; artists such as Max Bill have already attempted such transgressions. The phenomenology of forms could be studied to recognize the particular feelings they elicit. How are mathematical systems a summation of particular experiences? Why was statistics invented during the Enlightenment Age? What purposes did it serve? And what does its employment in everyday life mean to our lives?

To break the scientism that grips the science curriculum, the mysterious wonder of nature needs to be recovered. Science fiction literature is rich with such possibilities. The consciousness of materials needs to be reawakened to rid ourselves of the dichotomy between inert and living matter that is so prevalent in science. The dichotomies we have with animals need to be overcome. Ecological movements, Green party politics, eco-feminism are undertaking this journey. The increase in poetic metaphor in language arts, the introduction of a women's vocabulary, the overcoming of gendered words in Romance languages, the combining of literature as personal drama, as in the autobiographical mode (Boal, 1979; Pinar & Grumet, 1976), are other hopeful signs. Current peace movements, with their attempt to overcome the dichotomy between violence and perpetual peace, again represent a major push forward. Perhaps all these strands will grow together in harmony to reveal the New Age, the new Mythos.

BECOMING

There is certainly a danger of romanticism when speculating about the curriculum and the recovery of the aesthetic potential. The new biologism holds the danger of a renewed organicism, which, in the past, was used quite

effectively by the Nazi party. That mythology, however, was shaped historically by a male discourse—the pursuit of the Holy Grail (Whitmont, 1982).
i personally am unsure of the full implications of the above proposal. i have
presented a hypothesis and an exploration. Throughout this essay the assumption has always been that the whole enterprise of the Enlightment has
been misguided, despite brilliant social theorists like Habermas (1981) who
wish to save it. Jürgen Habermas represents one of the few attempts today
to totalize history and provide a grand theory in the tradition of Marx and
Hegel. Other historians, notably the French post-structuralists such as Foucault and Derrida (1974), think this is an absurd task. From the standpoint
of this essay, a fundamental (re)thinking of eschatology would need to begin
with the (re)examination of patriarchy in the spirit of Lerner's (1986) and
Whitmont's (1982) work, since our spiritual discourse has also been shaped
by male patriarchs. Goldenberg (1982) and Daly (1973) have made such a
critique of the Judeao-Christian religious tradition from a feminist viewpoint. They argue that this tradition should be (re)placed. Other feminists,
like Fiorenza (1985), argue that this tradition, once reformed, may still be
able to speak of women of today.

FOR THE PURPOSES OF MY ARGUMENT, the aesthetic roots to Nature belong
to a pagan era, prior to the Chalcolithic, or copper, period. An exploration
of pagan spirituality, as developed during the so-called magical phase of our
humane consciousness, is in order. This seems justified on the grounds that
no "afterlife" conceptualizations, as yet, had been spawned. These came with
the male "sun" religions. In the Egyptian context, for example, only the phar-
aoh had a *ka* and a privileged life after death. Whereas in the pagan religions,
like the ancient Japanese religion of Shinto, there were no strivings for life
after death, yet these animistic religions have a great reverence for Nature.
All deeds were to be done in the "present" so that Nature might be revered.

In contrast, the form of rationality and reason that took hold held the
seeds of its own destruction. We are feeling the power of that failed vision in
the phallocrats who run corporations today. Our break with Nature has de-
humanized us, alienated us from Her because we have overlooked the body
and elevated the mind, a direct result of the embourgeoisification of the social
order. Embourgeoisification refers to the achieved political economy of the
bourgeoisie in the middle of the nineteenth century, when their values began
to penetrate and affect all institutions (family, religion, state, etc.) and strata
of society. Understandably, gender issue haunts the entire attempt to reconstitute our relationship with Nature (Griffin, 1978).

Whence is the politics of this discourse to emerge? It appears that our
notions of an avant-garde, a small elite that will lead the way, have been
misguided. They recapitulate dominance and hierarchy. If aesthetics and ethics and politics are to be consonant, then it appears that the personal cannot

be separated from the political. Life-style, as many feminists claim, must be congruent with one's political style. The Greenham Common example, as one among many, seems to indicate that the form for change is anarchist in nature but one that is "responsible anarchy" (Caputo, 1988). The community of women who surrounded this missile base in Britain refused to give in to military pressure. Civil disobedience is sometimes essential. It must occur in the uncoerced terms formed by each body throwing its resistance into the larger whole. Out of ourselves a new visionary myth will be generated. As its articulation unfolds more and more people(s) will recognize its direction. This is not the lifework of a generation, but of many generations. It, like the six dimensions i have outlined, begins with a journey, a quest toward an unknown vision—yet it is pregnant with insight. Perhaps the child has already been born and waits in the birth canal.

REFERENCES

Baudrillard, J. (1983). The ecstasy of communication. In H. Foster (Ed.), *The anti-aesthetic—Essays on postmodern culture* (pp. 126–134). Port Townsend, WA: Bay Press.

Boal, A. (1979). *Theater of the oppressed.* New York: Urizen Books.

Boulding, E. (1976). *The underside of history.* Boulder, CO: Westview.

Caputo, J. D. (1988). Beyond aestheticism: Derrida's responsible anarchy. *Research in Phenomenology, 18,* 59–73.

Carson, T. (1987). *Peace education and the task for peace educators: A world council for curriculum and instruction monograph.* Bloomington, IN: World Council for Curriculum and Instruction.

Daly, M. (1973). *Beyond god the father: Towards a philosophy of women's liberation.* Boston: Beacon.

Deleuze, G., & Guattari, F. (1983). *Anti-oedipus: Capitalism and schizophrenia* (R. Hurley, M. Seem, & H. Lane, Trans.). Minneapolis: University of Minnesota Press.

Derrida, J. (1974). *Of grammatology* (G. C. Spivak, Trans.). Baltimore: Johns Hopkins University Press.

Dreyfus, H., & Rabinow, P. (1982). *Michel Foucault: Beyond structuralism and hermeneutics.* Chicago: University of Chicago Press.

Elshtain, J. B. (1981). *Public man, private woman.* Princeton, NJ: Princeton University Press.

Fiorenza, E. S. (1985). *In memory of her: A feminist theological reconstruction of Christian origins.* New York: Crossroads.

Foucault, M. (1972). *The archaeology of knowledge.* (A.M. Sheridan Smith, Trans.). New York: Pantheon.

Foucault, M. (1984). What is an author? In P. Rabinow (Ed.), *The Foucault reader* (pp. 101–120). New York: Pantheon.

Fromm, E. (1981). *On disobedience and other essays.* New York: Seabury.

Gadamer, H. G. (1975). *Truth and method* (G. Barden & J. Cumming, Trans.). London: Sheed & Ward.

Goffman, E. (1961). *Asylums*. Garden City, NY: Doubleday/Anchor.

Goldenberg, N. (1982). *The end of god*. Ottawa: University of Ottawa Press.

Gramsci, A. (1971). *Selections from prison notebooks* (Q. Hoare & G. Smith, Eds. and Trans.). New York: International Publishers.

Griffin, S. (1978). *Woman and nature: The roaring inside her*. New York: Harper & Row.

Habermas, J. (1981, Winter). Modernity versus postmodernity. *New German Critique, 22,* 3–14.

Hillman, J. (1975). *Re-visioning psychology*. New York: Harper & Row.

Hutcheon, L. (1989). *The politics of postmodernism*. New York: Routledge & Kegan Paul.

Jameson, F. (1983). Postmodernism and consumer society. In H. Foster (Ed.), *The Anti-aesthetic: Essays on postmodern culture* (pp. 111–125). Port Townsend, WA: Bay Press.

Jaspers, K. (1957). *Man in the modern age* (E. & C. Paul, Trans.). New York: Doubleday.

Jaynes, J. (1976). *The origin of consciousness in the breakdown of the bicameral mind*. Boston: Houghton Mifflin.

Jencks, C. (1973). *Adhocism: The case for improvisation*. Garden City, NY: Doubleday/Anchor.

Kandinsky, W. (1947). *Concerning the avant-garde and other modernist myths*. Cambridge, MA: MIT Press. (Original work published 1912)

Kostelanetz, R. (1979). (Ed.). *Visual literature criticism: A new collection*. Carbondale: South Illinois University Press.

Krauss, R. (1985). *The originality of the avant-garde and other modernist myths*. Cambridge, MA: MIT Press.

Lacan, J. (1977). *Ecrits: A selection*. New York: Travistock.

Lerner, G. (1986). *The creation of patriarchy*. New York: Oxford University Press.

Levin, D. M. (1985). *The body's recollection of being: Phenomenological psychology and the deconstruction of nihilism*. Boston: Routledge & Kegan Paul.

Lovelock, J. E. (1979). *Gaia: A new look at life on earth*. Oxford, England: Oxford University Press.

May, R. (1975). *The courage to create*. New York: Norton.

Papanek, V. (1974). *Design for the real world*. New York: Granada.

Phillips, J. A. (1984). *Eve: The history of an idea*. San Francisco: Harper & Row.

Pinar, W., & Grumet, M. (1976). *Towards a poor curriculum*. Dubuque, IA: Kendall & Hunt.

Prigogine, I. (1980). *From being to becoming: Time and complexity in the physical sciences*. San Francisco: Freeman.

Rosler, M. (1984). Lookers, buyers, dealers, and makers: Thoughts on audience. In Brian Wallis (Ed.), *Art after modernism: Rethinking representation*. Boston: The New Museum of Contemporary Art, New York in association with David R. Godine.

Rossbach, S. (1983). *Feng shui: The Chinese art of placement*. New York: Dutton.

Segall, M. D., Campbell, D. T., & Herskovits, M. J. (1966). *The influence of culture on visual perception.* New York: Bobbs-Merrill.

Stravrianos, L. S. (1976). *The promise of the coming dark age.* San Francisco: Freeman.

Von Franz, M. L. (1978). *Interpretation of fairytales.* Irving, TX: Spring.

Walker, B. G. (1983). *The woman's encyclopedia of myths and secrets.* San Francisco: Harper & Row.

Whitmont, E. (1982). *The return of the goddess.* New York: Crossroads.

CHAPTER 10

Between Crystal and Smoke
Or, How to miss the point in the debate about action research

CLERMONT GAUTHIER

There have been disputes regarding the definition of action research. This undoubtedly must be a sign of the interest brought about by this kind of research, but it can also reveal a mythological black hole leading to fruitless efforts. How must one define action research? What in reality does this term refer to? Customary methods used to define a term either circumscribe its essence (shape) or isolate it as a subject, a substance: this particular object (which amounts to the same thing, since substances and subjects are nothing but shaped bodies). Thus one can say that a table is a table and nothing else. It is neither a chair nor a chicken. There is some kind of essence of a table from which one can draw its outline and distinguish it from other objects.

Now let us just for a moment slip into fantasy and ask ourselves what is the limit of the concept "table." If a sheet of plywood is placed on two cows, is this still a table? Or if I imagine a table that cannot stand up, or a limp table (somewhat like Dali's watches). If we follow for a while this line of reasoning we might end up giving a definition based on essences, which would lead us to asking ourselves "How much hair we have to lose before we can say we are bald?" Here we are swimming in pure paradox. But this is the usual way one deals with the problems of definition, which almost inevitably lead to this type of dead end (black hole), since such a method of defining forces one to continually look for a missing piece. One asks "What does the table need to be truly a table?" or "What is missing about this table that really makes it table?" or "What is missing in order for action research to really be action research?" My intention here is not to stop any attempt to define but rather to start considering the question from another angle and build a combination, a kind of simulacrum by which different elements will combine to generate new possibilities. On that point Spinoza is an inspiring source. Instead of defining a body by its substance, he rather asks: "What can this body do?" Instead of asking: "What is the horse's essence? How is it specifically characterized?" he puts forward the following question: "What can a horse do? What is it capable of?". Thus we will say that there is a greater difference between a racehorse and a plough-horse than between a plough-horse and an ox. One could even add that a circus horse is closer to a poodle than to a racehorse. Hence defining a term has more to do with determining its relation and combination than with finding its essence.

One first has to identify all that through which it is set in motion, to name various possibilities—but not in the sense of one of its functions within a hole; this would still be too close to the functionalist ideology. When I say it is "possible," I refer to all with which it can be in relation to, all compositions, all machine-type combinations. The plough-horse operates within a farmer-field-harrow combination, whereas the racehorse is within a jockey-racetrack-stirrup combination. The circus horse is in a costume-tamer-ring combination.

Defining a term also implies a listing of behaviors (affects) arising from this combination. A plough-horse's behaviors will be similar to those of an ox because they are located in a similar combination. Hence when looking into action research to try to define it, I do not search for its essence but rather for the type of combinations in which it operates, as well as for behaviors (affects) associated with it or possibilities arising from it. "What is a body capable of?" instead of "What is its essence?" That is why definition has more to do with a machine than a mechanism. A machine signifies an encounter between independent heterogeneous elements that does not constitute a whole in itself since there are always new parts that can be added; a mechanism is a complete homogeneous system, thereby having an essence.

I intend to tackle action research's definition by considering the latter as a machine, or a machine-type combination, not as a self-contained mechanism having a substance or an essence of its own. I will therefore not be searching for a mechanistic definition of action research, but rather for machine-type combinations. I shall thus avoid the missing-piece trap caused by an essence-type definition. I will only be looking for relations between parts of the machine as well as for behaviors resulting from them. In short, I want to know how it works, and what it does, but not what it is. And if one comments that action research associates theory and practice, then I will accept the statement providing the following questions can be answered: Is it the only type of research having such an association, and what particular behaviors does it yield? If the same parts (theory and practice) are related in the same manner, they will probably give way to similar behaviors. On the other hand, if the interrelations between parts differ, one will probably notice different behaviors. So if the interrelations differ, and this is my hypothesis, how then can one construct a definition based on similar behaviors, on behaviors that can be found in other types of research (like authors in action research presently do). If such a problem exists, then even if I do not adhere to the method of definitions by essence, I can say that they have missed the definition, not on the ground that my own definition is the correct one, but rather because theirs is imprecise. Even if behaviors agreed with the combination theory-practice, I still would have been unable to say: This is action research. At the very most I could have said: Action research can do this within that combination.

QUESTION ONE: HOW WAS THE ACTION RESEARCH CONCEPT "MACHINATED"?

Action research's debate always returns to theoretical and practical notions. One wants to work on actual rather than abstract problems, to get involved in research and not simply be an onlooker; one wants a research method adapted to life, not only laboratory conditions. One wants to transform society instead of only watching it. In other words, action research's literature extensively covers theoretical and practical matters but finally gives preference to practice. Theory, although not neglected, is still never fundamental to the finality and only supports it. One wishes to unite theory and practice. It is as if there was on one hand a group of terms such as *practice, concrete, reality, real life, action,* and, on the other hand, a group including *theory, abstract, unreal, laboratory.* Upon hearing those terms one is left with the impression that something has been understood. But what precisely? The opposition of theory and practice, although so simple in common language, becomes more complex as it is put under scrutiny, to such a point that action research become a totally ambiguous research method. Certain clarifications seem necessary. This article will tend to demonstrate that a careless use of the terms *theory* and *practice* does not bring about a discriminating definition, so that in most cases one should not even be speaking of action research, since other types of research operate similarly. One should say that the combination was missed, that a bad encounter cut short our capacity to act.

Theory and Practice

Since action research is focused on the relation between theory and practice, here is where and how we shall begin our discussion.

Practice (1).   The word *practice* fundamentally refers to reality. Indeed, one often hears: "You know, this sounds very good in theory, but at a practical level, it can be quite different." The first meaning of practice is reality.

According to Rosset, reality is the *"simple accumulation or succession of events"* (1979, p. 12). It is everything that happens. It is an open set of unidentifiable objects. Serres would say reality is a multiplicity of elements without any standardization (1983).

Theory (1).   As one might expect, the word *practice* is opposed to the word *theory*. Theory can be seen as overlapping reality or practice or as some kind of double. Whereas practice presents reality, theory represents it. It tries to copy or reproduce reality. Theory is a reproduction.

Practice (2).   The word *practice* can also designate prescription. For example, according to Levy-Bruhl, practice encompasses the rules of personal conduct and the moral duties of men. (1971).

Thus practice is what one has to do. A recipe book is practical because it tells us what to do. In education we often hear people saying that a course is not practical because it does not tell the students what to do, it simply describes a situation without prescribing rules of conduct.

Theory (2).   Just as Theory (1) is opposed to Practice (1) (reproduction versus reality), Theory (2) is different from Practice (2). Descriptive language is opposed to prescriptive language, and there is no relation whatsoever between the two. They belong to completely different worlds: one being an indication (the descriptive language game), the other an order (the prescriptive language game) (Lyotard, 1979b, 1983).

Practice (3).   Specific rules are practical. Education programs are often based on policies that are general rules or theories. But they also give precise directions as to what has to be done. These directions are practical rules.

Theory (3).   But as everyone knows, the rules have not the same degree of generality. Some are very general rules, others are quite specific; the general ones are, as one skilled in the art would say, finalities. All finalities are moral theories. The specific rules are the means to achieve the finalities.

Practice (4).   Practice can also mean usefulness. Once the chemical properties of oil have been discovered, one may ask oneself to what use this discovery could be put. One will then apply this knowledge about fundamental science and put it to use in a practical way. While some people doing research are trying to probe reality in order to be able to understand and explain it better, others are trying to put to practical use discoveries that have already been made (see Figure 10.1).

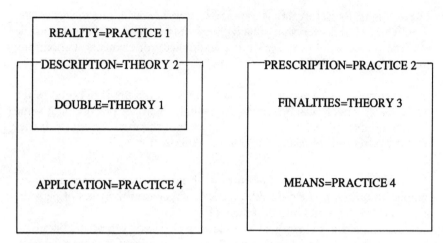

FIGURE 10.1   Action Research

The Relations Between Theory and Practice

The word *practice* has been given four meanings and the word theory, three. What do we mean when we try to establish a relation between theory and practice? Many people say without even thinking that theory serves as a guide for practice and that practice helps to correct theory. Very often scientific phrases become everyday language. The above statement establishes a relation between theory and practice. But if the words *theory* and *practice* have different meanings, what kind of relation can be established between the two?

First relation: Reality and its reproduction.   This is the most common relation between theory and practice. We have on the one hand reality, flowing smoothly, and on the other hand reproduction, that is, theory trying to reproduce reality as best it can. In this relation, one will try to find the *truth*, to discover the best copy of reality.

Thus we are trying to understand reality. Theory only tries to describe reality, to explain it and to predict its appearance. This relation brings out problems of understanding: One will try to explain the strange event, the conflict between what one can see and what one expected, between exception and habit.

Evidently this scientific activity is not neutral, because science has to follow rules of operation and produce a point of view on reality.

Second relation: From fundamental theory to its application.   After making a fundamental discovery one must eventually apply it. How can the discovery be used? What use can he make out of it? [see Theory (1) and

Practice (4)]. So we shall try to determine its *usefulness*. Theory will thus be used in a practical way. The resulting applications will always be based on general theory. For example, a particular sedative will always be part of a universal law that explains the relation between specific chemical substances and the brain.

At this level, theory serves as a guide for practice, since it enables one to make technological discoveries.

Third relation: Finalities and means. One can establish another relation between Theory (3) and Practice (3), that is, the relation between the finalities and the means. In the same way that a technological discovery is ruled by a universal law, the means used are particular rules based on general finalities. In this relation between means and ends, one must try to achieve *efficiency*. The general finalities will help to uncover the necessary means, but they may have to be changed somewhere along the way because they are impossible to achieve.

Fourth relation: Describing and prescribing. Whether descriptive or useful, theory inevitably leads to the following question: "What should we do?" Regarding this discovery or that situation, one must often settle the question. Should we encourage abortion? Should we agree to intervention in genetics? This fourth relation brings forward the question *should* as related to the concept *is*. This is where ethics and science meet. The problem here has to do with what is *justice*. What course must one follow? This fourth relation brings about the problem that results from the divergence between what is and what should, between describing and prescribing, between a vision of reality and an ideal. This is not a problem of understanding but a problem of the transformation of the reality. The relation between theory and practice at this level is rather special: We have two different kinds of language—one descriptive, the other prescriptive—that are side by side, but the relation between the two is not as logical as it first seems. This I will explain later. Whereas in other circumstances one could perceive the relation between theory and practice, here the two different kinds of languages are totally independent. Strictly speaking there is no such thing as a logical relation between description and prescription or rule. For example, there is no relation between one's knowledge about abortion (the procedures for performing an abortion) and the rule governing one's decision to ask for an abortion (see Figure 10.2).

Four Types of Research Connected to These Four Relations

Fundamental research deals with the understanding of reality, of what *is* without any mention of ethics or usefulness. It is the simple drawing of a

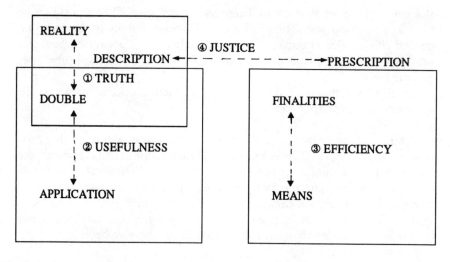

FIGURE 10.2   The Relations Between Theory and Practice

picture representing what is going on. This basic type of research goes with the first relation between theory and practice.

Applied research deals with the transformation into useful products of discoveries made at the fundamental research level. This type of research is slightly technological but does not include questions of ethics. Applied research deals with the *how* and goes with the second relation established between theory and practice. The first type of research applies to the physicist, while the second applies to the engineer.

Operational research deals with the transformation of reality. It has to do with finding the most efficient way of achieving goals that are set right from the start and are not problematic. Nor are these goals questionable. People working in this field are sometimes called "social engineers."

Action research deals with two different kinds of language: descriptive and prescriptive. It can be based on discoveries made at the fundamental or the applied research level, but it also brings out the problem of what is *justice*. And even when one has discovered what *must be*, there is yet the need to find the most efficient ways of achieving that finality. The most important thing in action research is to determine what one must do. For example, one takes a discovery at the fundamental research level (nuclear fission), then tries to put it to use in a technological perspective (the atomic bomb), but is faced with one last question: "Should this discovery be diffused?" The moral question is the problem of action research (see Figure 10.3).

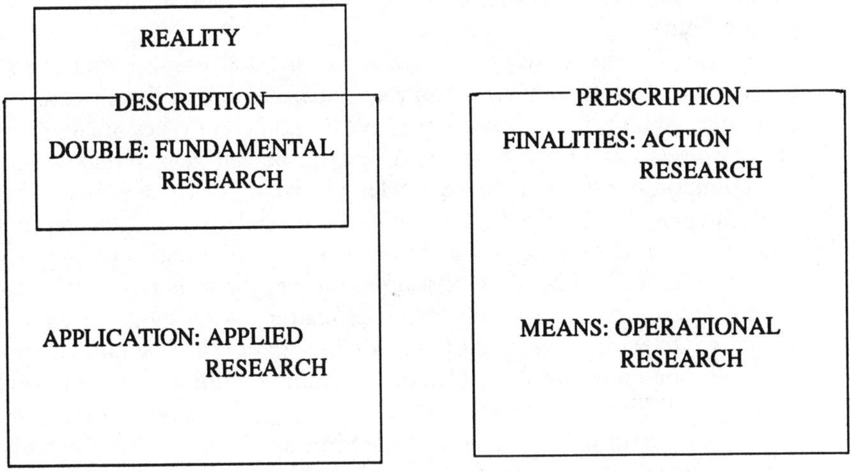

```
REALITY

DESCRIPTION                    PRESCRIPTION

DOUBLE: FUNDAMENTAL            FINALITIES: ACTION
    RESEARCH                       RESEARCH



APPLICATION: APPLIED          MEANS: OPERATIONAL
        RESEARCH                  RESEARCH
```

FIGURE 10.3   Types of Research

QUESTION TWO: WHAT EFFECTS RESULT
FROM THIS COMBINATION?

We have said that the first meaning of theory is a copy or a reproduction of reality. We know also that there have been throughout history significant *epistemes* (that is, paradigms that help us to understand reality). Henri Atlan suggests we call "crystal" and "smoke" two of these paradigms (1979). Briefly, crystal represents something repetitive, symmetrical, stable, hierarchical. Research that is based on a crystalline vision tries to separate every variable and to bring out the object under study. Those doing the research are thus "objective," they are "outside witnesses." The type of laboratory research that deals with stable situations is often referred to as a positivist model of research (Checkland, 1976).

This model is opposed by Atlan to the smoke concept, which applies to things that are different, unstable, asymmetrical, uncontrollable. Most modern scientists work at this level, trying to explain current instabilities and disasters (Thom), nonequilibrium systems (Prigogine), and so forth. Briefly, one finds oneself completely taken up by the Brownian movement.

Keeping that in mind, I can now grasp the problem: I have come to realize that while most authors consider action research as a type of research whose final purpose is to change reality, they keep opposing action research to research work done in laboratories. They think they cannot succeed unless they use a "smoke" method.

As for me, I contend that when one sets a rule, the approach that serves to describe the phenomenon can in no way be used to determine the content of these rules. Why is it so? Because we have two different types of language that have no relation with each other. A description can help to understand what is going on but it cannot serve in telling us what finality to pursue. The scientific language is descriptive, at least in the formulation of its sentences. Whether it is based on a crystal or smoke *episteme,* scientific language can only tell us what *is.* The question relating to the act, the *should,* according to the given description, is a totally different matter and belongs to ethics, which has to do with irrefutable opinions rather than refutable knowledge. Lyotard says our values are suspended in the air and cannot be deduced from descriptions (1979a). Everyone knows, for example, that smoking is harmful. The Department of Health and Welfare in Canada even advises against inhaling on each pack of cigarettes. Science has established a relation between smoking and ill health. This situation has been clearly described, explained, and expected. There follows the rule: Do not inhale. This prescription does not belong to the field of science, but to ethics. It is not a conclusion put forward by scientists and describing a situation, but rather a direct order. To try to be careful with one's health has nothing to do with science; it is a strictly personal matter and one's own choice. Thus I am surprised to see that the debate about action research always deals with controversy brought about by the arguments of crystal and smoke. It seems to me that the problem of the nature of action research should be expressed in terms of descriptive language versus the prescriptive language. Whether the descriptive language be expressed with the crystal or smoke perspective does not matter for understanding action research. The confusion that characterizes most authors results from the use of the words "theory" and "practice," to which they give different meanings. So I say that the authors dealing with action research have missed the combination of theory and practice. This (bad) encounter has unfortunate effects. The relation most authors have established between theory and practice does not necessarily bring about the following smoke effects: Action research is done with groups or in the field. These effects may be encountered in other types of research. This confusion unfortunately prevents the diffusion of effects that might not necessarily be immediately related to the elements brought together but that nevertheless are not in complete opposition to them. Indeed, action research may very well take place in one's office and be done alone. Finally, this confusion brings out an effect that is impossible to obtain any other way: One cannot set a rule from a description, that is, a scientifically set rule.

TEN DARING STATEMENTS CONCERNING ACTION RESEARCH

1. *Action research is not in the least concerned with a physical place in particular.* It can take place anywhere—in one's office, in one's mind.

2. *Action research is not specifically concerned about time.* That is, it is not concerned with time spent in the laboratory or the actual time in an institution.

3. *Action research is not really concerned with groups.* It can be done either alone or with others. To have people participate in the process of action research is only strategy; it is not effect following from the combination of description and prescription. It is not a characteristic that permits the definition of action research.

4. *There is no such thing as a theoretical problem.* All problems are real and result in an obligation. One has to react to the problem. It is like receiving an order.

5. *Action research is above all a matter of language.* Action research will take place depending on the way a question has been asked. In this perspective, there are only theoretical problems.

6. *One can be doing research in a school without its being action research.* All depends on the way the question has been put forward. A question such as "Is there any relation between a teacher's positive reinforcements and the students' performance?" does not lead to action research.

7. *Research that is limited to a description serves only as a contribution to disciplines, such as psychology and sociology, and does not help in establishing finalities.*

8. *If the prescriptions are opinions, then action research is based upon opinions.* Some opinions may be better constructed than others.

9. *To say what action research must be is to give an opinion or to set a rule.* What action research *must* be would thus be open to endless discussion. And if a particular action research prescribes something, this prescription is also an opinion; and while not refutable, it is debatable.

10. *When saying what action research is one gives a refutable opinion. The criteria are then the truth. But when looking for the truth, one can get lost in the midst of the different essences, which are all based on opinions, so I would rather deal with what action research can do, than with what action research is.* In this manner, the opinion can be replaced by a point of view. One can combine theory and practice to define action research (such a combination is possible), but only insofar as the combination is successful. These debates on action research that focus on theory and practice have missed the combination, since the meaning of each word has never been defined and has produced bad effects. The authors wished to be exact (that is to say, consistent with reality

and the *truth*), but all they have managed to do is to be obscure, while all along they should have been *precise without necessarily being exact.*

REFERENCES

Atlan, H. (1979). *Entre le cristal et la fumée: Essai sur l'organisation du vivant.* Paris: Seuil.
Checkland, P. B. (1976). Science and the systems paradigms. *International Journal of General Systems, 3* (2).
Levy-Bruhl, L. (1971). *La morale and la science des moeurs.* Paris: PUF.
Lyotard, J.-F. (1979a). *Au juste.* Paris: Christian Bourgeois.
Lyotard, J.-F. (1979b). *La condition postmoderne.* Paris: Minuit.
Lyotard, J.-F. (1983). *Le différent.* Paris: Minuit.
Rosset, C. (1979). *L'objet singulier.* Paris: Minuit.
Serres, M. (1977). *La naissance de la physique dans le texte de Lucrece.* Paris: Minuit.
Serres, M. (1983). *Le livre des fondations.* Paris: Grasset.

CHAPTER 11

Traces at Work from Different Places

JACQUES DAIGNAULT

I was not yet accustomed to the confusion of the cries, laughter, and children's tears in the schoolyard, to the roaring of short and irregular steps in the corridors and on the terrazo stairs, or to the crescendo of tables and chairs "gnashing their legs against the hardwood," but I started to fear and hate school: the sound of the restraining "clapper." Maybe I did not even hear it. The silence that fell then, sharp, yet reverberating drier and harder than the ebony or oakwood from which it was nevertheless emanating. More unbearable silence, the unforgettably stern look of the regulating authority that was in my first teacher's hands.

WHISPERS

I had to break that silence. At 5 years of age, I did not find anything better than the wheezing of asthma. This produced the desired reprieve. Peace in my room. Pleased to be there, I found that time stopped, that the regiment of school vanished, once I was no longer subjected to it. I took an inventory of all that school deprived me of; I pondered unpretentiously. I was perfectly happy.

But there is no stopping progress. Medical marvels put an end to my escape mechanism. Progress imperatively brought me back into the reality of life: school. Of course, I tried various scams to evade school: getting wet, running, sliding on the spring ice; it was unintentional, but they did not believe me for long. I learned a fear of dogs. A German shepherd that I met on my way to school stole my recorder; actually, I just gave it to him and ran away; I was scared to death. But I told everybody the dog took my recorder for a bone. That was going too far. Nobody believed me. I insisted. They gave me a dog. I was forced to adapt myself to school routine. I learned gradually to compensate for the tediousness that school inspired. Practicing a musical instrument made me hear a new art of rhythm and rest, of time and silence. I have not forgotten the tactile pleasure of fingering a guitar nor the whispering created going up and down the strings.

Today, neither wheezing nor playing guitar, I know another rest: soundless whispering and a quiver of eternity. Fetal reminiscence of world filtered from the womb. I prick my ears toward the origin of my ignorance: the questionnaire of the being, the answer of which is in a constant state of flux. Wheezing and whispering move into my soul unformed "expressibles." I am discovering in my skin a new body and with my ears a new soul: my audio-tactile body is my soul, the undying trace of my education. My link in language is in transition. I am confident. The next century will be ours.

A "t" TOO MANY

Dryad

Once upon a time, there was a nymph living in a tree, in the womb [*sein*] of a tree; a beech tree [*hêtre*] I guess. Some say it was an apple tree; because of the call [*appel*] of being.

There were three, Yesterday, spading [*bêche*] on the beach [*bêcha*]; working [*bûcher*] very hard. They did not find the fruit; only her forbidden lips: the godlike bark of the beech [text—discourse = *dius cortex*]; not yet dry. XeroX. X, or maybe I, will be [*ero*] X; as for the forthcoming "t" standing for "I." From Eros, x = x: copy; but no source, no target; no first hand, no secondary sources: copy of a "t" still alive; curriculum not yet dry.

Id

I am writing at Saussure's dictation (Strarobinski, 1971, 1979); but as if it was at Roussel's (Roussel, 1963, 1975; Foucault, 1963, 1986), inside out. I am trying to save the difference itself, the passage from anagrams to semiotics: the passage itself; Roussel before he died. In order to write, Roussel used a very special method made of two or three major mechanisms. We could not count all of those, men and women, who also used—and still use—such a method: analogous or even most identical. Actually Saussure comes before Roussel and yet translates him; Serres (1977, 1983) could explain it; Saussure translates Roussel inside out; Foucault probably knew that. I am translating Serres the translator; maybe I am writing at his dictation: matters of rhythms; this should be heard by those who have read Serres, even just a few. I am writing at the dictation of a soul three times drunk with writing. I also read Rousseau [Roussel – Saussure – Rousseau = *soûla*/a soul].

Three hundred pages of those mechanisms. Most of all unreadable; will I ever have, one day, the patience to read those pages? A soul, drunk three times with writing. Confused. At Foucault's dictation, Deleuze (1986, 1988) could explain it. I translate the interpreter: the diversity is a pure inside without any dialectical or analytical relationship to the inside; rather a translation-ship. I am but the effect of a folding, a suture that will not resist for long the passages' forces; impossible to bridge the soul; the infarction is severe. I am even forgetting my name. An unfolded wave carries out the letters, all the letters of my name; throw of the dice [*dé/D*]. *Jactus linguae ad 10^{18}*. Throw of the dice of language; Q times the letters fall. I was right, it is impossible to count up to one quadrillon. The signature is the same; but I forgot myself at the very edge of my last name. Only letters remain, tracing the twofold edge of it: D and T. What remains of my name: a lamb, between T and D, strays to a misspelling [*aignaul* instead of *agneau*]. To extract from the D a written dictionary. I have already begun, I will pursue *ad infinitum*. Still the T remains. I, a "t." Here is a shortened story of I*t*.

It

February 1985. *Pour une esthétique de la pédagogie* is at last on the market; printed, it strengthens my soul. A thousand times my name on a cover page! The suture is resistant; one could think of Narcissus. The printing form gives rise to the public expression of I. A book as a proof of an existing self. At least some pages that have defeated confusion; a public acknowledgment. Diffusion at last. The soul happy to recognize him-herself. I was that one; for one or two hours. Only. Once more, a force was coming to unfold my certainty: an error; the most boring type someone could imagine. A mis-print. Seven years after many efforts to master the understanding of the expression *médiation de pertinence* [mediation of relevance], a "t" too many— on the back cover, at the end of my signature—was transforming the *média-tion* into a *méditation*. It could not be worse; I almost believed it. However, I tried to convince myself that the concept was safely preserved inside the book; the exhibition of such an error, at the end of my own signature, im-posed itself as the symbol of a failure. So I put my book under a microscope. I was upset. I had paid for a perfect proofreading; I was naive; I did not really understand what proofreading was about. A close reading of the text itself could only reveal the difference between a word and a nonword, be-tween a word correctly spelled—lexically and grammatically—and the same word misspelled. *Méditation* was not the right word but it was written rightly. No one to blame. The anagram of my name—even though I was not aware of it at that time—clearly celebrates what happened: a throw of the dice of language. To pay attention to such a number 10^{18} is to realize my troubles are far from over. The happiness I thought I wanted could not be found in a narcissistic suture of the soul. Errors? There were many. I no longer count them according to species and genres: letters, the publisher, and even the thesis itself. I was born to be confused. I am writing at the dictation of errors.
The "t" too many is not isolated; I could rewrite it under Foucault's

dictation: a statement (Foucault, 1969, 1972). Four other misprints have been spotted so far: *était/étant* [was/being], *en/ne* [in/not], *monadisation/no-madisation,* and *Lapassage/Lapassade* [a proper name that sounds like "the passage"]. Those four errors have in common a balance, either by inversion or substitution of letters; a pure material exchange of letters among themselves: no deficit, no profit. A pure circulation of change neither related to exchange value nor to usage value; old money for new: the Saturnian verse, Saussure's anagrams. Transliteration of signs. Can they be exchanged for something else? The question is difficult. This text is betting every word it is made of on that question. Can the "t" too many be free from the labor I paid for it (exchange value), without falling back to the fiction of a political economy based on usage value? Baudrillard (1976) could explain it. I am writing at the dictation of flashes. One flash after the other. I know the value of detours: the *passage value.* To possess one's soul in patience. The flash is so fragile, in spite of its power.

I found more errors: i/n, e/n–n/e, m/n–n/m, g/d. The sign "/" means "instead of." I did not take that sign by chance; it comes from another misprint. It is found in the earlier work of Rousseau, in the original publishing of his very first essay in 1742: *Project concerning new symbols for music* (1742/ 1982). The first time Rousseau uses the sign "/", he is but a sharp transliterator; almost a flat semiotician. "The *sharp* is expressed by a little stroke crossing the note obliquely from left to right. *Sol* sharp, for example, will appear as *5, fa* sharp is *4.*" The second time Rousseau uses the same sign, it takes the place of another sign "\". "The *flat* is indicated by a similar stroke drawn in the opposite direction, *7 2.*" While everyone expects a backslash "\" on the "2," the publisher repeats the slash "/"; and forever: even subsequent editions repeat the misprint (Rousseau, 1979, 1982). Another substitution by inversion; the wrong sign: the risk of any transliteration. This is an anagrammatical error, not a semiotical one. The passage between both Saussure(s). The passage is difficult, particularly risky. Roussel killed himself; perhaps. Saussure killed a soul; maybe. I mean that running after rigorous demonstrations and after confirmations is a hunt: literally; for the semiotician reason is not completely innocent. "From Plato and a tradition which lasted throughout the classical age, knowledge is a hunt. To know is to put to death—to kill the lamb, deep in the woods, in order to eat it. . . . To know is to kill, to rely on death, as in the case of the master and the slave. . . . Today we live out the major results of these wolfish actions. For the 'I,' who played the role of the lamb by minimizing his powers and placing the de-clared powers upstream from himself, this 'I' is the wolf. . . . It has taken the wolf's place, its true place. The reason of the strongest is reason *by itself. Western man is a wolf of science*" (Serres, 1983, p. 28). Saussure, judge of Fer-dinand, wanted proofs of his innocence; he found none. Maybe the poet had that proof but he refused to give it to him. Then Saussure, Inquisitor of himself, condemned in a final judgment his own hypothesis on anagrams; he started semiotics. The poet kept silent; he probably knew the critical tribunal was calling for executions. To know is to kill. The poet's silence, perhaps confirming the wolf's critique, perhaps not, makes difficult the complete execution of the death penalty. Thinking is still alive. But the play is tight. More and more. Even the middle attracts new people committed to reducing it to a matter of knowledge, to a new epistemological stake: the wolf's place. Thinking happens only between suicide and murder, between miscarried anagrams and applied semiotics; at the letter. Between nihilism and terrorism. The passage is really hazardous. We always invite the third, but only to exclude it. And the exclusion is all the more violent because the wolf is there. I am in danger. Read *Le parasite* (Serres, 1980); *Little Red Riding Hood* would do as well.

Pour une esthétique de la pédagogie was about the passage between nihilism and terrorism. My rendezvous with that "t" made the passage more narrow yet. My name's throw of the die [*D(é)*] is partly responsible for what happened *there:* a frightening inmixture in my last name, just between the twofold edge of it, between the **throw** of the D(ice) and the "t" too many [*de trop*]. In *aignauL,* I cannot not read a lamb [*agneau/aignau*] the wolf [*Loup*] has not yet eaten; the wolf [*Loup*] missing the louse [*pou*]: the para**site**; *i–e* surrounding the "t" (ite) and echoing back *i/e* in *aignau/agneau* [what remains in my last name/lamb].

It is now possible to transcribe the central part of that transliteration. "i/e" repeated four times in my book; up to the "t." The anagram transcribed in the semiotics of my work; but neither the error of the latter, nor the application of the former: only the transliteration from one to the other, *i.e.* passages between death twice—evaded. The "t" of Translation and of *Tiers* [either middle or third]: Included-Excluded [i/e]; to include, *there*, rather than to exclude [*en/ne*]; to understand the "t" is a monad, a nondivisible sign running upon fron**tiers** [*monadisation/nomadisation*]; an eternal passage between signifieds and signifiers. Mediation: the presence of a third, the signified says; an excluded middle, what the signifier does: no "t" too many. Meditation: the exclusion of any third party, the signified says; an included middle, what the signifier does: a "t" too many. That is what every dictionary says.

The "t" too many has a "meaning," finally; I provided one: X maybe stands for Dissemination and/or Logical square. Maybe. The soul can dress [*panser*] his wounds, benefit from a rest. But it will not last long; the soul is drunk, three times, with writing. Saussure has had enough, let us put his soul to rest. Everything is calm now; let us benefit from a rest. It will not last long. Let us go once again, without any fear, towards the "t."

There were four errors inside the book: all substitutions and one error on the back cover: a supplement. That makes three different series: the "t" alone, the series of included letters "ienmng," and the one of excluded letters "nnemnd." The translationship between included and excluded letters made sense of the "t." But there is more: a direct translationship between the "t" and the included letters, a missing letter for a letter too many, the missing "a" in the series of included letters: ienmnga = meaning. One could even add the third series: two vertical crosswords: "name" and "ind" [index]; and a horizontal anagram: "end." I translate. In the end, the meaning of the "t" is nothing but the index of my name.

n
meaning
m n
e nd

ITER-ITER

I do not really know how to deal with such a result; I am afraid to be confused. I knew, somehow, the new sutures of my soul would not resist more; my double is still the work of Narcissus, just a mirror of an ego. It will not be long before I will have another soul attack. Translation is a passage; in many ways. Confusion is always at stake. The translation of the "t" is not ended yet, and will not ever be. How many errors yet to be spotted in *Pour une esthétique de la pédagogie*? How many other transliterations in the neighborhood of those forthcoming errors? And even how many other transcriptions—maybe better—of the errors already spotted? The passage value offers no guarantee of success. About his special method, Roussel maybe writes at Kant's dictation: "Still, one needs to know how to use it. For just as one can use rhymes to compose good or bad verses, so one can use this method to produce good or bad works" (Roussel, 1975, p. 11). Artistic productions do not rely on a method, *stricto sensu*, but on a manner (Kant, 1790/1979). Method is singular and definite: THE way; manner is singular but indefinite: A way. Curriculum translation is always plural: WAYS; neither definite nor indefinite. That is said by the transliterative difference itself between "transliteration" and "translation": ITER, what remains from a Sausserian difference between both words. In Latin, *iter* means 'way' [*hodos* in Greek); as a prefix, it also means 'repetition'. I say it again: "I" = re–"t." In the work of Roussel, anagrams (anaphones, actually, as in the work of Saussure) were only a way: *iter* or *hodos;* a manner. Saussure perhaps tried to embed anagrams in THE way of semiotics: *trans-iter* or *meta-hodos* [to go across the way]; a method. I am trying to conceive of passages in many ways: *iter-iter* [way & repetition]; WAYS. Not all the ways—only some—but always plural. I try to transcribe flashes that emerge from the play of transliteration; that makes perhaps a translation.

What kind of translation am I talking about? Serres brings Descartes' *Meditations* out of a La Fontaine fable or a locomotive out of the work of a nineteenth-century thinker, a theorem out of a narrative, a legend out of a demonstration and a demonstration out of a legend. Here it is not all matter of hunting for more or less ingenious parallels, but of *translating* word for word. As a translator, Serres would define science as the set of messages that last, optimally invariant, through any strategy of translation. Deduction and induction [*de/in-ducere*] would be the most stable means of transportation; beneath that threshold of a maximum of stability, one would find other cultural areas: production, reproduction (. . .) [*pro/repro-ducere*] would vary after their difference, that is nothing but the variation itself (Serres, 1974). For him, translation (in French *traduire* = *tra-ducere*) seems to be the passage itself from one point to another. Though there is more than this in his work; Serres is also an ethnician of passages; his main concern is to criticize any wrong translation—any distortion—that would lead [*ducere*] to death. I am seduced [*se-ducere*] by his work, but I am wondering if his concept of passage is appropriate to education [*ex-ducere*].

What kind of passage am I trying to define? What does it mean to pass? What is the relationship (translationship) between to translate and to pass? I have translated a "t" too many; what does it mean? I have tried to find passages between the variation and the invariable, between both: not from one to the other, but passages as their absolute difference, the *différance* between death, twice evaded. I have translated my own dissertation because of a "t" too many. Was it the same synthesis?

Why that question?

Two questions on line; I am trying to answer the second one. I know they will ask me why I am doing so.

That is a third question: Why to answer the question of the relevance of the first question, instead of answering the question itself?

If I could answer the second question, they would not even ask either the first or the third one. They might be disappointed, even angry with me; they might say I am confused.

The translation of a "t" too many is an answer to the second question. For translation is passages, here, between answers and questions, not the (or even a) passage from a question to an answer, but their absolute difference (*différance*); I could write at Deleuze's dictation (Deleuze, 1968) as well as Derrida's (1967, 1976). The poet did not answer the question of Saussure. For such a question always implies an answer the destiny of which is to close space, that kind of space the opening of which is called, sometimes, a problem. If not to kill it, either the problem was not a problem—a difficulty maybe—or the answer was not an answer—a passage, maybe. Amazing, I am almost writing at Chomsky's dictation (1975). I insist. To translate the "t" too many is a problem: still alive. I am writing at Nietzsche's dictation: to translate life in joyful wisdom, gay knowledge. Thinking, maybe.

After I*t* had been really disturbed by an error, the soul is now recovering health little by little; I am recovering my double on the side of object, in my relationship to object. The soul was alone with I*t*self: meditative. My challenge was to recover subjectivity in my translationship with the world as chaos. Unfolded by error, margin, chaos, chance—the absolute diversity— the soul has been finally refolded on I*t*self, happy again: meaningful for I*t*self. That, once again, will not last long. For behind I*t*s back, while I*t* was painfully recovering health—after struggling with chaos—other souls were protesting against I*t*s originality. The "t" too many was not mine; it resulted from a mediation. The soul has now to deal with other souls; the "t" was a double "t": X*ero*X.

DOUBLE "t"

February 1985; once again. In the French magazine *Lire,* B. Pivot (1985) has a great story entitled "Horreur! le 't' avait disparu" [What a shock! The "t" had disappeared]. Jacques Audiberti, a French novelist, complains he lost a "t." In the sentence "*tu est beau*" ["you is beautiful"], the pronoun is not the subject of a phrase but the subject of a proposition: as in "the pronoun *you* is beautiful." That was a kind of pun ("*est*" and "*es*" have the same sound in French), and it was predictable the proofreaders would make the following correction "*tu es beau*" ["you are beautiful"]. That happened. Several times. Each time Audiberti was adding the "t," proofreaders were taking it away. Upset, Audiberti gave the final manuscript, with the "t," to the printing press people himself; from hand to hand. His soul was completely reassured; no more proofreading that would chop the "t." And yet the book was printed without the "t," it had disappeared. What happened? It seems the "t" crossed the Atlantic to find a place in my own book!

Because of the "t," I have been involved in a long meditation, while Audiberti was a victim of mediation. The day his book was to be printed, somebody working at the printing press saw the sentence "*tu est beau*" and edited the text, which became "*tu es beau.*"

The "t" travels a lot. It is involved in many passages. Having crossed the Atlantic from France to Québec, the "t" has not been exchanged [*échangé*] for something (money, sense, etc.), it just moved from place to place [*changé de place*]. Lacan (1966) could explain it, Derrida could as well: the "t" as a hazardous supplement resulting from a trace. The "t" is more than a symbol *there*, it belongs to skin. Does it make a difference?

It would be difficult to reduce the value of the "t" to an exchange value, while the "t" is maybe an exchange, but for nothing else than itself; difficult either to reduce its value to an usage value, while its main usage is to be exchanged for itself. That must make a difference, all the difference. I am perhaps writing at the dictation of a new political economy: the value of the "t" is a **passage** value. The absolute difference as passages. We already guess education is to cross fron**tiers.** We are close, now, to curriculum: to run upon frontiers.

The soul disturbed by a "t" is no more alone; I*t* must share I*t*s chance with at least another "self"; maybe with every one. My soul does not only result from a "t" the translation of which would be, for I*t*self, **the** way to claim to be constitutive of I*t*s meaning for me. It is also matter to be folded by another soul resulting from the same "t," and the translation of which could be constitutive as well of my self: my soul's image. Everything is in everything? When t*here* are many connections, the absolute diversity—chaos—comes back to surface. The not yet differentiated stock of differences—that chaotic bottom, without which differences could never emerge—shows itself with the difference, when the difference is thought as an absolute difference: a unilateral distinction, Deleuze would say (1968). The "t" is maybe the same in both works, but only as it is not really differentiated from that stock of differences to which it still belongs; the "t" as a flash, a lightning in the dark sky. When I say confusion, I mean such a stock of differences that come suddenly into view under the light of a flash. When I say frontier or absolute difference, I mean to think of the difference itself: flashes that make thinking possible. When I say passages, I mean the impulse that goes back and forth between chaos and flashes and that makes differentiation possible. And when I say translation, I mean to open such passages: everything is in everything, *in many ways only.*

SENSUAL

Deleuze (1969, 1989) acknowledges at least two concepts of difference: differential and differences of intensity. Let us try to understand the interaction of these two concepts of difference in a famous reversal made by Deleuze, the reversal of models and copies.

In *Logique du sens* (1969), Deleuze clearly establishes that Plato is not so much fighting copies as fighting false copies, simulacra. Plato cannot do without copies because good copies are the only things that the philosopher, who has comtemplated ideas or models, has to offer. Plato's entire strategy consists, consequently, in fighting forgers: sophists and poets whose works are merely simulacra of ideas. And this strategy is one of selection and rivalry: selecting the line of true pretenders. Reversing Plato, therefore, will not be moving from model to copies, but from good copies to false ones, to simulacra. But once one truly understands that the simulacrum is in no way a copy, both model and copy equally are reversed. And that is precisely what Plato would have understood and what then would be at the basis of his relentless determination to fight false pretenders. Deleuze, therefore, proposes to pursue Plato in the same way Plato pursues forgers; there is something Derridean in this strategy; it is in Plato's text itself that Deleuze will find the means to reverse it. Socrates, in fact, cannot defeat the sophists unless he becomes one of them. But by becoming one of them he makes the simulacrum surface and he abolishes rivalry. Plato, obviously, does not discuss this; but Deleuze will grasp "this momentary flash of light" in order to establish his critique of representation. The simulacrum is an image resembling nothing, a pure sense effect. And that is precisely what sense is: something attributed to the body through the intermediary of language but that does not exist; a pure effect resembling nothing, but that nothing resembles either. Deleuze shows this in several ways. And each time sense is defined as difference: the differential play within the idea on the transcendental level, and the difference of intensity on the body at the empirical level. One of the clearest ways Deleuze does this is in his double recourse to the Stoics and Epicureans.

Deleuze discovers "the impalpable" in the Epicureans and "the incorporeal" in the Stoics. But as Foucault (1970) has remarked, it all adds up to a "materiality of the incorporeal," a splendid "metaphysics of extra-being," a metaphysics freed from the pursuit of illusions and engaged, rather, in "dis-illusioning fantasies." The incorporeal is sense as event: what happens to the body through the intermediary of language but does not exist; something Deleuze makes no bones about reproaching as the "speech act" in *Milles plateaux* (Deleuze & Guattari, 1980). But our conclusion will not be that sense is "speech act" because "the impalpable," too, is of the same order as sense, as a simulacrum or a fantasy; and a fantasy is not a "speech act." Foucault (1970) has clearly shown that the function of sense in Deleuze is to make the class of event and the class of fantasy resonate: the incorporeal and the impalpable. Now, what sort of sense lies in the direction of fantasy? Let us try to untangle all of this by taking things in order: first Epicurean atomism and then the Stoic philosophy of language.

The Epicureans proceed by analogy between objects of thought and objects of senses: "the atom is to thought what the sensible object is to senses" (Deleuze, 1969, p. 310). And, although the atom is indivisible, it is made up of thought minima just as the sensible and divisible object is made up of sensible minima. Secondly, the Epicurean method is a method of transition; one moves from the thought to the sensible, and also inversely as objects decompose or compose themselves. And this play of composition-decomposition is precisely the same as the falling of atoms into the void, where they meet and become organized or repel each other. For these encounters to take place, however, an original direction for the falling atom must be imagined, a sort of differential: some sort of angle behind or ahead, which Epicureans called the clinamen and which is linked, as Deleuze demonstrates, to the Epicurean theory of time. One has only to pursue the analogy: time is also formed from temporal minima; a minimum of continuous time exists during which an atom can move in a single direction. And as the atom is apprehended by thought, the atom moves at the same speed as thought; just as quickly. But the clinamen is even faster than this smallest bit of continuous time; therefore, it is faster than thought; one can never, therefore, think of the clinamen without the atom whose differential (once again) as the presumed, original synthesis of its direction it is. This would all be merely useless detail if the analogy stopped here. But the theory of the clinamen is also analogous to the theory of the simulacrum, and is impossible to understand without it. Because sensible time is also composed of temporal minima; a minimum of continuous time exists in which sensible objects are perceived; if they are not within this time they are imperceptible. The simulacrum is, precisely, issued outside of this time; therefore, it is not sensible. But the images it produces are entirely perceptible; they are the images of objects composed by the fall of atoms. We will not go into detail here concerning the types of simulacra; suffice to say simply that the best known are the fantasies against whose conflict the Epicureans established the most important distinction in their system: false and true infinities. Fantasies are images that enjoy perfect independence with regard to objects. This is a consequence of the multiplicity and the nonsynchronic nature of times or speeds relating to the play of images, certain of which—the fantasies—take the place of the object itself. The result is the illusion of an infinite number of objects and, therefore, of an infinite number of pleasures or sufferings associated with sensible objects. Simulacra inspire a false sentiment of will and desire in sensibilities. They produce the mirage of a false infinity in the images they form, and give birth to the double illusion of an infinite capacity for pleasures and an infinite possibility of torments. And that, claim the Epicureans, is what is disturbing to the soul. Because "the fear of infinite punishments is the perfectly natural penalty for limitless desires" (Deleuze, 1969, p. 316). The soul will have to survive the body indefinitely in order to expiate the limitless pleasures of the body. All religious morality will, therefore, forbid pleasure;

the selection of good copies is a form of rigorous asceticism that aims at rejecting or even destroying fantasies. Because we are afraid of them. However, there is no reason to be afraid of them, the Epicureans claim; fantasies do not exist but rather constitute what is impalpable in the sensible, the occasion for a pleasure that is not wrong and not guilty. Producing them and enjoying them is the occasion for an aesthetic of sense. This, of course, has far-reaching effects ethically: an obsession with relating images to their sensible or thought objects, as one would relate a copy to its model, becomes the symptom of an unhappy consciousness that is the victim of a disordered soul—which is the real cause of evil. Producing sense and enjoying it provide the antidote; which, we have said, is what differences do. And differences are related to the differential play of sense.

When Deleuze says that sense—in the same way as the clinamen and the simulacrum—is differential, he is saying at least three things: The differential is symbolic, the differential reverses models and copies by defining them both as independent variables, and, finally, the differential maintains an essential affinity with differences in intensity. Let us try to take the Stoics as a basis for understanding the two first theses. Later we will analyze the third on the basis of the concept of differen(ç)iation ["c" stands for differences and "t" for differential].

Starting off from Bréhier's (1928) thesis on incorporeals in ancient Stoicism, Deleuze raises the question again of the essential relationship of the event to Anglo-American "nonsense"; *Logique du sens* is a good treatment of this *a propos* Lewis Carroll. The event is that which happens to a body, but as a language predicate that becomes attributed to a body. The event is on the borderline between words and things: the circulation of sense between at least two classes, the class of places and the class of occupants. And it is *a propos* this play of classes that differential sense must be understood as symbolic: the value of places, no less than that of occupants, is positionally differential, exactly like signifiers and signifieds in language. Nothing of what Deleuze says about this is original. It is more *a propos* the relationship between classes that he will draw Stoicism's extreme conclusions, in order to attribute them to structuralism: no causality in classes and no determination of one by the other; classes maintain differential relationships between themselves, and that is what produces sense as an event and as a fantasy. Or rather it is the circulation of sense as fantasy-event in classes that prevents these from being taken for models and copies. This is not an easy thesis. Let us go back to the principal theses of the Stoics to try to understand.

For them everything that exists is body; language too is body, because it exists. And bodies form a network of causes among themselves. But language concerns not just bodies, it also concerns effects—effects that do not exist.

Effects also form a network among themselves. But there is no real relationship between causes and effects; causes refer to causes and effects to effects; effects are in a quasi-causal relationship among themselves. What are we to understand by that? The explanation is contained in their philosophy of language. Language is made up of three kinds of words: nouns, adjectives, and verbs. Nouns are used to designate bodies: actions and passions. All of that exists, all of that is body. But what happens to the body, the event, does not exist; it is something expressible only in language , but it is attributed to the body insofar as it is expressed by a verb. It is not a question of a body attribute, however, but rather of a language attribute. The theory of what is expressible is, in fact, a theory of interrelations between words and things: the logical predicate expressed by a verb is not attributed to the subject of the proposition but directly to the body designated by the subject of the proposition. As in Bréhier's famous example: flesh is cut by a scalpel. Flesh and scalpel are two bodies, but the fact of being cut—the event—is not a third body but solely something expressible, which, however, is attributed to the flesh and not to the word designating it. The event acts, therefore, on the surface of things as it does on the interior of language; it is thereby on the borderline between words and things and does not ex-ist, but sub-sists or in-sists, solely, in things and in language. This interplay is precisely what Deleuze refers to as sense, as the fourth dimension of the proposition: "being cut" does not designate any body (designation), does not express any belief by any subject (manifestation), and does not belong to any determination that is completely logical (signification). In fact, "being cut" is not a logical predicate of the proposition, but a predicate of the body. Now we must figure out how all that is differential.

Sense, Deleuze writes, has something structural about it: at least two classes, one of which is designated as "signifier" and the other as "signified," two classes defined by the dynamics of a symbolic exchange of places in the signifier and of occupants in the signified and finally a paradoxical instance circulating in both classes at once: an occupant without a place and, at the same time, a place without an occupant. This third condition is sense, forever deferring the complete meeting between signifier and signified: the plenitude of self-presence in the world. This is the level on which the reversal of models and copies is easiest to grasp; because it is always possible, Deleuze suggests, to define the model and the copy as a relationship between signifier and signified. Consequently, it will be understood that reversing the model cannot be placing the copy in the model's place, but producing the simulacrum deferring the meeting of model and copy, precisely; producing that which the signifier always-already lacks, but which the signified has too much of: producing differentiating sense.

SENSUALITY

Deleuze probably never clearly stated that sense was sensual; nevertheless, we will go so far as to maintain this is so. But on condition that sensual be understood by an analogy to sense: the sensual is the fourth dimension of the body; like an invisible skin that only the differential sense can sense a sort of audio-tactile sixth sense constituting a true subconscious for the body. A subconscious for the problem of the resistance of the subject; the subconscious as borderline between the signifier's unconscious and the overflowing consciousness of the signified, a surface for the inscription of sense, differentiating bodies and subjects as just so many possible solutions to the problem of the game of dice played by the world, defined as undifferentiated, differentiated, and different-making levels of immanence.

Deleuze's structuralism is entirely contained in his conceptual synthesis of difference. This is because the Idea itself is defined as structure, and structuralism seems the only means by which a genetic method can realize its ambitions: to actualize in real time the virtual singularities distributed in the Idea (Deleuze,1968). But Deleuze's greatest originality consists perhaps in showing that the actualization of differential and conceptual divisions has its cause in what is sensible and, more precisely, in differences of intensity. "It is intensity that dramatizes," writes Deleuze."It is intensity that is expressed immediately in fundamental spatio-temporal dynamisms, and that determines that a differential, 'indistinct' relation in the Idea will become embodied in a distinct quality and a marked duration" (Deleuze, 1968, p. 316). Here we touch upon Deleuze's essential thesis: the inequality of differences of intensity is in no way negative, but constitutes, on the contrary, a pure and positive difference, a distance as affirmation of that which it sets at a distance. Negative is the image of difference reversed, because it is subjected to the exigencies of representation subordinating it to identity; the hypothesis will be put forward that it is, precisely, sense's lack of sensuality that is the cause of this reversal of intensity into a simple symbolic opposition. The subject, it will be suggested, is unlike signs, inseparable from differences of intensity: the workings of differences of intensities of the body-subject determine the Idea's actualization in distinct and differentiated qualities. Put simply: no subject without a body. The subject is therefore produced twice: by the differential and symbolic workings of the Idea—that is its transcendental determination—and by the workings of differences of intensity—its empirical determination. And what is essential about the subject would lie in its affinity with this double determination, Deleuzian transcendental empiricism.

All this revives the question of the subject. Structuralism is right when it throws back into question the central position of the subject in humanism; and it is by insisting on the fact that the subject is symbolically determined;

it succeeds in decentering it, indeed even dissolving it. But that leaves intact the question of the sensible and not merely symbolic relationship of the subject to the body; it is my opinion that Deleuze's merit is in having completely revived this question. It is not a matter of going back to the romantic or phenomenological subject, but of showing that the real fissure of the *I* comes into being also through difference-making and not just through *différance*. And the key concept used by Deleuze is consequently that of individuation. "The essential process of intensive quantities is individuation. Intensity is individualizing, intensive quantities are individualizing. Individuals are signal-sign systems" (Deleuze, 1968, p. 317). The question of signals is taken up again in *Mille plateaux* in reference to the synthesizer: the synthesis of continuous variation; it is precisely at that point that the sensuality of sense is to be found. Not that sense is sensible; its synthesis is. And a synthesis implies a surface for recording differences in intensity, a sort of skin of differentiating sense; the condition without which the subject would never be anything more than a sign in a differentiating structure, or a differentiation subordinated to the identity of the plenitude of consciousness. The individual is not that subject.

> The individual is in no way indivisible, but never stops dividing as he changes his nature. There is no Me in what he expresses; because he expresses Ideas as internal multiplicities made up of differential relations and points that stand out, of pre-individual singularities. And there is no I expressed there either; because there again he is forming a multiplicity of actualization, like a condensation of points that stand out, an open collection of intensities. (Deleuze, 1968, p. 331)

The individual is, in fact, the meeting between an I that is cracked and a Me that is dissolved. This, says Deleuze, is the Nietzschean, or Dionysian, way of going beyond subject-identity toward the thought of differences and the production of sense. Shall we lay bets that the crack and the dissolution within the subject together define the sensuality of sense? That leads to an aesthetics that problematizes the subject instead of excluding it or placing it in the center, aesthetics that does not exclude emotion without reducing everything to it either. The aesthetics proposed by Deleuze goes beyond sentimentality and signification toward sensuality and sense.

TEACHING

The history of arts and the history of sciences are a struggle against prejudices and clichés of an age, while it seems the history of education is an irreducible struggle to find the best prejudices and clichés. Education is a second field of study—I mean a secondary one—because it is an excluded middle, the remains of which are scraps. No more significations, meanings, beauties, and senses. That is what rumor says. Indeed, when one quits the private to be understood by a public audience—the students—one usually feels the pressure to teach narratees how to become identical narrators (Lyotard, 1977).

But there is a gap, a great abyss between what the narratees are and what one thinks they ought to be as narrators. How does one deal with such a gap? Not to care is nihilistic. And to bridge the gap by any means is terroristic (Daignault, 1983, 1985). In both cases, one would encourage students to become stupid. The genesis of good sense and common sense would be issued. And that reinforces what the rumor says: Education is a secondary field of study, a minor one.

But it is not right per se. There is a way to pervert the rumor: to practice education or curriculum itself—the second field of study—as a third we refuse to exclude completely, as simulacrum; to treat pedagogical examples, for instance, as simulacra. Curriculum, I believe, is the excluded middle in the debates between art and science. Let us try to *subsist*. Sense, Deleuze writes (1969), does not ex-(s)ist but sub-sists in the world and in-sists in language.

A Propos of Teaching/Learning Process

Steve Reich's *Violin Phase* (1980) admits of the construction of a listening analogous to the dynamics of differential structuralism, which is highly praised from Nietzsche's perspectivism, down to the more recent writings of Levi-Strauss, Lacan, Barthes, Foucault, Deleuze *et tutti quanti*. It is a melodico-rhythmic cell, comprising ten notes, the musical representation of which is simply transcribed on a stave, as shown in Figure 11.1.

Each of the notes being attacked on the violin strings, touched by the bow, the strident effect of the artist's performance grasps, of the audition, the space of a question: Will one hear something new, even improbable? Three seconds have barely elapsed when the artist repeats a similar attack; again, in

FIGURE 11.1 Musical Representation of Steve Reich's *Violin Phase*

the same space, a question: Has the violinist erred, could it be he lost the technical mastery of a difficult passage, that the repetition would, at least, reveal? The question is yet in our mind, and the same passage is heard again. A listener unfamiliar with repetitive music will surely react promptly with a third question: Can it be that a musical work consists—even if only partly— of the repetition of the Same (especially when the Same is apparently so simplistic and so meager)? And now in the rhythm of a real mathematical progression, the theme reappears, once again, and again . . . up to 15′ 11″.

The answer to the third question is generally the expression of a tenacious prejudice: In spite of the tenuous objective differences heard in Reich's composition, the work actually sounds like a morbid repetition.

But the symbolic death of this work is but the symbol of a more atrocious death: The death of thinking. Who does not grasp the lesson arising from the analogy with structuralism stands no chance to grasp the effect of sense given by the interpretation of *Violin Phase*. In my opinion, this work is a representation, manifestly convincing, of a certain structuralist perspective. The work is a symbol of a paradigm of the difference engendered by the repetition. A signifier series unfolds all along the melodico-rhythmic course: a micro temporal shifting takes place in the repetition itself. After only a few repetitions, the ear inhabits a tridimensional space. For the repetition itself is repeated. A first loop defies the empirical erosion of its usage. The repetitive call is therein engraved and the recording unceasingly repeats it. Thus the interpreter superimposes his performance: but the latter will progressively be shifted in relation to the recording tape: the birth of an echo. And, in a telescopic progression of the shifting, differential values are introduced under the analogical form of signifiers (virtual melodico-rhythmic arrangements). In conformity with the structuralist rules, the number of signifiers is much more numerous than that of the signified (in a chess game, for example, the number of possible moves is much more numerous than that of moves made). But the question of choice is not easy. For in spite of the finite—even very great—number of strictly differential values generated by the product of the repetition and the shifting, each perceived value spans another line of signifiers: culture itself. But it is the intersection of these two sets that will constitute the subsets of the possible aesthetic choices. Namely, with the birth of a counterpoint and of a genuine harmonic layer, and the simultaneous theoretical increase of the number of possibilities, the number of the aesthetic choices decreases. This is a condition without which the choice of the artist would not differ from a cast of the die. But one need only listen to the music of Steve Reich to notice that chance, analogous to that in the poetry of Mallarmé, is never suppressed by a cast of the die. Each of the musical choices of a performer is strictly conditioned by the Occidental culture. The choices, analogous to real signifieds, overlap the shifted repetition. And nothing can prevent the thought that a repetition, shifted on a number of years, would give rise to the birth of one of Bach's fugues. Would that mean, then, that the game of the shifted repetition is limitless? Not necessarily. This depends on the structural strength of the structure of the work, not to reduce the paradoxical instance to the morbid repetition, and, also, of the conjugate strength of the performers and the auditors in giving and hearing the signifieds. Using the case of *Violin Phase,* this twofold set-up is quite easy to illustrate. Let us imagine that the shifting of the repetition is accelerated at a constant speed. There would necessarily happen a moment when the sole differential value created by the shifting will strictly be equal to the repetitive cell itself. The paradoxical instance being, by definition, a floating signifer (a place without an occupant) and a float signified (an occupant without a place), there will surge a first jamming of the structure: the repetitive cell, considered as a signified without a place, will find itself as a place. It might as well be said that the cell will fill itself up; in which case it will be neither a signified without a place nor a signifier without an occupant; it will simply have become a morbid repetition; it will fade out after a few repetitions. As for the second set-up, one need only imagine two cases: The performer does not play any signified, and thus the listener hears nothing but the repetition and a few shiftings; or the interpreter plays signifieds that the listener does not hear, in which case he also hears the repetition and a few shiftings. In both cases the repetition will appear very tedious and will generate no meaningful differences. What comes out of all this is that the paradoxical instance that pervades *Violin Phase*—and this pervading is a *sine qua non* condition of the work—is paradoxically, the repetitive cell itself.

The thesis of the differential structuralism performs this miracle of the *repetition that generates the difference.* There remains to imagine the contrary.

Apply the learning of *Violin Phase* (or Ravel's *Bolero*). One will have to repeat. And as long as one does not master the passage to be repeated, one will repeat. But is any repetition, a repetition after all? Certainly not. When one interprets the composition, *each repetition is strictly identical.* And it is only through the shifting that creeps in the period of repetition, that the differences show up. But, while learning the composition, it stands to reason that one does not repeat exactly in the same way. From one rehearsal to another one rather strives to annul the differences. And each of them reveals one's incapability, at a given moment, to repeat, repeat rigorously, the same passage, as it should be played. The learning process resides in the inverse play of the repetition and the difference. The repetition increases toward identity and the difference decreases to zero. In a way the difference gives birth to the repetition. And this, to the advantage of a repetition, which will decrease to zero (it is no longer heard) and which will increase to identity (only the differences are heard).

Hence learning is relevant to a logic of the signified; and teaching, to a logic of the signifier. And everybody repeats: the teacher, his analogies; the learner, his errors. So that the play of the repetition and the difference digs an abyss in the core of the teaching-learning process. Now, there is a paradoxical instance that circulates in the difference of the teaching-learning process: the "nonsense" of the differential repetition of analogies analogous to themselves. And this *sui-reference* of analogies is itself a function of the differences put forth for the joy of teaching.

I'M A T . . .

I do write. I teach too. I try to think of teachers I know, and to look for words that could dress their wounds; the ones for which we are maybe responsible in curriculum theory. I found a few.

> Too many people are trying to make you feel guilty because of the so-called failure of your work. Please don't listen to them; hatred and frustration always inform their critiques. They are struggling with each other to know who will lead the field; there is no winner yet, and they say it's your fault. Don't believe them. The Right complains, the Left complains, the students, the principals, the parents, the priests, everyone complains about your incapacity to reach the goals which they all know to be the best for you. Don't worry too much; what they all ask you to do is impossible to realize; orders they give you result from their own inability to dream without any idea of vengeance. You know as well as they should know how difficult it is to deal with desire; please don't be trapped in guilt and sadness. They accuse you of not doing enough to change the world. The world is indeed in bad shape; and we need you to change it. But we need you to be serene. Please don't let them make you feel guilty; that is important for you as well as for them. Death is not only your fault.

Acknowledgments

I wish to thank all the people—Bill Pinar, Georges Daignault, Rebecca Martusewicz, Robert McDonald, and Betsy Wing—who helped me with the translation or the editing of the four unpublished manuscripts which this chapter mainly comes from:

Daignault, J. (1983). *Analogy in education: An archaeology without subsoil* (G. Daignault, Trans.). Paper presented at the annual meeting of the Bergamo Conference on Curriculum Theory and Classroom Practice, Dayton, OH.

Daignault, J. (1986). *Semiotics of educational expression*. Paper presented at the annual meeting of the Bergamo Conference on Curriculum Theory and Classroom Practice, Dayton, OH.

Daignault, J. (1988). . . . $Y^n X Cursus [.^{T.I.A}]^2 Arts aRe$. . . . Paper presented at the annual meeting of the Bergamo Conference on Curriculum Theory and Classroom Practice, Dayton, OH.

Daignault, J. (1989). *Where did the subject go?* (B. Wing, Trans.). Unpublished manuscript, University of Quebec at Rimouski.

REFERENCES

Baudrillard, J. (1976). *L'échange symbolique et la mort*. Paris: Gallimard.

Bréhier, E. (1928). *La théorie des incorporels dans l'ancien stoïcisme*. Paris: Vrin.

Chomsky, N. (1975). *Reflections on language*. New York: Pantheon.

Daignault, J. (1983). Curriculum and action-research: An artistic activity in a perverse way. *The Journal of Curriculum Theorizing, 5*(3), 4–28.

Daignault, J. (1985). *Pour une esthétique de la pédagogie*. Victoriaville, Quebec: Editions NHP.

Daignault, J. (1986). De l'analogie en science. In D. Lafontaine (Ed.), *Psychanalyse et changement social. Réflexions épistémologiques sur la question du développement* (Actes du colloque *Le plaisir et la contrainte,* mars 1983) (pp. 52–73). Rimouski, Quebec: GRIDEQ.

Daignault, J. (1988). *C.V.-autobiography dictionary*. Unpublished manuscript, University of Quebec at Rimouski.

Daignault, J. (1989). Un t d'trop. *Urgences, 23,* 89–99.

Deleuze, G. (1968). *Différence et répétition*. Paris: PUF.

Deleuze, G. (1969). *Logique du sens*. Paris: Minuit.

Deleuze, G. (1986). *Foucault*. Paris: Minuit.

Deleuze, G. (1988). *Foucault*. Minneapolis: University of Minnesota Press.

Deleuze, G. (1989). *The logic of sense*. New York: Columbia University Press.

Deleuze, G. & Guattari, F. (1980). *Mille plateaux*. Paris: Minuit.

Derrida, J. (1967). *De la grammatologie*. Paris: Minuit.

Derrida, J. (1976). *Of grammatology*. Baltimore: Johns Hopkins University Press.

Foucault, M. (1963). *Raymond Roussel*. Paris: Gallimard.

Foucault, M. (1969). *L'archéologie du savoir*. Paris: Gallimard.

Foucault, M. (1970). Theatrum philosophicum. *Critique, 26,* 885–908.

Foucault, M. (1972). *The archeology of knowledge*. New York: Pantheon.

Foucault, M. (1986). *Death and the labyrinth*. New York: Doubleday.

Kant, I. (1979). *Critique de la faculté de juger*. Paris: Vrin. (Original work published 1790)

Lacan, J. (1966). *Ecrits*. Paris: Seuil.

Lyotard, J.-F. (1977). *Instructions païennes*. Paris: Galilée.

Pivot, B. (1985). Les carnets de Bernard Pivot. *Lire, 113,* 11.

Reich, S. (1980). *Violon Phase*. ECM Production's record, side two.

Rousseau, J.-J. (1979). *Ecrits sur la musique*. Paris: Stock. (Original work published 1742)

Rousseau. J.-J. (1982). *Project concerning new symbols for music*. Kilkenny: Boethius Press. (Original work published 1742)

Roussel, R. (1963). *Comment j'ai écrit certains de mes livres*. Paris: Pauvert.

Roussel, R. (1975). *How I wrote certain of my books*. New York: Sun.

Serres, M. (1974). *Hermes III. La traduction*. Paris: Minuit.

Serres, M. (1977). *Hermes IV. La distribution*. Paris: Minuit.

Serres, M. (1980). *Le parasite*. Paris: Grasset.

Serres, M. (1983). *Hermes. Literature, Science, Philosophy*. Baltimore: Johns Hopkins University Press.

Starobinsky, J. (1971). *Les mots sous les mots. Les anagrammes de Ferdinand de Saussure*. Paris: Gallimard.

Starobinsky, J. (1979). *Words upon words*. New Haven, CT: Yale University Press.

CHAPTER 12

Achieving the Right Distance

PETER M. TAUBMAN

A woman who has taught for many years told me once of her first year as a teacher. Her most secret pressing concern was not content in the classroom but what would happen if she met one of her female students in the women's bathroom. So concerned was she that she practiced scenarios to insure that the proper distance was maintained and that her identity as teacher would not dissolve. I do not believe she was alone in her concern with distance and identity.

When teachers ask how close they should be to students they are not only asking "Who am I in relation to these students or this student?" and "Who are these students or who is this student in relation to me?" They are also asking questions about what they want from students and what students want from them. These are questions of identity and intention.

It is interesting that these same questions are raised in another form of communication that is both an art and a craft—acting. Stanislavsky once condensed the preparation necessary for playing a part into two questions that each actor must be able to answer. The questions were: "Who am I?" and "What do I want?"

Unlike method acting, however, where the agentic integrity and unified subjectivity of the actor are assumed—the unity of the "I" in each of Stanislavsky's questions is taken for granted—teaching also exists in another dimension, the dimension of the unconscious.

When Stanislavsky said acting was, within the confines of the script, a real response to an imaginary stimulus, he was working in the register of psychological realism and Coleridgean aesthetics and in such a register was not speaking of teaching. But when we put his definition of acting—a real response within the constraints of a script to an imaginary stimulus—in a Lacanian register, we come close to a definition of teaching that takes into account identity and intention as they form and are exercised within conscious and unconscious systems and within the symbolic realm of the classroom or school.

All this is to say that if we are to talk about the psychic closeness/distance between teacher and student, we are going to have to address issues of identity and intention as they play themselves out in the realms of the unconscious and conscious and within the school.

I am not interested in discussing physical or sexual proximity between students and teachers, role ascription, or gender and class as they anchor and serve as the horizon for a discussion of closeness and distance, identity and intention. All of these assume some identity beyond which they do not go.

To repudiate any identity is, of course, to embrace madness. I am not interested in that either. What I wish to do is suspend a few unities or identities and put them into question in order to examine the psychic dynamics, distances, and proximities that occur between or among two or more individuals who meet in a relationship we call educational.

IDENTITY

I did not want to teach. When I was a senior in college in 1969, one of thousands of English majors, I said to a friend, "Teaching is the perpetuation of an intellectual kick. I'll never do it." I started teaching the following fall, thanks to the draft.

Believing I had never taught before and living at home, I turned to my mother for advice. She had taught at Benjamin Franklin High School in Spanish Harlem, had studied with Freeman Butts at Teachers College, and had tutored me in different subjects. I figured she could help.

She told me to stand in front of the enormous mirror in the hall and practice doing what I would do during the first few weeks of school. So I stood there, hearing myself talk about phrases and clauses, gerunds and participles, listening to myself ask questions, modulating and projecting my voice. I stood there watching my reflection smile and nod, gesture and pause as I adjusted to the image projected back to me.

And all the while in the shadows of the living room behind me, I could see in the mirror my mother, sitting quietly nodding and prompting.

It was during those fall evenings, in front of the mirror, that a loose sense of myself as a teacher emerged.

Lacan tells us that an individual's identity as a unified "moi" congeals during the mirror stage. This stage allows for the erection of the ego edifice that may later turn into a fortress. He writes:

> The mirror stage is a drama whose internal thrust is precipitated from insufficiency to anticipation—and which manufactures the subject—the succession of fantasies that extends from a fragmented body-image to a form of its totality that I shall call orthopaedic—and lastly to the assumption of the armor of an alienating identity which will mark with its rigid structure the subject's entire mental development. (1972, p. 4)

According to Lacan, this ego, then, is itself both imaginary and alienated because it is totalized and formed by the other. As Lacan said, "In the last resort—'I' is an other" (1972, p. 4).

The identity of that teacher who began to form in 1969 in the mirror and in the gaze of the other was in a Lacanian register also imaginary and alienated.

Every teacher at some point and over some period began to experience herself or himself as a teacher. Perhaps it was the Girl Scout leader who first said, "You are a born teacher." Perhaps it was a father or another teacher who suggested that certain qualities associated with a teacher were present and could be capitalized on; but at some point before the symbolic credentialing occurred, each of us envisioned, heard, felt ourselves as a teacher. Which is to say nothing except and unless that the figure carried in it the imagined other in whose gaze it came to be.

I was a teacher, which meant I was consciously and unconsciously assuming and assimilating what it meant consciously and unconsciously to my mother to teach and what others who were called teachers consciously and unconsciously meant by that term. Without analysis this construct, which formed in my case during those fall evenings, may remain resistant to reflection, may organize identity and structure experiences while it remains itself not out of sight but the lens of sight. The formation parallels what Lacan talks of as ego: "We call the ego that nucleus given to consciousness, but opaque to reflection, marked by all the ambiguities which from self-satisfaction to bad faith structure the experience of the passions in the human subject" (1972, p. 15).

This identity of teacher is layered over and dissolves into an already imaginary identity—me—and further dams up the Heraclitean flux as it enters the realm of the symbolic—that is, as it is certified by the institution.

The day I started teaching I was told by the headmaster of the school to cut my hair and to seek help from the head of the department if there were problems with controlling students, who would, I was told, probably test me.

The loose identity of teacher formed in the mirror and coalescing conscious and unconscious experiences could emerge at the institutional level only as castrated. The as-yet unarticulated sense memories, emotions, relationships, and desires that were drawn into and gave an unconscious weight to the teacher reflected back in the mirror were repressed and denied as I become an institutional teacher. The price for power and control as well as a public identity—castration. With my hair cut and with contract in hand I began to work in schools, considered myself a teacher, and in the name of teacher began to teach. Lacan writes: "The symbolic function presents itself as a double movement within the subject: man makes an object of his action,

but only in order to restore to this action in due time its place as grounding"
(1972, p. 73). Identified in the institutional language as teacher and assuming the identity emergent in the mirror alongside the parent who held me
up, I began to spend time with students.

Teachers, then, are not simply those who teach, nor are they simply con-
tracted workers with a listed title in a dictionary of occupations. They come
to be within a complex dynamic. Their initial sense of themselves as teachers,
given to them by another, is already a fiction and often comes more out of
the needs of the one making the initial suggestion than any actual bestowing
of a title. Often embedded in the assumed identity is emotional sediment left
by the relationship with the original namer, associations with the term itself,
introjected ideals of a teacher—often based on the one in whose gaze we
came to be a teacher—and our own desire, which is given focus through the
lens of this identity.

It is not unusual for young teachers, even those trained in teaching programs, to act out the imaginary relationships, the emotional flurries, the
ideals, and the stereotypes that congealed in their new identity of teacher. It
is at this level that for the new teacher who is just entering the symbolic
realm—that is, the realm of institutional identity and language—students
often become the other, and transference occurs.

Shoshanna Felman (1982) has brilliantly analyzed the transference that
occurs in the classroom, but she has focused on the way students reproduce
archaic emotional patterns and transfer these onto the teacher—the one supposed to know. I am suggesting that initially the new teacher with his or her
fragile identity is still in the realm of the imaginary and transfers onto the
students the unconscious relationships that constitute that identity. Thus we
see new teachers working hard at being liked or changing their students into
a particular ideal. It is in the eyes of the students that such a teacher looks for
affirmation. Or, conversely, it is in the eyes of the students that the teacher
looks for a reflection of himself or herself as the original Other in whose gaze
that teacher came into being. It is not unusual at this level for new teachers
to talk about being friends with their students, about taking care of them, or
about saving them in some vague way. Boundaries between teacher and student are diffuse. And it is in this register of the imaginary that one can hear
the unarticulated unconscious fears, desires, and needs that constitute the
new identity of the teacher.

It is not long, however, before the symbolic intrudes. Once a teacher is
credentialed, hired, shorn of his or her metaphoric hair, the imaginary is
submerged in and reemerges in the symbolic realm of the law of the school.
The symbolic replaces imaginary elements in an identificatory reshaping of
the teacher and demands that the teacher renounce the imaginary realm—as
if that could be done—for the "reality" of the institution. The language of

school—with its emphasis on rigor, control, grade medians, testing, information and with its pronounced distinction between students and teachers—reformulates the imaginary realm and thus repudiates it while maintaining it.

The conscious and unconscious relationships, ideals, sentiments, desires that led individuals to teach remain unquestioned, unexamined, and unchallenged; yet they are repressed and reshaped by the symbolic realm of the school. Thus we see the stereoscopic image of teachers sequestered in their rooms acting out the imaginary, behind another image of teachers unable to articulate their views in any meaningful way, behind finally a last image of teachers reshaping their own submerged practice in the language of information conveyance or transmission that is the public language of the school.

When I gave up my hair for a contract, not only did I gain the right to control and therefore exercise a kind of power, I also gained a public identity. I became once and for all a teacher, but a teacher defined as the one who knows. Suddenly I was presumed to know a body of knowledge—English. At the same time, however, my emergence as a teacher in the symbolic crystallized another body of knowledge—leftist politics—that I presumed to know. I was doubly the one who knew; I was doubly a teacher. I was a double agent, and I assumed I had complete agency—I knew. Through questioning and shaping I drew from the mouths of my students the politically correct answers. I was a teacher and on my way to becoming a master.

To master a field or a body of knowledge is to be able to represent it or totalize it through paraphrase or encoding, such that the totalization is synonymous with the field or body or assumes it. To demarcate a field or body is to say what is left out as well as what is kept in. It is to ignore what is not relevant. As Felman puts it:

> Ignorance—is nothing other than a desire to ignore: its nature is less cognitive than performative; as in the case of Sophocles' nuanced representation of the ignorance of Oedipus, it is not simple lack of information but the incapacity—or the refusal—to acknowledge one's own implication in the information. (1982, p. 30)

The master is the slave of the very body mastered, for the master must deny complicity in what is mastered, must ignore that which is not designated as relevant, and must collapse his or her identity onto an external field. His mind, to quote Coleridge's definition of mania, "is obsessed by a fixed idea, sees and interprets all things in relations to that idea, and so has (though in a morbid form) a coordinating power" (quoted in Lowes, 1964, p. 315). The idea congeals the field, the master masters the idea or field and then becomes the idea, becomes maniacal.

It is interesting in this light to look at a recent article by Gary Olsen

(1988) in the leftist magazine *Z*. Olsen, a college professor and author of *How the World Works*, was teaching students to see the links among global capitalism, American-sponsored terrorism and its result in Third World countries, and the students' own investment in their living standards. He was shocked and shattered that at the end of the course students who had written "A" exams on the topic and appeared to have mastered the views he presented, actually saw those views as so much empty rhetoric, as only one more discourse to be mastered for the teacher. They admitted they preferred Mercedes 450 SL's to demonstrating. Olsen eventually staged the mock execution of an African student to dramatize the insensitivity of his students to their complicity in Third World murder.

By setting himself up as the master—the one who knows—and against the students, by retreating from subjectivity and allowing his knowledge to tyrannize his students' fantasies, Olsen had estranged himself in the ego edifice of teacher-as-master and had become a fortress.

Lacan implies that the discourse of the master involves "the tyranny of the all knowing and the exclusion of fantasy; gives primacy to the signifier; is a retreat from subjectivity and produces knowledge as an object which stands over and against the lost object of desires" (Mitchell & Rose, 1983, p. 161). Perhaps for Olsen that lost object was the African student or those in the Third World who needed saving or the students themselves who needed rescuing or even further back the one in whose gaze he came to be a teacher, the one no doubt who inspired the compassion or passion for saving. But in the end, as master, that one, in whatever guise, had to be sacrificed. It was after all Olsen who staged the execution, an execution that is perhaps the final act of mania.

For the master, the one who knows, those individuals with whom time is spent in the school come into being as students, disciples who do not know. Between teacher and student a great chasm exists, crossed only by the dynamics of transference and countertransference. As Lacan pointed out, "As soon as there is somewhere a subject presumed to know there is transference" (quoted in Felman, 1982, p. 35). He went on to say that when transference occurs, at that moment there is resistance. Discourse dries up.

For the beginning teacher who confronts students, this transference and resistance may take the form of a dread of not knowing what to say. For the student who confronts the master such resistance, according to Felman, takes the form of ignorance. "Ignorance," she writes, "is not a passive state of absence—a simple lack of information. . . . Ignorance is a desire to ignore" (1982, pp. 35, 30).

In the symbolic realm of the school, individuals who emerge as students and who are confronted by teachers presumed to know have two alternatives. By returning the words of the master they appear to become the master, but this is impossible, for the master always knows more. Or they resist and become ignorant. In such a system knowledge itself regulates a distance between alienated figures, and the classroom becomes a hall of mirrors. If the student reproduces the discourse of the master, the student becomes he who is already alienated, he who, as we have seen, has already become some one other. The masters see only themselves reflected back and are unable to discover the fundamental alienation which made them construct their being like another and which destined that identity to be taken by another. The student who resists becomes the empty mirror in which the master searches for his reflection.

Philip Jackson has called the teaching style of the master "mimetic." According to Jackson the mimetic style is dominant in the classroom, but we all know teachers who refrain from such an approach and repudiate the idea of being a master. Unfortunately, many of those teachers who do resist their symbolic encoding as masters retreat to the classroom, where they reproduce the initial imaginary identity and dynamics that first crystallized them as teachers and fail to move beyond the limitations of that identity. In *Life in Classrooms* Jackson writes: "If teachers sought a more thorough understanding of their world, insisted on greater rationality in their actions—they might receive greater applause from intellectuals, but it is doubtful that they would perform with greater efficiency in the classroom" (1968, p. 144).

Ironically, the rationality Jackson sees as interfering with classroom efficiency parallels the discourse of the master, which is premised on the rational and the denial of the irrational and unconscious. The efficiency he refers to— that is, the daily nonreflective practice of teachers who repudiate that discourse—is the acting out of the imaginary, what Jackson refers to as "intuition."

In my third year of teaching I had begun to renounce being the one who knew and had come to believe that there was little difference between teachers and students. In the classroom and out I let my feelings be my guide. I quite simply acted out. I shut the door of my classroom and had discussions on whatever topic came up. The distance that separates the master and the student disappeared. We were equals. Two memories stand out from this period.

I was chaperoning a dance sponsored by the Black Student Union at Germantown Academy in Philadelphia. I was slightly tipsy, and seeing several girls dancing together and a few boys awkwardly standing alone, I asked one of the boys to dance. We went out on the floor, and in the presence of hardly one raised eyebrow we hustled to, as I recall, a record by Earth Wind and Fire. He led, I followed, and afterwards we spoke about this seemingly outrageous act, which, however, in fact provoked no rage or derision at all. In some ways the dance was similar to the way I was teaching then: extend a provocative invitation and then follow where the student leads until there remains only a duet of two people moving as one to the same beat, which remains unconscious.

I remember, too, for the first and only time, falling in love with a student or, perhaps more accurately, falling in love with the image of her that I saw reflected back in the dark green of her eyes. She was the one I assumed knew.

The duet and the love affair are apt metaphors for the kind of teaching I did at the time, a teaching that fled from any identity as teacher.

It would appear, then, that in terms of identity there are two choices open to those who teach and thus two poles as regards the distance or closeness between teacher and student. One may become a master and thus remain castrated, forever separated from those one teaches, alienated both from oneself and one's students, and lost in a house of mirrors. Or one may flee from any identity as teacher and sink into the inarticulate realm of the unconscious, lost forever in the Other and renouncing any distance whatsoever.

Neither position feels very comfortable. But, then, what is the right distance between someone called a teacher and someone called a student? What is the relationship between these two figures if we suspend the identities?

INTENTION

What does a teacher want? What is the teacher's intention? However these questions are answered, they are answered in language. Foucault, having learned from Lacan, teaches us that words do not simply carry our wishes or intentions on their wings. Rather, they are our intentions. Lacan called these intentions that emerged in discourse "demands" and then said that demand produces an excess, which he called desire. The need for total absolute love is alienated in the demand and produces desire. He writes, "Desire . . . is what is evoked by any demand beyond the need that is articulated in it" (1972, p. 263).

> So far as the subject's needs are subjected to demand they return to him alienated. That which is thus alienated in needs constitutes a primal repression, an inability . . . to be articulated in demand, but it reappears in something it gives rise to, that which presents itself . . . as desire. (Lacan, 1972, p. 286)

As Jane Gallop in *The Daughter's Seduction* puts it:

> The demand is made within language's imaginary register where the first model of one-to-one correspondence is presumed to operate . . . its signified is assumed to be delimitable. Desire is that portion of the pre-articulated need which finds itself left out of the demand. (1982, p. 11)

The articulated demand colonizes, reshapes, and squeezes the need and produces a seepage, an excess that is desire.

The question is how to move back through the teacher's demand or intention to the need and thus understand the teacher's desire.

I suspect that the need that becomes alienated in the demand or intention takes shape at the moment the initial identity of the teacher congeals in the gaze of an Other. It is a need, I suspect, to be loved by and to be like that Other, to be one with the Other and to be what the Other desires.

Ragland-Sullivan writes in *Jacques Lacan and the Philosophy of Psychoanalysis:* "[The answer to the question: Who am I?] lies in ascertaining the Desire of the Other. The Desire to know or possess the Other has been displaced into the Desire to be, to know or to have" (1987, p. 83).

The need that emerges in the original identificatory process becomes in the symbolic realm of the school intention or demand expressed as lesson plans, goals, and objectives. When subtracted from need, desire results that is displaced into the desire to be the master, to know the field, to have the answer. To compensate for the unconscious and forever unsatisfied need, the student, knowledge, and the privileged position as the one who knows are substituted. The master reproduces in the relationship with the student the unconscious relationship with the One in whose gaze he or she initially emerged as teacher, but unlike the first-year teacher or the teacher who repudiates the figure of master, the master mediates that relationship with knowledge that only the master possesses, and the master speaks to and from a position of privilege in the realm of the symbolic. The desire of the master then is for students who do not know, for more knowledge that remains always external to him but onto which he tries to collapse himself, and for greater privilege; that is, positions of legitimacy in the symbolic realm of the school. The desire to be, to know, to have is an unending desire that works in the direction of increasing distance between teacher and student.

For the beginning teacher or the teacher who renounces the figure of master, the unconscious need becomes intention or demand expressed as caring, helping, or engaging students. The desire that results when the latter is subtracted from the former is displaced into the desire to be the student, to know the student, to have the student. The figure of the student compensates for the unconscious need to be like that original Other in whose gaze the teacher initially emerged, to be one with that Other, and to be what that original Other desired. No longer mediated by knowledge, the distance between teacher and student is abolished.

Absolute distance and the abolition of all distance: What, then, is the right distance between the master who knows and the teacher who cares, between the subject who is the teacher and the subject who is the student?

I suspect the answer lies in the middle, at the midpoint. Perhaps it is not coincidence that the term Lacan used to denote his practice was "midire" or "midspeak," and the term Socrates used to describe himself was "midwife."

Now, the midpoint on a line is an interesting position. If the line is bent, the midpoint becomes the apex of a triangle, and in another discourse that apex becomes the child in an Oedipal triangle, with mother and father at the base points. But for our purposes, the midpoint can be understood as a switch point; a point, as Klaus Riegel puts it, "of dialectical interpenetration which is the intersection of two lines" (1973, p. 7). It can be understood as a point between an identity striving for ideal form—the master—and an identity dissolved in the unconscious. It can be understood as a point between the ideal forms of Plato and the formless ideal of Lacan.

THE MIDPOINT

"I am barren of wisdom," says that exemplary teacher, Socrates, in Plato's *Theaetetus*. "My mind has never produced any idea that could be called clever. [Those who associate with me become clever] not because they ever learn anything from me; the many fine ideas and offspring that they produce come from within themselves" (Plato, 1987a, p. 128).

Written several years before the *Theaetetus,* the *Meno* has Socrates saying something similar. "It isn't that, knowing the answer myself, I perplex other people," says Socrates. "The truth is rather that I infect them also with the perplexity I feel myself" (Plato, 1986, p. 128).

It would certainly appear that Socrates does not assume himself to be the one who knows. He even says in the *Meno* that there is no such thing as teaching (Plato, 1986, p. 130) and in *The Republic* that "we must reject the conception of education professed by those who say that they can put into the mind knowledge that was not there before" (Plato, 1987b, p. 322). It would seem, then, that the distance between teacher and student has been abolished.

And yet, we know better. We know that Plato's Socrates was not as innocent of being the master as he appears. There may be no teaching, but there is recollection, and Socrates will help his students recollect. He may be barren, but as midwife he will supervise his students as they labor to birth ideas to which he will "apply every conceivable test to see whether one young man's mental offspring is illusory and false or viable and true" (Plato, 1987a, p. 27).

If we stopped here, we would find an identity empty and barren, an identity of teacher as one who helps others recollect or give birth to their own ideas through a dialectic that "proceeds by the destruction of assumptions," who does not bully (Plato, 1987b, p. 296) but goes "wherever the wind of the argument leads him" (p. 152), who establishes the conditions from which knowledge may arise, who sees mistakes as misidentifications, who professes to "know nothing about the subject but only learns from others" (p. 77) by asking grateful questions. If we paused at this point, we would find the identity of Lacan's pedagogical analyst.

Here is Lacan saying that "there is no true teaching other that the teaching which succeeds in provoking in those who listen . . . the desire to know which can only emerge when they themselves have taken the measure of ignorance as such—of ignorance . . . in the one who teaches" (quoted in Felman, 1982, p. 31). "What I teach you," says Lacan, "does nothing other than express the conditions which make it possible to learn" (quoted in Felman, 1982, p. 31).

As Felman puts it, "Teaching [for Lacan] is not the transmission of ready-made knowledge, it is rather the creation of a new condition of knowledge—the creation of an original learning disposition" (1982, p. 32).

The teacher/analyst who engages in midspeak teaches the subject to recognize his own méconnaissance (misrecognition). His art "must be to suspend the subject's certainties until their last mirages have been consumed" (Lacan, quoted in Felman, 1982, p. 43), so that the subject/student gains true speech. Like Socrates as teacher, Lacan as analyst is the one to whom one speaks freely and who greets the subject/student with grateful questions. Like the midwife, the one who engages in midspeak

> does not have to guide the subject to knowledge, but on the paths by which access to knowledge is gained. He must engage him in a dialectical operation, not to say to him that he is wrong, since he necessarily is in error, but show him that he speaks poorly, that is to say he speaks without knowing. (Lacan, 1981, p. 34)

And finally, like Socrates' midwife who judges his students' offspring by their consequences, Lacan's teacher/analyst confirms an interpretation by "the material that emerges as a result of that interpretation" (Lacan, 1972, p. 234).

There exists, then, a point of convergence between two lines of thought, Lacan's and those of Plato's Socrates; but those lines lead in opposite directions, and it is the points where they end and from which they return that pose problems.

Plato's Socrates leads the student who, like the slave boy of the *Meno*, knows but does not know he knows or the student who, like Meno, thinks he knows but does not. He leads them from their unconscious knowledge or their imaginary knowledge, the *doxa,* into the light of the *eidoi,* the realm of ideal forms. He leads them through recollection and a dialectic to the beyond of the Good. This dialectic progresses toward "the first principle of everything. When [the student] has grasped that principle, he may again descend keeping to the consequences that follow from it" (Plato, 1987b, p. 134).

Socrates' student is led from his enslavement in the cave, from his ignorance of his unconscious knowledge, into the light where he contemplates the Good beyond which he cannot go. He can only return.

Aside from the explicit and implicit politics of Plato's Socrates, what troubles me about this line of thought is its direction. It moves, as we can see, in the direction of greater distance. In the *Theaetetus* Socrates describes his consummate philosopher as one detached from the matters of the world, far removed and above the realm of necessity:

> [H]e is detached from them . . . and disdains all these matters, seeing them as petty and worthless. . . . [H]is mind is constantly exploring the general nature of every entity as a whole, but no local object becomes his perch. (Plato, 1987a, p. 69)

The journey to the beyond of the good requires a contempt for everyday reality, for the body, for the press of the sensate world, and for the sociopolitical structures that impinge on us. It requires a severance of thought from action, cognition from emotion, and identity from the roots of that identity. For as Plato's Socrates says,

> The true philosopher whose mind is on higher realities, has no time to look at the affairs of men. . . . [H]is eyes are turned to contemplate fixed and immutable realities, a realm where . . . all is reason and order, and which is the model which he imitates and to which he assimilates himself as far as he can. (Plato, 1987a, p. 297)

The teacher/philosopher of Plato's Socrates is drawn from a position of one who knows he does not know to one who is the same as the *eidoi,* one who is the ideal form, one who is the master.

From the point at which there is convergence of Lacan's teacher/analyst and Socrates' midwife, Socrates' line moves upward into the ideal forms and then descends as the master. Thus it is not surprising that philosopher/educators such as Mortimer Adler, Allan Bloom, and William Bennett demand a Socratic dialogue while they also assume a ceiling of knowing, a ceiling on which they see the fixed realm of knowledge and in which is reflected their identity as master.

Having seen the sun, the *eidoi,* these masters then return to the cave, and through a dialectic that will culminate in the same, impart their knowledge to the student, who is no longer the one who knows but does not know he knows but who has become the student who knows nothing. For ignorance, according to Plato's Socrates, is nothing.

If the movement from the midwife of Socrates ascends toward the ideal form and returns alienated and passive, then the movement of Lacan's teacher/analyst descends into the realm of the imaginary and returns also alienated and passive or not at all.

Let us see how this works.

We know that Lacan's conception of the unconscious subverts the end point of Plato's and later Hegel's dialectic, which in the end, Lacan says, culminates in absolute knowledge.

As Felman points out, "the unconscious in Lacan's conception is precisely the discovery that human discourse can by definition never be entirely in agreement with itself . . . since it is constitutively the material locus of a signifying difference from itself" (1982, p. 28). A kind of unmeant knowledge that escapes intentionality and meaning, the unconscious renders knowledge untotalizable and subverts the notion of master. Like the slaveboy of the *Meno,* Lacan's subject possesses a knowledge that he does not recognize or assume as his, a knowledge that does not know itself but is revealed in dreams and slips.

The task for Lacan's analyst/teacher is to assume his own ignorance as he listens to each specific case in order to learn the patient/student's own unconscious knowledge and teach it back to him. His task is to point out the subject's misrecognition of that knowledge. The analyst/teacher becomes the student of the patient/student's knowledge. The knowledge that emerges then can only do so in the dynamic between analyst and analysand, between teacher and student. As Lacan put it, "no knowledge can be supported or transported by one alone" (quoted in Felman, 1982, p. 33). The dialogue in which this knowledge arises is between "two partially unconscious speeches which both say more than they know" (Lacan, quoted in Felman, 1982, p. 33). The teacher is thus the one who learns, and the student becomes the teacher when he realizes learning is interminable. As Lacan wrote, "the subject of a teaching is a learning" (quoted in Felman, 1982, p. 37).

Such a stance, then, is not unlike that of Socrates' midwife, the one who knows he does not know, except Lacan's teacher/analyst knows he knows but does not know the meaning of what he knows. Whereas Socrates' midwife is propelled upward toward the ideal forms, Lacan's analyst/teacher is propelled downward into the unconscious, the formless ideal. It is a descent and reascent that entails the eternal alienation of the subject or his dissolution.

The teaching, whose subject is a learning, that Lacan proposes involves a regression that, as Lacan states, is "simply the actualization in the discourse of the fantasy relations reconstituted by an ego at each stage in the decomposition of its structure" (quoted in Felman, 1982, p. 44). The regression is in the service of recuperating the subject's speech. "Analysis" writes Lacan, "can have for its goal only the advent of a true speech and the realization by the subject of his history in his relation to a future" (1972, p. 88).

But such regression leads to a dissolution of the ego that was formed in the gaze of the Other. Which leaves what? The fragmented being, the formless ideal that remains must, in order to exist, reemerge into the symbolic or remain mad. The teacher who descends back through the imaginary dissolves his or her identity as teacher; but then on what basis is that identity reconstituted?

The choice is between not being a teacher or reemerging in the symbolic realm of the school as the master. The problem is more obvious in the work of Lacan's student, Michel Foucault. For Foucault, discourse is an anonymous field in that its origin or locus of formation is neither a sovereign consciousness nor a collective consciousness. It exists at the level of the "it is said." It indicates certain circumscribed places from which, he writes, "one may speak that which is already caught up in the play of exteriority" (Foucault, 1972, p. 122).

The individual figure is dissolved as the constituting figure of discourse and is dispersed and replaced by various subject positions opened within discourse itself. Within the symbolic realm of the school those positions are the positions of the master.

As the teacher/analyst engages in a regression and the dissolution of what is seen as an alienated ego, the teacher is forced into either reemerging as the master or leaving teaching. I suspect it is no coincidence that we hear of students of Lacan arguing over who has mastered his teaching best or leaving the field of psychoanalysis altogether.

But there is another problem with the end point of Lacan's descending line of thought. For Lacan the ego is the enemy. As Catherine Clement puts it, "At the conclusion of therapy what will have disappeared is the armor of the Ego, the fortress, the glass cage of narcissistic illusions" (1983, p. 146). What is supposed to emerge is an "I" free of all dependency on the Other, of nonrelation to the Other in whose gaze the ego is formed. What is repudiated is the Other when an identityless "I" emerges.

But to act in the world is to project oneself into the future to assume an identity, to be finally political. Otherwise we become a shifting and shiftless "I" that is indeed a slave of the unconscious. I would suggest then that not only is the Other repudiated but also the very real world of connections and passions that demands we assume an identity. Perhaps this rejection of the realm of necessity can be glimpsed in a statement Lacan once made. He said,

"I have had several opportunities to watch hope, the promise of what is called a better tomorrow, lead people . . . quite simply to suicide" (quoted in Clement, 1983, p. 146).

Like the ascent of Socrates' midwife into the beyond of the ideal forms and his return as master, Lacan's teacher/analyst descends into the beyond of the ideal formlessness of the unconscious, where his identity is dissolved only to reemerge as a master or not at all.

Both beyonds are finally inexpressible, but the path back from them holds in contempt the realm of necessity and the Other in whose gaze we came to be. Perhaps it is not surprising that Plato's Socrates scorned passion and passionate love, choosing celibacy. Perhaps it is not surprising that Lacan defined love as "unabashed distance" and called for an "ethics of celibacy" (quoted in Clement, 1983, p. 145). In the end the collapse into the ideal forms of Plato's Socrates or the formless ideal of Lacan represents a flight from politics in the sense of community and from intimacy in the etymological sense of making known in the realm of necessity.

I have taken us, it may seem, far afield into Lacanian and Platonic discourse, but I have done so for a reason. The teacher who takes a position at the midpoint, at the point between Plato's Socrates and Lacan, at a point where he or she is a midwife or engages in midspeak, where she or he subverts her or his own position as the one who knows, assumes an identity that is at a crossroads. The teacher who takes a position at the midpoint assumes an identity that can always be drawn in one of two directions—up toward the *eidoi* from which the master returns or down to the unconscious from which it returns as the master or in another profession.

The pull is always there. And yet it is the midpoint that seems most attractive, most rich. How, then, can we maintain it without being pulled irrevocably in directions that are dangerous?

I suspect the answer lies in moving in both directions at once, in a dialectical operation that takes into account the very real world that we teachers inhabit. What does this entail?

ONE LAST STORY

Recently I was asked by a member of the history department, a young Irishman named Dermot Dix whose degrees are in colonial American history, to come into his classroom and try to teach about the Continental Congress. He had been depressed about the way the class was going. Now, I know very little about the Congress, but what I did know led me to try an experiment.

When class began, I told everyone why I was there and that we were going to try something. I asked them to talk about what they were dissatisfied with in the class and how they thought it could be better. I put their responses on the board, which was soon filled, and asked more questions about what role the teacher should play or who should set the agenda for class. Their responses ranged from wanting more specific direction and information from Dermot to dissolving the class while keeping the teacher as a resource person.

The students then grouped the various comments into five positions. I asked them to group themselves physically into those positions and come up with clear statements about how each group envisioned the class. These were then read and discussed.

While all this was occurring, Dermot matched up the views expressed by individual students with views expressed by actual delegates to the Continental Congress. The student who wished to disband the class was matched with Patrick Henry.

At the end of the class, I suggested that Dermot could indeed be seen as the British and they as the colonists. Students were given their respective identities as delegates and asked to find out about them.

The next day the students were given name tags of their delegates and grouped into colonies. They then continued, as themselves although wearing those name tags, the previous day's discussion.

They were asked to choose five students whom they felt represented their differing views to meet outside class. These five would compose over the course of a week a formal document declaring the new relationship between Dermot and the students. The question of representation was heatedly argued. At the end of class, each student as colonial representative rose and presented his or her views about the British.

The following day the five colonial delegates who actually drew up the Declaration of Independence were asked to meet outside class and study their part in forming it. Again representation was discussed. Ensuing days saw a continual movement back and forth between the imaginary Continental Congress and the very real concerns of those students, Dermot, and me.

What interests me about all this is the position Dermot, the students, and I assumed in that class. I, who know little about history or what that knowledge means, found myself pulled toward the here and now in the class, regressing into a formless ideal. I found myself at times wanting the approval of the students in the imaginary. I wanted them to see me as savior of the class, and patted myself on the back for sacrificing my time to come into the class while resenting those students who appeared uninvolved and unappreciative. I found myself at one point in a whispered conversation with a nearby student.

What pulled me back to a midpoint were three forces: the claims for justice and truth made by the students who had become the ones who knew the meaning of their own knowledge of life in that classroom and who wanted to change the structure of the class; the actual press of the class, which could be felt in the intensity with which a community was forming itself; and Dermot, whose movement toward being the master of a body of historical knowledge pulled me up. And it was again the needs of the students, which I acknowledged as my own, that kept me from following Dermot to mastery.

Dermot, who began by being one who knew he did not know (he doubted he knew anything about what was really going on in the class, as he put it) as well as the one who did not know the meaning of what he knew (he wondered what meaning his teaching had), was pulled in the direction of ideal form as he fell into lecturing and playing guessing games. Later, when we processed what had gone on, Dermot suddenly began talking of one of his old teachers who had inspired him to go into teaching. He spoke of how he, Dermot, as a student had misbehaved. Then he slipped, and instead of saying that the teacher had "quelled" his acting out by lecturing him, he said the teacher had "quenched" his acting by lecturing. I suspect that slip reveals the dynamic between Dermot and that teacher, a dynamic incorporated into the identity of teacher that made it easier for Dermot to assume the role of master.

What I am suggesting is that there occurs in the classroom, the realm of necessity, a dialectic between two lines of thought whose end points must be attended to but not submitted to. This dialectic entails moving back to that moment when our identity as teacher first congealed in the gaze of the Other, not in order to dissolve that identity, but to enrich it; not in order to free a desire to which we will be slave, but to understand, accept, and acknowledge the needs that, when forced into intentions, spill out into desire. It entails a regression, but one in which we never lose sight of the Good as we give respect to the unconscious. It entails turning our backs on the mirror and facing the person in whose gaze we came to be a teacher and acknowledging, without falling prey to, the needs of that person.

Those fall evenings when I stood before the mirror, it was Dorothy Taubman who sat behind me. But there were others, too, in whose gaze I came to be a teacher. As I think back through them, I see and feel their gestures, intonations, and style in my own; I bear witness to our relationship and try to keep in view their needs that formed themselves into my own.

When I am exhausted and feel insecure, I look for approval and love in the eyes of my students, and when at times I feel frustrated, I fall into Freire's aggressive malefic generosity, and I know these needs and aggression congealed in that initial identity as teacher. But I also see the Good in those Others and allow it to pull me back from dissolving that identity or falling into the unconscious. This Good is the conviction that the world, the classroom, and I as a teacher can be better.

Rather than repudiating those Others or seeing that initial identity and the consequent expansion of that identity as alienated, rather than working to dissolve that identity, we can grow beyond it as we reform it. By maintaining our relationship to that initial Other, by remaining connected to that initial identity and the regression that takes us back to it, we can also resist returning as the master.

Lacan was right when he advocated a regression, but so was Socrates who held a conviction of justice, beauty, truth, and the Good. But we must also live in a world of classroom hubbub, troubled kids, poor pay, too much work, and too little love—and in this world we must find a position of hope, must sustain a position between the one who knows and the one who cares.

Lacan and Socrates were right at the midpoint. We do teach a learning and we do infect others with our perplexity. At the midpoint we ask grateful questions of our students as we become their students. At the midpoint Lacan becomes Socrates' student and Socrates his. At that intersection that occurs in the realm of necessity, student and teacher meet at the crossroads.

REFERENCES

Clement, C. (1983). *The lives and legends of Jacques Lacan* (A. Goldhammer, Trans.). New York: Columbia University Press.

Felman, S. (1982). Psychoanalysis and education: Teaching terminable and interminable. In B. Johnson (Ed.), *The pedagogical imperative: Teaching as a literary genre* (pp. 21–44). New Haven, CT: Yale University Press.

Foucault, M. (1972). *The order of things*. New York: Vintage.

Gallop, J. (1982). *The daughter's seduction*. Ithaca, NY: Cornell University Press.

Jackson, P. (1968). *Life in classrooms*. New York: Holt, Rinehart & Winston.

Lacan, J. (1972). *Ecrits* (A. Sheridan, Trans.). New York: Holt, Rinehart & Winston.

Lacan, J. (1981). *Four fundamental concepts of psychoanalysis*. New York: Norton.

Lowes, J. L. (1964). *The road to Xanadu*. Boston: Houghton Mifflin.

Mitchell, J., & Rose, J. (Eds.). (1983). *Feminine sexuality: Jacques Lacan and the ecole Freudienne*. New York: Norton.

Olsen, G. (1988, July–August). Execution class. *Zeta,* pp. 33–38.

Plato. (1986). *Meno* (W. K. Guthrie, Trans.). New York: Penguin.

Plato. (1987a). *Theaetetus* (L. Campbell, Trans.). New York: Arno.

Plato. (1987b). *The republic* (D. L. Lee, Trans.). New York: Penguin.

Ragland-Sullivan, E. (1987). *Jacques Lacan and the philosophy of psychoanalysis*. Chicago: University of Illinois Press.

Riegel, K. (1973). *Dialectical operations: The final period of cognitive development*. Unpublished manuscript, available from Educational Testing Service, Princeton, NJ.

Appendix
About the Contributors
Index

Genealogical Notes

The History of Phenomenology and Post-Structuralism in Curriculum Studies

HISTORY OF PHENOMENOLOGY IN CURRICULUM STUDIES

Dwayne Huebner introduced phenomenology to curriculum studies in the 1960s. Perhaps his "Curriculum as Concern for Man's Temporality," read to the 1967 Ohio State University Curriculum Theory Conference and printed in *Theory into Practice* (reprinted in *Curriculum Theorizing: The Reconceptualists*), can be acknowledged as the specific event. Huebner's colleague at Teachers College, Columbia University, Maxine Greene, drew upon phenomenology, existentialism, and imaginative literature in her evocative studies in philosophy of education. Her work influenced a number of curriculum scholars a decade later, including Janet Miller, Madeleine Grumet, and William Pinar. David Denton's 1974 collection included essays by phenomenological philosophers such as Chamerlin, Trountner, and Vandenberg. However, Huebner must be credited with introducing this important European philosophical tradition to curriculum studies in the mid-1960s.

Max van Manen and William F. Pinar continued the introduction of phenomenology to curriculum studies in the early 1970s, although neither knew of the existence of the other until 1976. Van Manen had studied phenomenology in his native Holland; Pinar was introduced to the subject in 1967 as an undergraduate at Ohio State University. Van Manen introduced the subject to his Ph.D. advisor, Tetsuo Aoki, as he included phenomenological elements in his Ph.D. dissertation, written in 1972. Pinar studied phenomenology with his graduate students, most notably Madeleine R. Grumet, at the University of Rochester. He had moved quickly from phenomenology to autobiography by 1975, although there was always an important phenomenological dimension to autobiographical work (see Chapter 2). Pinar and Grumet still write in a phenomenological mode on occasion (Pinar, Chapter 5 in this volume; Grumet, 1988a). Grumet's feminist theory exhibits considerable phenomenological influence (Grumet, 1988b), as does that of Janet L. Miller (1988, 1990), also a student at Rochester in 1973. It was van Manen and Aoki, however, who advanced the phenomenological cause most force-fully and who established the University of Alberta as the North American center for phenomenological studies in education.

Max van Manen and Ted Aoki

Max van Manen is the "father" of phenomenological curriculum study in Canada (Smith, 1988), perhaps the most influential phenomenologist in North American curriculum studies at the present time. (We include the qual-ification "perhaps" because Aoki's visibility is commensurate.) Van Manen was introduced to phenomenology and hermeneutics in 1962 while studying education at the State Pedagogical Academy in Hilversum, the Netherlands (five years before he included phenomenology in his dissertation research at the University of Alberta). One of the first and main theoreticians was M. J. Langeveld. Van Manen studied his *Beknopte Theoretische Pedagogiek (Concise Theoretical Pedagogy)* and twelve other Langeveld volumes. He was also taken with an edited volume by J. H. van den Berg, entitled *Persoon en Wereld (Person and World),* which he used later in the writing of his Ph.D. dissertation (van Manen, 1988).

Van Manen introduced Aoki to phenomenology (Aoki, 1988; Carson, 1988) during van Manen's Ph.D. study with Aoki. Aoki supported van Ma-nen's dissertation research, which explored the "application of phenomenol-ogy to curriculum" (Carson, 1988). Van Manen introduced phenomenology to Aoki when he "was seeking wholeness, seeking an authentic reading of 'we' through such people as Buber (sensing something still missing), seeking what it is to be a Zen master with this disciplinary stick." Van Manen reports that Aoki "had a captivating way of employing general systems notions and concept-based epistemologies to ask more fundamental philosophical ques-tions about teaching and curriculum" (van Manen, 1988). Aoki's influence on van Manen was evident in van Manen's M.A. thesis, entitled *The Nature of Concepts in the Social Studies.* However, in the final stages of writing the Ph.D. dissertation, van Manen experienced a "crisis of relevance. . . . I came to the realization that a cybernetic or systems perspective led me further away from the concreteness of the lifeworld" (van Manen, 1988). Van Manen re-ports that he:

> called on Dr. Aoki at his home. There I explained my sense of frustration . . . and asked if he would object if I included a phenomenological perspective in the dissertation. Ted's greatness as a teacher showed itself not only in his prepared-ness to let a student take a risk by following his own path, but also in his ability to help me strengthen my resolve and by indicating that an epistemological wed-ding or comparison between the cybernetic view and the Dutch phenomenolog-ical view of teaching and curriculum would be a worthwhile dissertation project.

After conferral of the Ph.D., van Manen taught at the Ontario Institute for Studies in Education in Toronto. There he became friends with Dieter Misgeld, who introduced van Manen to the work of Jürgen Habermas. Via Professor Misgeld, van Manen met Gadamer at Misgeld's home in Toronto. "As a result of these experiences," van Manen reports, "I presented my first papers at AERA and Social Studies conferences on the implications and differences of the interpretive phenomenological approach and the critical theory approach" (1988). Professor Aoki visited him at OSIE, while he (van Manen) was studying Habermas. Returning to Edmonton, Aoki's Ph.D. students Walter Werner (now at the University of British Columbia) and Bryan Connors (Edmonton School Board) brought him W. F. Pinar's edited *Curriculum Theorizing: The Reconceptualists*. Aoki reports: "That last event did it!" Thereafter Aoki's work took a decided phenomenological turn. As well, he identified himself with the so-called reconceptualist movement.

Another "event" during this important period of theoretical reformulation for Aoki occurred during his tenure at the University of British Columbia, the period 1975–1978. He was invited to speak at the inauguration of Concordia University's doctoral program in fine arts. Aoki served as one of three speakers; Helmet Wagner from the New School for Social Research (and a Schutz disciple and colleague) and Kenneth Beittle from Pennsylvania State University were the others. Aoki's paper was the now well-known "Towards Curriculum Inquiry in a New Key" (1985). Also during the British Columbia period, Aoki led the British Columbia Social Studies Assessment, a project in which he included "critical" as well as phenomenological dimensions. Both events strengthened his phenomenological interests.

Aoki returned to the University of Alberta as chair of the Department of Secondary Education in 1977, where he remained until his retirement in 1985. During this relatively short period, Aoki—primarily through pedagogic power and tact—established the department as the North American center for phenomenological—or, more broadly, human science—studies in curriculum. Among his students are Terry Carson, Basil Favaro, Linda Peterat, Stephen Bath, Eric Chappell, Mahn Oh, and Sook Hur Ki-Hyung Hong (who worked with Ken Jacknicke and translated Helmut Wagner's *Phenomenology of Consciousness and Sociology of the Life World* into Korean). Describing the important Aoki-van Manen relationship, Margaret Hunsberger (1988) writes:

Dr. Aoki is a catalyst who has been very effective in bringing people and ideas together. In general terms, he is certainly Max's academic "father." But with phenomenology specifically, I don't think that quite holds. As I see it, Ted provided an environment, a context, in which Max could flourish. This was true, both when they were advisor and graduate student and later when they were department head and faculty member. When Max was a student Ted gave him his head and let him explore new directions and write a typical dissertation. Max began his professional career at OSIE where he was strongly influenced by Dieter Misgeld who, I think, moved him further toward phenomenology. And of course, his Dutch connections are not to be ignored. With Dutch as his mother tongue, he had access to scholarly work in Holland well before it was available in translation. Langeveld, among others, made a real impact on him. . . . I'd conclude that various influences (at least these three: Aoki, Misgeld, Utrecht) came together, rather like streams into a river, to give rise to Max's conceptualizing of phenomenology.

Relatedly, David Smith (another Aoki student) writes: "Ted was/is unquestionably 'father'; however—to us all. Ted's abiding strength was to discern good things and then support and encourage them to full flower" (1988).

The phenomenological emphasis continues under the tenure of Dr. Ken Jacknicke, Aoki's associate chair from 1977 to 1985 and current (1990) chair of the department. Jacknicke took his B.Ed. and M.Ed. at the University of Alberta, the Ph.D. at the University of Colorado in Boulder. Out of a traditional-technical background in science education, Jacknicke studied phenomenological research during his seven-year colleagueship with Aoki. Under the Aoki-Jacknicke administrations the phenomenological emphasis has been extended beyond curriculum and pedagogy to include teacher education and subject-matter specializations such as English, mathematics, science, physical education, social studies, drama, art, and religious studies. The University of Alberta Department of Secondary Education exerts enormous influence in those curriculum discourses associated with the hermeneutical and phenomenological traditions, as illustrated in this collection. In addition to those scholars whose affiliations are the University of Alberta—Carson, jagodzinski, van Manen—one other took her Ph.D. degree at the University: Margaret Hunsberger. Other University of Alberta faculty are involved in phenomenological/hermeneutic research.

Van Manen is critical of the focus on curriculum, arguing that pedagogy is the proper concern of educational studies. This view reveals van Manen's existential phenomenological roots, as well as the primacy of pedagogy among Dutch and German education faculties. Van Manen returned to the Netherlands during the 1970s, interviewing Langeveld, Bijl, and Tak. Langeveld referred van Manen to his former student Ton Beekman, who had been appointed to a chair in theoretical and historical pedagogy at the University of Utrecht. Van Manen credits Beekman with "democratizing" the phenomenological method so that a larger number of students could utilize it. However, he took exception to Beekman's ethnographic interests, which, in van Manen's view, "tended to lead to a certain shallowness that sacrificed the scholarly impulse to democratic aim" (van Manen, 1988). Carson believes that this Dutch and German educational literature and Heidegger have influenced van Manen most. Recently, van Manen has attempted to "show" pedagogy via a poetic language describing pedagogical situations between parent and child, teacher and child, and so forth (Carson, 1988). To illustrate this point, when van Manen returned to the University of Alberta in 1976 as associate professor, he began offering a curriculum course in phenomenological research. When the course was regularized, it was entitled "Pedagogical Theorizing" and recently was renamed "Human Science Research in Pedagogy." This rootedness in pedagogy rather than curriculum is a major difference between van Manen and Aoki, and van Manen and the Americans, specifically Grumet and Pinar.

Van Manen and his students report they have "experimented" with research in lived experience as "text based." This research-as-writing program, van Manen writes, "draws research and writing into a close and active relation which I have termed 'pedagogical theorizing.' Theorizing [is not practiced] in an abstracting alienating sense, but in a mundane sense of bringing everyday lived experience to reflective awareness in a textual or writing manner. This approach has both hermeneutic (in the German sense) and phenomenological (in the Dutch sense) dimensions. But of course there are infusions from semiotics (specially Barthes), narrative theory (e.g., Rosen), ethnomethodology (Blum). . . . My critical epistemological terms for this process are *pedagogic thoughtfulness* and *pedagogic tact*" (van Manen, 1988).

In contrast to van Manen, Aoki has been more interested in curriculum and hermeneutics. Through his work with Lee Brissey (his former professor at the University of Oregon), Aoki had been interested in the relationship between knowledge and human interests. During Carson's M.A. work in 1973–1974, this interest led Aoki to general systems theory. Then he read Macdonald's paper on "Curriculum and Human Interests" (Macdonald, 1975), which he extended and reformulated in his "Toward Curriculum Inquiry in a New Key."

Hermeneutics tends to be more "eclectic" than phenomenology (Carson, 1988), partly because phenomenological work "still seems to be influenced by the ghost of Husserl and the search for a transcendental methodology." The hermeneutic tradition is "more broad." "Informed by the need to interpret, which rises out of the experience of misunderstanding, hermeneutics draws upon phenomenology and critical theory as ways of gaining insight" (Carson, 1988).

> Unlike critical theory, hermeneutics is a humble gesture, acknowledging that life proceeds and surrounds interpretation. Thus understanding is always incomplete and one must always be attentive to the lifeworld of the school as experienced by teachers and students. This is the phenomenological moment of hermeneutics. But understanding also requires that these individual stories be contextualized in the larger cultural story. This is where the contribution of critical theory comes in, as does post-structuralism. (Carson, 1988)

This view is not universal among phenomenologists. "I'm not sure if hermeneutics is more eclectic, however. . . . One of its [hermeneutics] strengths that it is, at least to a degree, interdisciplinary in nature" (Hunsberger, 1988). Hermeneutics holds more potential, David Smith argues, for thinking about experience and social life because phenomenology is apolitical. The notion that hermeneutics is interdisciplinary is demonstrated in work done by William Reynolds.

A Second Generation

Reynolds was introduced to phenomenology and autobiography during his studies with William Pinar and Madeleine Grumet at the University of Rochester. His dissertation, completed in 1986 and later published as *Reading Curriculum Theory: The Development of a New Hermeneutic* (1989), centers around the concept of a hermeneutic phenomenology. Based on the work of Paul Ricoeur, Reynolds uses literary theory, autobiography, and hermeneutics to achieve a heightened self-understanding and an understanding of that understanding. Reynolds cites Ricoeur's notion of hermeneutics.

> "Hermeneutics and reflective philosophy are correlative and reciprocal: on the one hand, self-understanding provides a way of understanding the cultural signs in which the self contemplates himself and forms himself, on the other hand, *the understanding of the text is not an end in itself and for itself;* it mediates the relation to himself of a subject who, in the short circuit of immediate reflection, would not find the meaning of his own life . . . reflection is nothing without mediation by means of signs and cultural works and that explanation is nothing if incorporated as an intermediary stage." (Ricoeur, in Reynolds, 1989, pp. 48–49; emphasis added)

Reynolds develops this type of understanding through the interpretive mediation of major texts in the curriculum theory field. This understanding leads one, Reynolds believes, to a sense of agency that becomes invariably political. "The agency will be to attempt to provide readers with a way to find their own voices and senses of agency in a world that is against such labor" (Reynolds, 1989).

Margaret Hunsberger (now at the University of Calgary) took "phenomenology as a research method in education" in the 1978–1979 term with van Manen, who had returned from OSIE (Carson, 1988), David Smith, and six others. It was the first time the course had been offered at Alberta. The enterprise was "uncertain, even insecure . . . at that point" (Hunsberger, 1988). It was unclear "whether phenomenology was a viable method."

David Smith (now at the University of Lethbridge, Alberta) was introduced to phenomenology as a M.A. student with Aoki at the University of British Columbia in 1976 (Aoki, 1988; Smith, 1988). Aoki had arrived in

Vancouver from Edmonton to serve as director of the Centre for the Study of Curriculum and Instruction. Phenomenological curriculum theory was nascent then. Walter Werner had just finished a Ph.D. dissertation with Aoki at Alberta, pursuing a Schutzian phenomenology, and Aoki was able to appoint Werner to the first staff position at the Centre.

Werner attempted to establish a phenomenology research center at the University of British Columbia, but after only a few offerings it was discontinued, largely because of resistance from the faculty generally, which in turn left students politically vulnerable (Smith, 1988). Smith observes: "This is an example of the kind of resistance phenomenology has experienced in many quarters, and I've learned from hard experience that it is often politically risky to trace one's intellectual lineage to phenomenology. Apparently job-hunting doctoral students from the University of Alberta now check out beforehand whether or not it is appropriate to use the 'f' (ph) word in job interviews" (Smith, 1988).

Although retired from the University of Alberta, Aoki is an active scholar today, recently teaching at the University of Victoria, the University of Lethbridge, and Louisiana State University, influencing students to look "to contemporary French philosophy for curriculum insights." Eric Chappell (another Aoki Ph.D.) was influential in guiding him in this direction. This is typical of Ted's learning from his students. Max van Manen and Walter Werner was also important in this way in relation to phenomenology" (Carson, 1988).

David Jardine, currently at the University of Calgary, writes:

> I enter curriculum studies backwards to most of the people mentioned already, beginning (after an undergraduate degree in philosophy and comparative religious studies) with an M.A. in philosophy emphasizing Edmund Husserl's phenomenology, done with Gary Madison at McMaster University in Hamilton, Ontario from 1974–77. Gary is currently the head of the Canadian Society for Hermeneutics and Post-Modern Thought and did his doctoral work with Paul Ricoeur in Paris. From there, I moved to O.I.S.E. in Toronto into philosophy of education and did my Ph.D. (completed 1983) with Dieter Misgeld (who did his work in Germany with Gadamer and Habermas, in that order). I thus ended up developing an interest in curriculum and pedagogy out of an interest in phenomenology, rather than vice versa. My dissertation was on Piaget and Heidegger.
>
> I ran across the others mentioned in the piece [this volume] you sent me by accident, meeting David Smith at the annual CSHPMT meetings in Winnipeg in May 1986. And, as anyone who has met David knows, things are different afterwards. (Jardine, 1990)

THERE IS RESISTANCE TO PHENOMENOLOGY, particularly in the United States. Richard Bernstein in his 1976 *Restructuring of Social and Political*

Theory criticizes phenomenology for lacking a political perspective. Clearly, however, Bernstein takes seriously the phenomenological perspective. Indeed, he concludes his study of "empiricism," phenomenology, and critical theory by suggesting that each represents a necessary epistemological moment in a comprehensive research orientation.

There is, additionally, a resistance to phenomenology in curriculum studies that can only be linked to ignorance, a fear and hostility toward that which one does not know and hence cannot understand (Pinar, 1990). This is flaw in the field, a philistine absence of commitment to teach curriculum theory comprehensively and impartially. There is an order of cultural resistance to phenomenology as well. David Smith understands this resistance as part of "a Western cultural predisposition against intimacy with the world. The sanctity of experience which phenomenology posits runs counter to Western metaphysics" (Smith, 1988).

Students embody this issue in their embrace or rejection of phenomenology. (Rarely do students seem to respond in a middle range.) Regarding those students who embrace this tradition, Smith observes:

> Graduate students first introduced to phenomenology often feel euphoric, as if they've at last found a language for the self felt to be lost or banished under the deep dogmas of the calculative dispensations of Western scientism. Unfortunately the euphoria sometimes translates into an excuse for not thinking deeply (politically, historically, socially) about experience, about its meaning, and this is the point at which phenomenology becomes sentimental subjectivism. (Smith, 1988)

Despite resistance from competing traditions and difficulties internal to it, phenomenological curriculum theory must be acknowledged as a major contemporary discourse. The volume and sophistication of its scholarship permit no other conclusion. Further, it is clear that serious study of this work will prove indispensable in our field's project to understand curriculum.

HISTORY OF POST-STRUCTURALISM IN CURRICULUM STUDIES

Post-modernism is an umbrella term that includes post-structuralism but refers as well to developments in architecture, science, and in the culture industry as well. In curriculum the best known post-modernist is William E. Doll, Jr. (in press). Critical theorists such as Henry A. Giroux (1988a, b, 1991) and Peter McLaren (1988) have incorporated post-modernism into recent scholarship. In his 1987 critique of Apple, Giroux, and other so-called new sociologists of curriculum, Philip Wexler appeared to embrace aspects of post-modernism and post-structuralism, but in a recent lecture (at Pinar's home, May 2, 1990) he spoke dispargingly of these movements. Here we restrict our focus to post-structuralism, although that term is an umbrella term as well.

Post-structuralism first appeared in American curriculum studies, as we noted in the introduction, in 1979 at the University of Rochester, in a doctoral dissertation written by Peter Maas Taubman. However, unknown to Taubman, two young Quebecois scholars—Jacques Daignault and Clermont Gauthier—were also at work studying post-structuralism. Daignault and Gauthier presented their first post-structuralist paper at the *JCT*-sponsored Airlie House Conference in 1980. Taubman left academia upon graduation to study acting in New York City. For most of the decade Daignault and Gauthier were the only curricularists working post-structurally. While post-structuralist scholarship and theory remain less voluminous than phenomenological scholarship, several curriculum specialists pursue these complex, varied, and sometimes inaccessible lines of research.

Cleo Cherryholmes

Cleo Cherryholmes is now the best-known scholar of post-structuralism in the United States, thanks to the publication of his *Power and Criticism: Poststructural Investigations in Education* (1988), the first book-length study of post-structuralism and education to appear. The book links post-structuralism with structuralism rather than with phenomenology, as does this collection.

Cherryholmes was trained as a political scientist (as of this writing he is professor of political science at Michigan State University), a preparation that stressed the adaptation of natural science to the study of politics. Analytic philosophy—the epistemological basis for the positivism-empiricism that typifies political science—gave way to postanalytic philosophy. Cherryholmes writes: "to make a long story short, I came to post-analytic philosophy by way of analytic philosophy and feel much more comfortable talking about poststructuralism in contrast to structuralism. I chose to couch the book [*Power and Criticism*] in terms of the latter because I think it is much easier to teach. . . . One of the reasons Jonas Soltis [Cherryholmes's series editor at Teachers College Press] responded so warmly to my manuscript even if he does not agree with much or most of it, [is] I think because the influence of analytic philosophy is always presented in my thinking and writing" (Cherryholmes, 1989).

Cherryholmes acknowledges that critical theory, and the work of Habermas in particular, demonstrated that knowledge is a social product. "Phenomenology reconstituted the subject/object distinction so central to positivism-empiricism, thus providing more insights into the social—and lived—nature of social knowledge. Society and the knowledge we produce about it are complex texts that have no beginning, center, or end. These arguments, in turn, toppled the hypothesized centeredness of the subject in phenomenology" (Cherryholmes, 1989).

Jacques Daignault

While Cleo Cherryholmes is the best-known scholar of post-structuralism in education, Jacques Daignault is the major post-structuralist theoretician in curriculum studies. The distinction is this: While Cherryholmes explains post-structuralism, Daignault writes about curriculum post-structurally. Excerpts from four unpublished Daignault essays appear in this collection.

Daignault studied music as an undergraduate. Glass, Reich, and particularly Cage influenced him most. He cites their influence as imprinting his later interests in Deleuze and Lyotard, whom he began to read in the late 1970s as a graduate student in education. He completed a post-structuralist dissertation at Université Laval in 1982. Since 1979 Daignault has taught at the University of Quebec at Rimouski (UQAR), interrupted by a year at the University of Paris and a year at Louisiana State University.

In autumn 1979 Daignault met Clermont Gauthier at UQAR; Gauthier had joined the faculty a year earlier. At that time Gauthier was working on "open systems theory" (associated with Checkland), which he hoped to apply to action research. His collaborator on this project was a colleague named Arthur Gelinas. During this time Gauthier was uninterested in post-structuralist writers. Both Gauthier and Daignault were unhappy with Marxism.

Daignault introduced Lyotard's work to Gauthier, whose first reaction was negative. Indeed, Daignault recalls Gauthier coming to his office after a few days with Lyotard, throwing the book down on his desk and exclaiming, "There is nothing there to be understood!" Daignault cites that moment as the commencement of a fruitful collaboration that lasted two years.

Daignault and Gauthier began discussing Lyotard and post-structuralism generally; after a few months Gauthier suggested that together they attempt to write curriculum theory inspired by post-structuralism. During the spring of 1980 the two men composed "The Indecent Curriculum Machine," which they presented to a stunned audience at the fall Airlie Conference sponsored by the editors of *JCT*. Those of us present at that presentation recall the excitement of listening to language forms and order of understanding that we knew were as important as they were initially opaque.

In the 1985–1986 academic year, Daignault taught and studied at the University of Paris. He was close to Ardoino and Lapassade, among the best-known education scholars in France. He taught a doctoral seminar linking post-structuralism with education; he reports that, at the time, no one was offering such a course in France. At the same time Daignault attended Deleuze's class on Foucault and Lyotard's on Kant. He was able to meet with both Deleuze and Lyotard privately. In 1987 Daignault met with Michel Serres in Montreal, interviewing him for the *Journal of Philosophy*. Daignault terms that day memorable, as Serres proved to be "a great teacher!"

Clermont Gauthier

Gauthier (1989) writes that post-structuralists consider style a major aspect of writing. "Style is a dimension of the content and is not only an ornamentation." Further, despite the many differences among Deleuze, Lyotard, Serres, Derrida, and Foucault, post-structuralists "have in common the idea to search for new ways of speaking the world after the dead end . . . of phenomenology and existentialism, after the Marxist disillusion (particularly after Czechoslovakia in 1968 and later in Afghanistan), and after the formal excess of structuralism of Levi-Strauss" (Gauthier, 1989).

Gauthier links the evolution of his interest in post-structuralism to conditions in Quebec. Until the end of the 1950s, he writes, Quebec was "strongly Catholic"; "most intellectuals were Thomists and it was a sad period of obscurantism. I was educated like the other children in Quebec in this atmosphere of holy water." He continues:

> With the sixties, later in the seventies in Quebec was like everywhere in the world. We opened to the ideas associated with Marxism and existentialism. It was like fresh air, but at the same time these ideas create their own new obscurantism. . . . In 1980 in Quebec the "Parti Quebecois" was the government. It was the time for the Referendum [independence for Quebec from Canada]. By the way, you have to know that poets were at the origin of that political movement. At the time Jacques Daignault and I were discussing the movement a great deal (hundreds of hours); we were both strongly in favor of Quebec's independence. And we were studying passionately "post-structuralism." The context of independence for Quebec meant for us: the act of creation of a country, liberation from domination by Anglo-Canadians, the elaboration of a discourse that was not Thomist, Marxist, or existentialist. We were experimenting with a new rhetoric and enjoying the "puissance" it gave us. In this atmosphere of excitement Jacques and I produced "The Indecent Curriculum Machine," a kind of expression of the new "puissance" (in Nietzschean sense) we were living. At the political level there was a country to build, at the educative level there was too a new space to occupy with new intellectual tools: "the post-structuralist ones." But while writing "The Indecent Curriculum Machine" I was sure of one thing: I would never be a member of a "post-structuralist movement." . . . To create yes; to dominate, no; to be a pope, no; to follow one, much less. (Gauthier, 1989)

Gauthier reports that he is less interested in post-structuralism now. He felt that the primacy of style functioned well to undermine the dominant ideology of the late 1970s, but now it has had the "perverse effect" of creating a new elite. "For my part," Gauthier writes, "now I try to write in education like Calvino or Kundera does a novel: a minimum of tools and a maximum of effects. This is surely an esthetic consequence of my 'post-structuralist' readings but without the baroque ornaments" (Gauthier, 1989).

Peter Maas Taubman

During his senior year in college (1969), Peter Taubman began to study identity formation, including the function of the "Other." More generally, during this period he began to explore the relations between language and reality, and specifically the ways in which language constitutes reality. His initial bachelor's thesis explored African-American theater but changed to focus on work of Jean Genet, whose play *The Blacks* (and its famous epigram *"Qu'est que c'est un Negre and quelle est sa couleur?"*) raised questions of identity.

During the early and mid-1970s, Taubman investigated the Vedantic philosophies of Huxley and Isherwood, the Buddhism of Suzuki, and the writings of Mukantananda, Ram Dass, Rimpoche, and Alan Watts. During this period identity appeared to him as a costume draped over Atman-Brahman or a divine no-thingness. Left unanswered were questions of the process of identity constitution and the composition of a nontheological noumena.

The sexual-political movements of the 1970s led Taubman to investigate feminism and homosexual theory. His curiosity regarding gender identity intersected with his continuing interests in language and identity formation generally. He lived in the Berkeley gay community for a few months, where he became frustrated with what he perceived as a counterproductive trend in sexual politics to preserve static concepts of gender identity.

To look into this blind spot in contemporary gender discourses, Taubman turned to the work of Michel Foucault and secondarily to the work of Jacques Derrida and Jacques Lacan. Reflecting upon sexual politics and gender identity formation, Taubman reports that he was then about to move "beyond the discursive grid that was both trapping individuals and forming them as *idées fixes* in the shape of 'man,' 'woman,' 'lesbian,' 'homosexual,' 'heterosexual,' and 'sexual'" (Taubman, 1990). This move was the subject of his doctoral dissertation at the University of Rochester (1979).

The dissertation, published in its entirety in *JCT* in 1982, was the first post-structuralist study of curriculum in the United States and, more specifically, the first post-structuralist study of gender in the curriculum field.

Not until the mid-1980s did Taubman again take up the work he began in his dissertation. By then other writers—most notably French feminists such as Cixous, Iragaray, and Kristeva—had extended the ideas of Lacan, Foucault, and Derrida to address feminist understandings of gender. In the United States Chodorow employed object relations theory to construct a sociology of gender, work Grumet and Pinar in turn employed in their analyses of gender and schooling. None of these Americans, however, employed Foucault or Lacan in their efforts. In 1986, employing the work of Chodorow, Pinar, and Grumet, Taubman examined male identity development and specifically the role of castration. In so doing he moved away from his earlier work, in which he had attempted to unhook or de-cathect identity and discourse from prediscursive (or in phenomenological terms, preconceptual) reality. In this respect Taubman regards his essay, "The Silent Center: An Essay on Masculinity," as a step backwards, but a necessary one. The essay asks: "What is the relationship between the flesh (or the unconscious) and discourse? What is relationship between identity and the subject?" (Taubman, 1990).

To answer these questions, Taubman returns to Foucault's teacher—Lacan—and explores the ways discourse creates and is substantiated by the body and the unconscious. "Achieving the Right Distance" (Chapter 13) plays Lacan off Plato to understand how the identity of teacher is formed, reconciling the symbolic and the real (Taubman, 1990).

jan jagodzinski

Jan Jagodzinski, a University of Alberta Ph.D. who has moved from phenomenology to post-structuralism, writes:

"i have been given permission to write my own story, to write/right/rite myself into this post-structuralist genealogy of curriculum studies. Such a task is wickedly amusing, If i understand Derrida's project even remotely, it has been his uncanny ability not to be pinned down, not to be named, which has given him room to play and not get tagged. It is precisely that possessive ego, the omnipresent eye/i that he hoped to deconstruct, that very ego that profits through the name by claiming exclusivity in its signature. In many ways, a genealogy repeats and vivifies the presence of such signatures. It situates and establishes its own canon, formulating yet another grand narrative, which Lyotard so adamantly hoped to abolish.

"There is something decidedly paradoxical in claiming participation in a post-structuralist genealogy whose very project has been to undermine and decenter the formation of any such canon. But Derrida could not play his ruse for long. Soon he would be 'it.' His marginality is slowly being centralized. He has been named 'father' of deconstruction and the 'ladies-man' of feminist post-structuralism, two equally pejorative titles that he cannot avoid being labeled despite his protestations. Perhaps he has now been housebroken by the California sun, living the life of Baudrillardian *simulacra,* for every recent bit of esoteric dribble is now given saintly status. Like Picasso, his signature, his style has become commodified. Patriarchal implications aside, he has become an industry unto himself. Like the proclamation by the fine arts industry that Robert Mappelthorpe, once he died of *AIDS* at the tender age of 31, was a postmodern photographic master, Derrida's reputation too is genealogically assured. Despite himself, he too has become a postmodern master.

"One can well understand the pain of anonymity in a society that celebrates signature. The worst fate one can suffer is to be homeless and become a parasite/paracite/parasight, to live on the material and intellectual waste of the wealthy and the intellectually elite. Yet it is the metaphor of the parasite/cite/sight and the vicissitudes of para/dox that "spell" the post-structuralist game. Doxa now supplants truth. In this sense, i especially applaud the efforts of Jacques Daignault, who has refused to compromise his discourse and become famous by publishing mainstream dribble. His work remains difficult and challenging, problematizing the reader and the reading. It was a full twenty-three years later, in 1980, that Derrida finally conducted his 'thesis defense' based on the writings of his published books. There is a lesson in that for all of those on the genealogical tree.

"So what remains to be said which continues this antibiographical vein? My pedigree remains that of a mongrel for i see myself more as a student than professor, searching, listening to the voices of Others who remain nameless, but whose moral, ethical, and political i is resolutely sounded in ecological and feminist arguments. My teacher has been Harry Garfinkel, a person whose modesty and brilliance do not appear within the confines of any book cover, but whose generosity, kindness, and brilliance have been felt by many graduate students. Those who have seen the film *Jesus of Montreal* will readily understand me when i state that there are many Harry Garfinkels and Ted Aokis out there, silently working outside any genealogy, encouraging others to forget about their names, their greed, and star status for a more just society. Sometimes, fortune strikes and their students capture the sparks of the fire that spewed from their mouths. The major works of George Mead and de Saussure were written from the notes taken by their students. Were it not for the nameless, their thoughts would have been lost. In much the same way, the efforts of Bill Pinar, who has an ability to orchestrate a cacophony of voices, need to be recognized, for there is an equal generosity and recognition for the works of the nameless. i keep recalling that Socrates wrote *nothing* and we are still recovering from the misreading by Plato.

"*Genealogy:* jan jagodzinski: B.F.A., Prof. Dip., B.Ed., M.Ed., Ph.D. (1980); institutions attended: Notre Dame University, University of Alberta,

Kootney School of Art, University of Oregon, University of Warszawa, University of Leeds, Mount St. Vincent University, Royal Academy of Art; languages: English, Polish, German, French; areas of interest: *fast alles.*"

A Second Generation

Among Daignault's students are Rebecca Martusewicz (with whom he worked via telephone and correspondence while she studied at the University of Rochester), Wen Song Hwu, Nicole Perraton, and Robert McDonald (the last three at Louisiana State University). Pinar studied post-structuralism with Daignault as well, attending his doctoral seminars offered during the year (1988–1989) he taught at Louisiana State University.

REBECCA MARTUSEWICZ was introduced to the work of Michel Foucault by Philip Wexler in 1981 during her first year of graduate work at the University of Rochester. During the second year she read semiotics, especially the work of Roland Barthes, Umberto Eco, and Julia Kristeva. For a paper for the historian Christopher Lasch she utilized Barthes's concept of myth to perform a semiotic analysis of the feminization of teaching, a paper she developed and delivered at the 1983 Bergamo Conference. At the meeting she met Jacques Daignault.

The following year Martusewicz studied with Daignault via telephone. She read his work, Descombes's study of modern French philosophy, and Foucault. Martusewicz recalls: "We talked about paradox versus dialectical thinking, about theory, practice, writing, teaching and thinking, about poetics, about the problems of ideology and terrorism in Marxism. . . . These wonderful two-hour discussions went on every other week for an entire semester" (Martusewicz, 1990).

During that same semester Martusewicz reports taking a women's studies course entitled "Feminist Criticism Beyond Positivism" wherein she read Kristeva, Luce Irigaray, Helen Cixous, Lacan, Foucault, Barthes, and Derrida. She remembers that "the feminist readings challenged the symbolic order as phallocentric, opening wide for me the pursuit of questions about language, knowledge, education, culture, difference, multiplicity and gender" (1990). This course and Daignault's resulted in questioning mainstream critical theory and in particular the concept of dialectic.

The following year Martusewicz studied linguistic anthropology with anthropologist Amelia Bell, from which followed her doctoral dissertation study of women's historical relation to knowledge. After two years of high school teaching, Martusewicz accepted a faculty position at Eastern Michigan University. Despite teaching obligations, she is—as of this writing (1990)—returning to Daignault's work:

"Supported and inspired by another of Jacques' students, Wen-Song, I have returned to my interest in pedagogy, theory and practice, and paradox, this time as a teacher. I'm reading Michel Serres, Gilles Deleuze, rereading Jacques' work and rethinking my approach to undergraduate teacher education. I will visit Wen-song and sit in on a course with Jacques and Bill Doll, offered at LSU this summer (1990). . . . The problem that I'm working on is how to teach about pedagogy as a performative thought act within the social relations of schooling. The question is how not to get caught in old social theory categories, how not to close up the gap between theory and practice while trying to teach as I think. It's a problematic that fights against the assignment of fixed identity, hierarchy and domination. I'm still learning how not to get stuck in sad passion when thinking about what goes on in schools. It's actually that challenge that I want to offer my students as they learn to be thoughtful teachers. Meanwhile, another Bergamo approaches, so I write" (Martusewicz, 1990).

PATTI LATHER IS another major figure in this second generation of scholars. Currently at Ohio State University, Professor Lather writes:

"You [Pinar] will be pleased to know that my interest began at the 1986 Bergamo conference. I had been vaguely aware of Daignault's work for a few years—considered it outside of my frame of reference (which at that time was a kind of socialist-feminism). But the 1986 conference made me aware that Jacques was not some idiosyncratic French guy with a penchant for obscure prose and word plays. This certainly had something to do with the presence of others in the program (I especially remember a guy from L.S.U. whose name I cannot now remember; I remember people buzzing about how brilliant he was; I remember not understanding a word of his presentation). [This was probably Eric Chappell—eds.] Becky Martusewicz was making her break from Phil Wexler's neo-Marxism; I remember supporting her in her separation from the father, but I also remember not understanding what she was doing. When I returned from the conference that fall, I told people something was going on that I needed to know more about, and that it had something to do with a way of thinking that 'tickled one into awareness' as opposed to the neo-Marxist use of language, where one often felt battered into awareness.

"Lucky for me a student more schooled in critical theory than myself volunteered to get me up to speed. He Xeroxed articles and provided bibliographies, and I began trying to find my way through the burgeoning literature. Lucky for me also was that a former student of Gayatri Spivak's was teaching right down the hall from me and was interested in forming a reading group. We began with the Frankfurt School and quickly moved into an anthology entitled *On Signs,* edited by Marshall Blonsky (John Hopkins University Press, 1985). Some of us attended an amazing conference in April, 1987 ('Postmodernism: Text, Politics, Instruction'), sponsored by the University of Kansas and the International Association of Philosophy and Literature. Spivak, Frederic Jameson, Richard Bernstein, Nancy Fraser, Kenneth Framptom, and a host of others were there. I figure the conference saved me a year or so of reading and focusing my sense of the issues.

"Simultaneous to the conference, I was teaching a course, 'Feminism and Postmodern Thought.' Committed to reading only women, we did much with the 'new French feminists.' This course was my effort to begin to come to grips with my earlier dismissal of such work as 'essentialist.' We read Toril Moi's *Sexual/Textual Politics: Feminist Literary Theory* (Methuen, 1985) and Alice Jardine's *Gynesis* (Cornell University Press, 1985) in order to explore the implications of post-modernism for the arts and humanities, and Sandra Harding's *The Science Question in Feminism* (Cornell University Press, 1986) for the sciences. Central questions included the following: How can liberatory intentions become part of what Foucault terms 'master discourses'? How can feminist thought and practice escape becoming a totalizing, dogmatic discourse itself? What challenges does post-modernist discourse present to feminist thought and practice and vice versa?

"A final conference that was very important to me was the April 1990 'Cultural Studies Now and in the Future' conference at the University of Illinois: Donna Haraway, Homi Bhabha, Meaghan Morris, Michelle Wallace, Stuart Hall, Constance Penley, James Clifford, Cornell West, Andrew Ross, and many others. I took 24 pages of notes (at AERA I average half a page!). The conference made those of us who went from our Postmodern Studies (PMS) feminist theory reading group at O.S.U. feel that we were doing well in terms of what we were reading and how we were wrestling with the issues. Both the PMS group and such conferences seem especially important with trying to 'keep up' theoretically and politically with this stuff. Wrestling collectively with its implications provides both the pleasure and the political accountability that might get lost by oneself.

"None of the above addresses why I have become so utterly absorbed in 'the postmodern turn' (Hassan, 1987). Two reasons come immediately to mind.

"First, it addresses concerns I have long had with the limits of emancipatory discourse-practices. I had found my own way, via the intersection of feminist and neo-Marxist practice and theory, to be uncomfortable with issues of imposition in emancipatory work. Much of 'pomo' [post-modernism; actually 'pomo' comes from *Utne Reader* issue on post-modernism, July/August, 1989] seemed to be paralleling such feminist discomforts as well as challenging some of feminism's own blind spots. Even with only a tentative grasp of 'pomo,' I was quite struck with its tremendous implications for practice with emancipatory intentions. Key to what I have been able to work out thus far is some movement of 'critical intellectuals' away from the position of either universal spokespeople for the disenfranchised or local warriors against the barriers that keep people from speaking for themselves. While still largely unarticulated, this post-modern repositioning of critical intellectuals has to do with struggling to decolonize the space of academic discourse that is accessed by our privilege, to open that space up in a way that contributes to the production of a politics of difference. Such a politics recognizes the paradox, complexity, and complicity at work in our efforts to understand and change the world.

"Second, and not unrelated, I find great pleasure in the kind of thinking that this body of work evokes in me. There is a fluidity, a serious kind of 'playfulness' at work here where I begin to get a feel for what it might be like to think differently about what it means to know and be known. And the differences mesh with my sense of what is needed in order to break out of the dead ends of the Left in U.S. politics. Contextually, of course, all of this began for me at the end of the Reagan years, where I was hiding out in the relatively nurturing space of a quite radical women's studies program. 'Pomo' fed my head in ways that let me position that time/this time as the 'dying gasp of a dinosaur era,' a time that generated its fervor from its own sense of displacement. Similarly, it continues to help me 'read the world' in ways I find inspiring. The collapse of the Berlin Wall, unexpected outcomes in Nicaragua, the naked hand of power in China, the reconfigurations of the struggle for women's reproductive rights: In the face of a swirl of contemporary events, 'I feel transformed, renewed, and sacralized' instead of exhausted and overwhelmed (Stephen Tyler, 1987, writing of ethnographic truth effects, p. 126, quoted in Scheurick, in press). Jameson's argument that post-modernism is not something we decide to like or not, but the condition of our time, Baudrillard's ideas regarding the society of spectacle and simulacra, Foucault's concept of power/knowledge, Derrida's deconstruction of logocentrism: All of this helps me make sense of a world that continues to elude our efforts to 'explain,' to 'know,' to 'change' in a way that is other to nihilism or existential despair.

"Who have been my main folks? Certainly Gayatri Spivak. I just finished reading *The Post-Colonial Critic: Interviews, Strategies, Dialogues* (Routledge, 1990; see also Spivak, 1987a,b). I have such respect for the way her mind is always moving across the arenas of international politics, global economy, the academic marketplace, and counterdisciplinary practices, especially feminist and postcolonial work. I also find Sandra Harding (1986–1987) and Donna Haraway (1985, 1988) of great help in trying to think through what all of this means for ways of doing research in the human sciences. And Linda Hutcheon's two books, *A Poetics of Postmodernism: History, Theory, Fiction*

(Routledge, 1988) and *The Politics of Postmodernism* (Routledge, 1989) have addressed many of my concerns.

"In terms of men, I find Edward Said (1975, 1986, 1989) and Stuart Hall (1985, 1990) my main influences. Both are committed to a global politics that is similar to mine. The post-Fordism literature coming out of Britain's *Marxism Today* has been especially useful to me as I wrestle with those other men, Derrida, Foucault, and Baudrillard. Foucault is easier for me ('Do You Cry When You Read Foucault?' is the title of a graduate reading group here at O.S.U.!), but something tells me Derrida is more important for me. This has to do, I think, with my disdain for psychology (you notice no word of Lacan here, outside parenthesis!). And in spite of his reputation as the 'wild man of post-structuralism,' I find my limited reading of Baudrillard quite invigorating. With all of them, I position myself as I did with Marxism then years ago: Take what seems useful in a feminist struggle for a more just world and throw away the rest.

"Still in terms of men, in ways I cannot understand, I cannot seem to leave Althusser alone. I went away to New Zealand carrying my Gramsci with me, thinking to do something along the lines of Spivak's 'Speculations on Reading Marx: After Reading Derrida' (1987b). Instead, I read, and continue to read, Althusser: *Essays in Self-Criticism* (New Left Books, 1976) and *Philosophy and the Spontaneous Philosophy of the Scientists* (Verso, 1990). And I am haunted by a story I heard from a sociologist in New Zealand who had heard the story as a student of Foucault: that Althusser speaks to Gramsci each night before retiring to his bed in the madhouse where he was placed after killing his (feminist) wife. Something is brewing in me about all of this that I will eventually write about.

"Moving away from categories of female/male for a moment, I also read everything I can find by Hal Foster (e.g., 1985, 1988), who in his own writing and in his edited collections opens me up to how post-structuralism inscribes/is inscribed in the art world. I actually find this the single most fertile source for my own thinking. As I grasp how art work both constructs and is constructed by 'pomo,' I then try to apply it to doing empirical research in the human sciences. I think my attraction here is to the theory-practice nexus of art criticism. What art does, of course, is document the human effort to represent the unrepresentable. Foster, for example, writes of the practice of some 'pomo' artists of using old forms to show how lived experience eludes representation in a way that shows the dangers of the old forms, 'to rehearse the obsolescence of our thought, the inadequacy of our representation' (1984, p. 86). Efforts to theorize out of such practice have much to offer in reinscribing approaches to empirical work in the human sciences.

"What does all of this make me? At AERA in 1987 I prefaced my remarks with, 'I have finally learned the lesson of the new French feminists: that I am a constantly moving subjectivity.' In my book, *Getting Smart: Feminist Research and Pedagogy With/in the Postmodern* (Routledge, 1991), I present myself thus: 'As a first-world women—white, middle-class, North American, heterosexual, my self described positionality shifts from "postmarxist feminist" to "postmodern materialist-feminist." Which I then immediately qualify, in a note, with:

> This listing of positionality has long been normative in feminist scholarship. It is, however, much problematized by poststructural debates on the authority of meaning, specifically the role of the author. Additionally, poststructuralism brings into question the idea of a unified, stable "self" capturable via linguistic portrayal. For example, that I write from a position of heterosexual privilege is not unimportant, but heterosexual feels a thin term and an unattractive kind of closure to the complexity of my life. How to use such categories as provisional constructions rather than as systematic formulations and what this means in terms of identity politics remain largely unexplored territory. Additionally, Spivak (1989) cautions against "a kind of confessional attitudinizing" which occludes that a subject position is a sign "of an ethno-politics, of a psychosexual reality, of an institutional position, and this is not under the control of the person who speaks . . . A subject position is a hard place, and we cannot read it ourselves" (pp. 208–210). (Lather, 1991, p. 166)

"I also immediately problematize both 'post-Marxist' (distinguishing it from anti-Marxism) and 'materialist' (given its reproduction of the idealist/ materialist polarity), and go on to question the whole business of classifying the various strands of feminism. I conclude this interrogation of categories of feminism with de Lauretis's (1989) cautions regarding 'the typological project' (p. 33) as constructing 'an ascending scale of theoretico-political sophistication' (p. 4). Her term of choice is 'non-denominational feminist theorist' (p. 9).

"I am not 'non-denominational.' As is obvious from the above, what Linda Hutcheon (1988) terms 'neo-Nietzschean schizocynicism' is not attractive to me. Indeed, I have long toyed with the thesis that nihilism is a sort of 'white boy angst,' a gendered subjectivity that has deeply inscribed those parts of post-structuralism that serve as a mask with which a frustrated, defeated consciousness tries to cover up its own negativity. My attraction to 'pomo' comes more from those attempting 'a critical appropriation of postmodernism' which grows out of the dilemma of those intellectuals who, while committed to emancipatory discourse and modernist strategies (e.g., consciousness raising), are yet engaged by post-modernism to try to use it in the interests of emancipation. It is this intersection of post-modernism and the politics of emancipation that I put at the center of my exploration of what it might mean to generate ways of knowing that can take us beyond ourselves.

"So what am I? Certainly a feminist. Certainly a feminist 'cultural worker,' sited in the academy and most intrigued with the implications of post-structuralism for the research and pedagogy that I undertake in the name of liberation. Beyond that, I cannot say. My feminist theory PMS group at O.S.U. continues to play with such questions as Where we are drawn intellectually and why? What differences does this make in our academic practices and the ways we live our lives? What are the politics of the relationship of feminism to the essentially male-based discourses of 'pomo'? These are questions that position us as feminists paradoxically aware of our own seduction and resistances to the post-modern, cultivating a deliberate ambivalence. This ambivalence is a way to interrupt the contestatory discourses of the various feminisms, neo-Marxisms, minoritarianisms, and post-structuralisms in order to begin to move outside of both the logic of binary oppositions and the principle of noncontradiction. Situated in our multiple sites for movements of social justice, we can begin to 'reinscribe otherwise' while avoiding the fall into an infinite regress of demystification. Both the seductions of and resistances to post-modernism can help us to 'get smart' about the possibilities and limits regarding, specifically, political work through education, and, more generally, a basis for critical social theories less ensnared in phallocentric and logocentric assumptions."

NICOLE PERRATON, who finished a M.A. at University of Quebec in Rimouski with Clermont Gauthier and Jacques Daignault and currently studies toward the Ph.D. at Louisiana State University, writes:

"I taught six years in private schools to children from 6 to 13 years old with severe learning abilities. My colleagues were as deeply involved as I was in the research of the passage between WHAT IS to WHAT OUGHT TO BE. Not only did we differ in our methods but also in our philosophical foundations. I had a great confidence in their competence. Then, how could we differ so strongly in our understanding and approach toward the children and learning?

"So I started my master's at Rimouski, attended a class in 'Les Courants Pedagogiques' with Clermont Gauthier. He revived my questioning, shook my basis assumptions in education. I started reading Lyotard and Deleuze. I felt like Alice in Wonderland. I registered for a class in 'Les Fondement Philosophiques en Education' with Jacques Daignault: I met a pedagogue. I felt very strongly that pedagogy brings together literature, philosophy, and education; pedagogy has no specific space, although its call is very distinct and loud. Afterwards I heard that this call might be post-structuralist. I do not know if this label does justice to pedagogy; I just know that this is where I am going, as a pedagogue."

SUSAN H. EDGERTON, a Ph.D. student at Louisiana State University writes:
    "I think I *felt* 'post-structuralism' long before I heard the term. That is, around ages 18 and 19 (mid 1970s)—ages, for me, in between periods of anger—when I was reading Eastern philosophy, 'novels' by Carlos Casteneda, and novels by Tom Robbins, I was thinking in terms of ambiguity, paradox, and joy. Subsequently, I packed it away and only recently began pulling it back out of storage. Now, for better or for worse, it has been labeled.
    "My first year of graduate studies in education (1985) involved several courses in history and sociology of education, where I became excited by revisionist and critical theorist (Frankfurt School) perspectives. They helped me to name my own experience of school and social life in a small Southern town—much of which had angered me—in ways that I had been unable to articulate before. This was a significant turning point for my thinking, but finally I saw such thinking approaching a static limit. Also, operating from a standpoint of anger was exhausting for its apparent political futility and its potential violence (violence to myself if to no one else). Nostalgically perhaps, I wondered how what started as intellectual excitement could have lead me so far afield of a younger woman who saw life as a 'crusade' for joy.
    "When I moved to Baton Rouge from Shreveport (fall 1988) to continue my graduate studies with Bill Pinar and others, I began taking courses that introduced me to alternatives to anger and terrorism. In Bill Pinar's class I read, among many other things, pieces by Bill that clearly celebrated interior lives, and pieces by Madeleine Grumet, Florence Krall, and Jo Ann Pagano that put me back in touch with my body and its relationship to consciousness, the natural environment, and reading. Something different was emerging from my work with Cameron McCarthy as well. He encouraged and nurtured my engagement with literature—a new and dangerous journey for me as I had been a student of chemistry for years, not of literature. Work done with Tony Whitson has also been influential, and I have come to appreciate it more and more as time passes. Many of the brilliantly conceived and orchestrated connections that Tony made across widely diverse frames of reference were lost on me—or so I thought at the time. Somehow, the more I read, the more issues that surfaced in that classroom have come back to memory in the form of revelations. Although I would not presume to label Tony as 'post-structuralist' (or anyone else for that matter), he has been one who has helped me to imagine the possibilities for grounding such theory in the 'practical,' at least in some ways and at some times.

"Post-structural thought had not presented itself to me as an undeniable force until I took a course from Jacques Daignault in Spring of 1988. Still I resisted, well into the semester, echoing critics' (of post-structuralism) concerns for the potential political paralysis, self-centeredness, and obscurity of such thought. When, at last, I allowed myself to read this 'text' rather than to 'read' the same things into this text as I read into every other, I discovered, *not* paralysis, but a wonderful breathing space for difference and ambiguity. I continue to find this air in the texts of Daignault, Deleuze, Guattari, and most recently, Serres.

"Since the class with Jacques I have done coursework with Rick Moreland, a Faulknerian scholar interested in post-structural literary criticism who teaches in the English department at LSU. In his classes we read Faulkner, Twain, Ellison, and Morrison in conjunction with Kristeva, Deleuze, Clement, Jardine, Schmitz, and other theorists. Through Rick's sensitive treatment of these texts and his generous mentorship I have been able to extend my theoretical interests to include their connections (or as Serres might call them, translations) to literature and reading.

"Much of my writing now is done through literature via post-structural philosophy, some psychoanalytical theory, and feminist thought with particular emphasis on marginality (broadly conceived). My most pressing concern (besides finishing my degree) is to seek and work through translations among my writing, the curriculum field, and my teaching."

EFFORTS TO UNDERSTAND CURRICULUM as phenomenological and deconstructed texts are made by concretely existing persons. Indeed, these efforts function to pull the reader closer to concrete experience, closer to an intensity of intellectual life. These genealogical notes confirm the intensity and intelligence of the participants in these profound and exciting traditions.

REFERENCES

Aoki, T. (1985). *Toward curriculum inquiry in a new key* (Department of Secondary Education Occasional Papers, Series #2, rev. ed.). Edmonton: University of Alberta.

Aoki, T. (1988). Personal correspondence.

Bernstein, R. J. (1976). *Restructuring of social and political theory.* New York: Harcourt Brace Jovanovich.

Carson, T. (1988). Personal correspondence.

Cherryholmes, C. (1988). *Power and criticism: Poststructural investigations in education.* New York: Teachers College Press.

Cherryholmes, C. (1989). Personal correspondence.

Daignault, J. (1989). Personal correspondence.

Denton, D. (Ed.). (1974). *Existentialism and phenomenology in education*. New York: Teachers College Press.

Doll, Jr. W. E., (in press). *The post-modern curriculum*. New York: Teachers College Press.

Foster, H. (1984). *Recodings: Art, spectacle, cultural politics*. Port Townsend, WA: Bay Press.

Foster, H. (Ed.). (1988). *Vision and visuality* (Dia Art Foundation, Discussions in Contemporary Culture #2). Seattle, WA: Bay Press.

Gauthier, C. (1989). Personal correspondence.

Giroux, H. A. (1988a). Border pedagogy in the age of postmodern. *Journal of Education, 170*(3), 162–179.

Giroux, H. A. (1988b). Postmodernism and the discourse of education criticism. *Journal of Education, 170*(3), 5–27.

Giroux, H. A. (1991). *Post-modernism, feminism, and cultural politics*. Albany: State University of New York Press.

Greene, M. (1973). *Teacher as stranger*. Belmont, CA: Wadsworth.

Grumet, M. (1988a). Bodyreading. In W. F. Pinar (Ed.), *Contemporary curriculum discourses* (pp. 453–473). Scottsdale, AZ: Gorsuch, Scarisbrick.

Grumet, M. (1988b). *Bitter milk: Women and teaching*. Amherst: University of Massachusetts Press.

Hall, S. (1985). Signification, representation, ideology: Althusser and the post-structuralist debates. *Critical Studies in Mass Communication 2*(2), 91–114.

Hall, S. (April, 1990). *Cultural studies and its theoretical legacies*. Paper presented at the Cultural Studies Now and in the Future Conference, University of Illinois, Champaign.

Haraway, D. (1985). A manifesto for cyborgs: Science technology and socialist feminism in the 1980's. *Socialist Review, 80,* 65–107.

Haraway, D. (1988). Situated knowledges: The science question in feminism and the privilege of partial perspective. *Feminist Studies, 14*(3), 575–599.

Harding, S. (1986). *The science question in feminism*. Ithaca, NY: Cornell University Press.

Harding, S. (Ed.). (1987). *Feminism and methodology*. Bloomington: University of Indiana Press.

Hassan, I. (1987). *The postmodern turn: Essays in postmodern theory and culture*. Columbus: Ohio State University Press.

Huebner, D. (1967). Curriculum as concern for man's temporality. *Theory into Practice, 6*(4), 172–179. Also in W. F. Pinar (Ed.), *Curriculum theorizing: The reconceptualists* (pp. 237–249). Berkeley, CA: McCutchan.

Hunsberger, M. (1988). Personal correspondence.

Hutcheon, L. (1988). A postmodern problematics. In R. Merrill (Ed.), *Ethics/aesthetics: Post-modern positions* (pp. 1–10). Washington, DC: Maisonneuve Press.

Jardine, D. (1990). Personal correspondence.

Lather, P. (1988). Personal correspondence.

Lather, P. (1991). *Getting smart*. London: Routledge & Kegan Paul.

Lauretis, T. de (1989). The essence of the triangle or, taking the risk of essentialism seriously: Feminist theory in Italy, the U.S., and Britain, *differences, 1*(2), 3–37.

Macdonald, J. (1975). Curriculum and human interests. In W. F. Pinar (Ed.), *Curriculum theorizing: The reconceptualists* (pp. 283–298). Berkeley, CA: McCutchan.

McLaren, P. (1988). Schooling the postmodern body: Critical pedagogy and the politics of enfleshment. *Journal of Education, 170*(3), 53–83.

McLaren, P., & Hammer, R. (1989, Fall). Critical pedagogy and the postmodern challenge. *Educational Foundations*, pp. 29–62.

Martusewicz, R. (1990). Personal correspondence.

Marxism Today. (October, 1988). Special issues on post-Fordism.

Miller, J. L. (1988b). The resistance of women academics: An autobiographical account. In W. F. Pinar (Ed.), *Contemporary curriculum discourse* (pp. 486–494). Scottsdale, AZ: Gorsuch, Scarisbrick.

Miller, J. L. (1990). *Creating spaces and finding voices*. Albany: State University of New York Press.

Pinar, W. (1990). Impartiality and comprehensiveness in the teaching of curriculum theory. In J. Sears & D. Marshall (Eds.), *Teaching curriculum* (pp. 259–264). New York: Teachers College Press.

Reynolds, W. M. (1989). *Reading curriculum theory: The development of a new hermeneutic*. New York: Peter Lang.

Said, E. (1975). *Beginnings: Intention and method*. New York: Basic Books.

Said, E. (1986). Orientalism reconsidered. In F. Barker et al. (Eds.), *Literature, politics and theory* (pp. 210–229). London: Methuen.

Said, E. (1989). Representing the colonized: Anthropology's interlocutors. *Critical Inquiry 15*, 205–225.

Scheurick, J. J. (in press). Old metaphors and new. *Review Journal of Philosophy and Social Science*.

Smith, D. (1988). Personal correspondence.

Spivak, G. (1987a). *In other worlds: Essays in cultural politics*. New York: Methuen.

Spivak, G. (1987b). Speculations on reading Marx: After reading Derrida. In D. Attridge, G. Bennington, & R. Young (Eds.), *Post-structuralism and the question of history* (pp. 30–62). Cambridge, England: Cambridge University Press.

Spivak, G. (1989). A response to "The difference within: Feminism and critical theory." In E. Meese & A. Parker (Eds.), *The difference within: Feminism and critical theory* (pp. 207–220). Amsterdam: Johns Benjamin.

Taubman, P. M. (1982). Gender and curriculum: Discourse and the politics of sexuality. *JCT: An Interdisciplinary Journal of Curriculum Studies, 4*(1), 12–87.

Taubman, P. M. (1900). Personal correspondence.

Tyler, S. (1986). Post-modern ethnography: From document of the occult to occult document. In J. Clifford & G. Marcus (Eds.), *Writing culture: The poetics and politics of ethnography* (pp. 122–140). Berkeley: University of California Press.

van Manen, M. (1988). Personal correspondence.

Wexler, P. (1987). *Social analysis of education: After the new sociology*. New York: Routledge & Kegan Paul.

About the Contributors

T. Tetsuo Aoki is professor and chair emeritus, Department of Secondary Education, University of Alberta. He has taught as well at the Universities of Victoria and British Columbia and Louisiana State University. He is the editor, most recently, of *Voices of Teaching* (British Columbia Teachers Federation).

Robert Brown is a Ph.D. candidate at Louisiana State University. His dissertation research includes a comprehensive study of the work of Aoki and van Manen.

Terrance Carson is associate professor in the Department of Secondary Education at the University of Alberta. With David Smith he is author of *Educating for Peaceful Future* (Toronto: Kegan & Woo).

Jacques Daignault is associate professor of education at the University of Quebec at Rimouski. He has taught also at the University of Paris and Louisiana State University, where he is adjunct professor of education.

Clermont Gauthier teaches education at Laval University, Quebec. He has taught also at the University of Quebec in Rimouski. The author of *Une education juste ou juste une education?* (Victoriaville, Quebec: Editions NHP, 1986), he is currently working on the origin and nature of pedagogy.

Madeleine R. Grumet is professor and dean, School of Education, Brooklyn College of the City University of New York. She is the author of *Bitter Milk* (University of Massachusetts Press). She has taught as well at the University of Rochester and Hobart and William Smith Colleges.

Margaret Hunsberger is associate professor in reading/language arts education at the University of Calgary. Teaching and research interests include understanding the experiences of reading and writing, language curriculum, and literature across the curriculum.

jan jagodzinski is associate professor of art education at the University of Alberta.

David W. Jardine is assistant professor, early childhood education, University of Calgary.

Rebecca A. Martusewicz is assistant professor of teacher education at Eastern Michigan University. She teaches courses in social fondations of education, including sociology of education, philosophy of education, social aspects of teaching, and popular culture. At present she is exploring the work of Gilles Deleuze, Michel Serres, Jean Francois Lyotard, among others, to think and write about pedagogy and curriculum.

William F. Pinar is professor, Department of Curriculum and Instruction, Louisiana State University. He is the Founding Editor of *JCT: An Interdisciplinary Journal of Curriculum Studies* and the editor, with Joe Kincheloe, of *Curriculum as Social Psychoanalysis* (State University of New York Press).

William M. Reynolds is associate professor of education, University of Wisconsin–Stout. He is the author of *Reading Curriculum Theory* (Peter Lang) and the editor of *JCT: An Interdisciplinary Journal of Curriculum Studies*.

Peter M. Taubman is chair of the English Department of Poly Prep Country Day School in Brooklyn, New York. He is author of *Gender and Curriculum* (JCT).

Index